The AntiTerrorist Handbook

velluminous

Published by Velluminous Press
www.velluminous.com

ISBN: 978-1-905605-17-0

COVER DESIGN
HOLLY OLLIVANDER

THE ANTITERRORIST HANDBOOK

to

MU
*for showing me just how insignificant illusion and material
things are in the face of true love and acceptance.*

my Parents
for their unconditional love and guidance.

my Children
for choosing me, I love you more than life itself.

&

HEO
*my muse; for loving me, for seeing possibility in me,
and for helping me remember who I really am.*

THEANTITERRORIST HANDBOOK

When TheAntiTerrorist asked me to write the foreword to this book and to include a little ditty I had written on the stages of emotional, educational and spiritual awakening, I was pleased to accept, but before we come to the piece in question, I would like to take a moment to introduce the author of this book. The best way I know to do so is to quote a comment by one of his channel subscribers,

> *'It's great to have someone talking like it's natural to think this way—which it is.'*

It *is* the most natural thing in the world to desire freedom, and the line above simply and eloquently sums up the attraction and appeal of TheAntiTerrorist's message.

As moving as I found the quote above, the next—in response to a comment posted by another viewer—made me laugh out loud:

> *'TheAntiTerrorist could bend you in half with his mind. Get a clue, you idiot.'*

The people in our lives who leave the best and longest-lasting impression tend to have one particular trait in common: the ability to state aloud what we all have locked away in our secret hearts, to bring it out into the light and to communicate it in a way that seems natural, straightforward and clear. This is the way one changes the world for the better—not by coercion, cajolement or the manipulative technique of lies, but by reacquainting humans with the concept of common sense, to awaken someone to who they truly are: not victims, not slaves, but sovereign souls who have allowed themselves to fall into the trap of trusting others to fix the world for them.

The stages of waking up to a new view of reality are remarkably similar to the stages of grief. In either case, an individual can—and should—spend some time mourning for what has passed on—whether grieving the loss of a loved one or an outmoded belief. Each of these stages are necessary mileposts on the journey to becoming a complete human; fully aware, fully alive, shorn of illusions, cooking on all burners, playing with a full deck and aflame with a passion to make their world a better place.

The book you hold in your hands was written by a man who is decent, kind, humourous, generous and honourable. In a world filled with tin heroes, he is a man of gold.

TheAntiTerrorist is a messenger and the message—like any gift—can either be cast away, or grasped like a flaming torch and carried aloft on your journey.

In this spirit, may you take what you can use from this book and light your own way to freedom.

WAKING UP, A HUMAN EXPERIENCE
For Timothy

You're tootling along, you think you have a pretty good bead on things, but something's not right somewhere, something just doesn't add up. Something… is about to change.

It's like a constant annoying drone or a splinter too small to pick out easily. The world is out of joint but you cannot seem to put your finger on exactly what it is that's bothering you. It's fairly easy to ignore, so you do. For a while.

The thing about systems crumbling is that tiny bits begin to fall off at first. These tiny bits are very easy to dismiss, as in 'There's more homeless people downtown than I remember seeing last year,' then you put your pedal to the metal and drive on. You see prices beginning to rise in the shops because your currency is buying less and less every season, but the head of state is on the box saying the economy is fine and things are only getting better, so you change the channel. Then, larger chunks begin to break off—someone you actually know gets laid off or loses their house or gets arrested on a charge completely out of proportion to the offence they allegedly committed and it all seems to be a bit more personal and closer to home.

Then one day it reaches a critical mass. Someone or something brings the truth home to you—and you immediately shut down. It's too horrible to think about, but still, despite all the mental evasions, the rationalising, the justifications, you inexorably find yourself moving to…

Anger

Some are enraged at anyone bringing a new view of reality. They demonise those seeking truth, characterising them tin-hats, liberals, crazy people, idiots. They cling to the status quo but something has shifted in their lives at a molecular level. The new view isn't comfortable, but they find they are no longer at ease with their old, accustomed reality, either. It doesn't feel like home anymore.

They now have two choices; stay angry at the messenger, or move on to feel anger at the people in power.

Loads of people get angry at the people in power—and get stuck there. They are the ones bitching away on blogs and forums—griping, moaning, shit-stirring—never actually doing anything apart from endlessly rehashing the problem. Once in a while, a few make it out and generally find themselves at…

Despair

People self-medicate or commit suicide or bore the socks off people at parties who generally aren't ready to have their world rocked. People in despair sometimes find it's useless to trumpet their beliefs to all and sundry because they suspect nobody's really listening anyway. We are all assaulted on a daily basis by entities willing to spend vast sums of money and effort to capture and command our attention; from the major media, to organised religion, to every commercial enterprise you can think of. There's no point in competing with them, yet if someone asks what you think and believe about the world, you should answer as simply and as truthfully as you can. You cannot persuade anyone to accept at face value what you know, you can only point them in the direction where they can discover the truth for themselves, and you accomplish this most effectively by the example of how you live your own life.

Despair is a very lonely stage. Many people never move beyond it. The ones who do, find themselves washed up on the shore of...

Doing Something

You are a living, breathing soul; this makes you powerful. So, break the pattern of history—don't wait around to be told what to do, or where to stand, or how to think. Don't wait on others with empty promises to do it for you. It's up to you to claim the power to change your own destiny.

To really *do something*, you must be willing to risk everything you possess. I am not saying that price will be extracted from you at the end—but you should be prepared for it to be. You must get yourself into the mindset of *I am willing to risk everything for what I most desire.*

The world is what we make it, one individual at a time. I want to add to the sum total of beauty in it. A little at a time, if that's all I can manage to accomplish. I decided a long time ago that I would be doing that anyway no matter what else was going on.

and finally...

Wake up. Create as you go. Keep on your toes. Fly by the seat of your pants. Don't forget to breathe. Be happy anyway.

Most of all, remember you're in it for the adventure.

HOLLY ELSPETH OLLIVANDER
10 August 2009
Sir Gaerfyrddin • Cymru

Enlightenment is man's emergence from his self-imposed immaturity.
Immaturity is the inability to use one's understanding without guidance
from another. This immaturity is self-imposed when its cause lies not in
lack of understanding, but in lack of resolve and courage to use it
without guidance from another. 'Sapere Aude! Dare to know!
Have the courage to use your own understanding!'
That is the motto of enlightenment.
IMMANUEL KANT

The natural progress of things is for liberty to yield
and governments to gain ground.
THOMAS JEFFERSON

PROLOGUE

'Hello Friends, I am TheAntiTerrorist. Please excuse the mask and the theatrics but in a country where you can now be thrown into a cell for merely speaking your mind or questioning the 'status quo,' I am afraid it is entirely necessary.'

The above was a statement I made in my first video introducing myself as a 'conspiracist' on YouTube. Theatrical those words may seem, but the overwhelming evidence of a burgeoning Police State makes them seem less and less frivolous as the days go by.

I was initially inspired to broadcast based on events I had witnessed outside Parliament in 2007, concerning a certain anti-war protestor named Brian Haw.

Brian doesn't know me, but I've been an advocate of his stand since it began. He lawfully occupies an area of five square meters outside Parliament and has thwarted all attempts to remove him since he made camp there over six years ago, in protest against the illegal and unlawful invasion of Iraq.

He's a thorn in the side of the establishment, to say the least. His anti-war display is makeshift and certainly not pleasing to the eye, but is highly effective nonetheless. In fact, thanks to the Internet and the power of his message, he's become something of a tourist attraction, much to the consternation of the politicians who drive by his encampment in their polished black Daimlers and Bentleys.

The Police have tried every dirty trick in the book to remove him. I've been witness to bullying, coercion, violence and threats of imprisonment but there he remains, undaunted. Brian is a passionate but peaceable soul and—to the best of my knowledge—has never raised a hand against another. He has my profound respect.

Most recently, in 2008, several 'officers' wearing SWAT-type apparel accosted him. He was dragged into the back of a waiting van and was—allegedly—the test dummy for a bout of 'truncheon practice.' He emerged some five minutes later, bloodied and battered, but as defiant as ever. I wasn't there to see the event with my own eyes, but there are hundreds of photos and several video recordings of the incident available on the net.

What disgusted me most was the general reaction of the onlookers; they walked by as though nothing of any significance had happened. Once Brian had been carted off in an ambulance, the Police stationed around Parliament nonchalantly continued to direct human traffic—Nothing to see here folks, move along now.

The general level of apathy in this once great country is so pervasive and so apparent that I despair for our future. And 'The Powers that Be' are thriving on it.

> *All that is necessary for evil to persist*
> *is for enough good men to do nothing.*
> EDMUND BURKE

I remember feeling profoundly helpless at the time. Despite my growing knowledge of the law and 'the system', it seemed as though there was nothing I could do, until I discovered YouTube and the knowledge that I was not alone in my rejection of the current establishment.

In the days that followed, I must have watched hundreds of videos, from very credible sources, containing evidence of corruption, subversion and malpractice, and realised that this was a way I could make a difference in fighting the ignorance and indifference—if I could make the information accessible—bring it closer to home, so to speak. At least then I would be part of the solution and no longer part of the problem, which is how I see the majority of the people in this country at the moment: blissfully unaware of the stealth politics that will have them under draconian, Machiavellian rule within the next two to three years. Yes, that bad and that soon.

At the risk of saying too much about my private life, my profession requires that I keep a low profile, politically speaking. If my employers were to become aware of me denouncing the current system, it would certainly mean the end of my career; hence the clandestine façade. I'm well aware that for some the mask might be off-putting but I hoped it would grab their attention long enough for the information to hit home.

Although I have strong views on many subjects and was committed to sharing them, I wasn't about to jeopardise my ability to feed and clothe my family. I was also acutely aware that—should it turn out I was just a misguided nutcase and that all was actually well with the world—I could drop the project like a hot potato and blend back in with no embarrassment to those who associate with me on a regular basis.

Also, there was the small issue of HR1955, a bill (currently being bounced around Congress) nicknamed 'The Thought Crime Bill'. The Violent Radicalization and Homegrown Terrorism Prevention Act of 2007 effectively empowers The Powers That Be to arrest you as a suspected terrorist for publicly expressing your anti-establishment views. Freedom of speech really is a thing of the past.

Anything that happens in the UNITED STATES happens here in the UNITED KINGDOM within a short space of time, and I wasn't about to be carted off to some British version of a FEMA camp before I'd at least managed to wake a few sleepers, or 'sheeple' as they're commonly referred to in conspiracist circles.

I pride myself on my diligence and meticulousness, and I always have. Call it an obsessive-compulsive disorder if you like, but it has always served me well. I also have an over-developed sense of curiosity, which has gotten me into trouble every now and then, but that too has been a great asset in most cases.

In viewing others' presentations on YouTube, I found myself becoming increasingly frustrated seeing relatively intelligent people with valid arguments blathering on and wildly digressing whilst trying to make their point, and decided I was going to make my own as crystallised and as accessible as possible. My presentation in the videos became highly edited in order to distil the information and—hopefully—hold the viewer's attention.

In all modesty, I believe I discovered a formula that works well. From time to time, I do feel as though I am preaching to the choir but every now and then I will get a fresh insight from a viewer who sends an email thanking me for 'waking them up'. It is this which spurs me on.

It's been said that all truth passes through three stages; the first stage being denial, the second being violent opposition and the third being widespread acceptance as common knowledge. As you read this book, keep in mind that you'll probably fall into one of those three categories. One group of people will absolutely deny that what they are reading could possibly be true. The second group of people will be violently apposed to this information being released and do whatever they can to discredit the messenger, rather than pay attention to the message, and there is a third group who will sit back in their comfy chair and say, 'I'm not surprised, I knew it all along.'

With this in mind, let's begin by playing a little word association. I will say a word and you think of the first word that comes to mind:

'Conspiracy...'

'Theory' is what most people think of. We've all been conditioned to associate the word 'theory' with the word 'conspiracy' because, after all, no conspiracies could possibly be true; they're all just theories, aren't they?

Well, in the phrase 'conspiracy theory', the second word is the active word. By definition, a theory is a supposition, an idea, a concept, a hypothesis.

Let me give you an example: In theory, if I purchase a raffle ticket I could win a prize. If I don't purchase a raffle ticket, my win is only theoretical, but once I actually have that ticket, winning becomes a possibility. The more raffle tickets I purchase, the more possible—and probable—my win becomes. Such is the case with a conspiracy theory; as long as there is no evidence, it is a conspiracy theory. However, once you have a piece of evidence, no matter how circumstantial, it becomes a possibility. The more evidence that is gathered, the more probable the conspiracy is.

You will be looking at evidence in this book and it will be up to you to decide whether what is presented is conspiracy theory, or indeed a conspiracy.

LEGATUS NON VIOLATUR

WE'RE ALL GOING TO DIE...

...not 'Someday', or quietly in our sleep at the end of a fulfilling life, unfortunately, we're all going to be unceremoniously snuffed out together on the 21 December 2012. Just after teatime.

I spent a great deal of time wondering how to begin this book since conspiracy theories are rife and there are many intriguing points of view on any given subject. After much deliberation, I decided to begin with the granddaddy of them all, Nibiru, since it really doesn't get much more serious than the 'There's a Big Frickin' Rock Headed This Way And We're All About To Be Crushed Like A Discarded Toy Under A Petulant Toddler's Shoe' conspiracy

Planet X, Eris, Wormwood, Nemesis—call it what you will—it's heading this way and there's no escaping it, or so the proponents of this particular conspiracy would have us all believe. The story goes like this...

The term 'Nibiru' comes from Sumerian cuneiform tablets and writings dating from 5,000 years ago. The term means 'Planet of the Crossing'. The 'Nibirans', have graced us with their presence on at least two previous occasions after swinging by on their 3600-year elliptical orbit that traces a path from far out beyond Pluto to within spitting distance of Earth. They genetically engineered us to serve as a labour force way back when, and will be checking in once more in 2012 to do a major cabinet reshuffle and to remind us who is calling the shots round these parts. Apparently, this is the only theory that accounts for 'the missing link' and other flaws in Darwinian theory.

All religions—including Christianity—are built upon a foundation derived from memories of The Shining Ones—the people of Nibiru. There are countless statues and carvings from every era and nation on Earth depicting spaceships, astronauts and The Shining Ones themselves. The Nibirans are also credited for the universality of angel myths, despite archaeologists and historians ignoring or suppressing all evidence that suggests anything other than the conventional view.

The first sign of Nibiru's approach will be a meteor bombardment, initiated as the dwarf star passes through the asteroid belt between Earth and Mars; millions will perish. The second effect will be a reversal of the Earth's magnetic field caused by Nibiru's proximity to Earth, initiating mega-tsunamis and planet-wide earthquakes. The third and final event will be a UFO invasion.

Earth will be colonised and the human race will be openly (rather than covertly) enslaved, while Nibiru continues on its orbit back from whence it came.

Even now, Nibiru is visible in the heavens from the southern hemisphere. By late 2009, it will be close enough to be seen with the naked eye all over the world, and will grow steadily larger as 2012 approaches. Our leaders and scientists are aware of Nibiru's approach, but remain silent because there is nothing they can do.

Nibiru was also known to the Mayans, who associated it with the end of their calendar in December 2012, give or take a year. The Mayans didn't elaborate on what 2012 will manifest, but the possibilities being forecast by modern day interpreters include:

- Major changes in human DNA
- An enormous leap in Consciousness
- Dimensional shifts
- The cessation of linear Time
- An evolutionary human pinnacle
- A huge surge and multiple breakthroughs in technology
- The end of Money
- Astonishing genetic mutations
- Massive earthquakes and volcanic activity due to sunspot activity and unique planetary alignments.

So—in a nutshell—there you have it.

I have lost count of the number of messages I have received on this topic but—invariably—the ones sent by believers were all tinged with a sense of depression, despair and hopelessness… or jubilation, ecstasy and longing depending upon their belief system.

Here's a typical, unedited example from a British teenager:

Hi AT,
Why haven't you spoken about Nibiru? Do you know that we only have five years left before the Annunaki come to kill us all? I've been trying to warn my friends but they tell me I'm crazy and just laugh. They don't know what's going to happen in 2012 and I want them to take it seriously. I know that if you talk about it they will listen. Please think about it. If you want me to send you some links, let me know. There is so much proof to show that we will all be killed. What can we do?

Peace out.
Matrixson1

And another from an American:

Hello blessed one,

I am very grateful for your videos on youtube, they have certainly opened my eyes to a few things I can tell you. I have to say though that you're missing the point somewhat. In 2012, all of the topics you have been discussing will be moot, as we're coming to the End times. Wormwood is the angel of death, sent by God to cleanse the earth of all Sinners and it will be here in 2012. Did you know? Have you made your peace with God? Have you accepted Jesus Christ as your Lord and Saviour? The great cleansing will begin as all of God's angels tear the sinners from this earthly plane and send them to fiery damnation. I sincerely hope you will not be one of them. Repent while there is still time.

God go with you.
Blessings
Angelwings212012

I have a commitment to keeping my mind wide open. In fact, some of my friends often say I could do with closing it a little, as there's clearly a crazy draught blowing through, so I don't know whether those two are bonkers or not... and neither do you, if we're honest. Let's face it, our so-called 'leaders' have said and done crazier things. What I do know is there's a growing feeling that 'something's about to give.' There is a distinct sense of *dis*-ease in the collective unconscious and people are reacting to it in all sorts of ways.

As an aside, a new term has been coined to describe what I feel is prevalent amongst some of the believers of this particular theory: Demoralization Syndrome.

Hopelessness, loss of meaning, and existential distress are proposed as the core features of the diagnostic category of Demoralization Syndrome. DS can be differentiated from depression and is recognizable in palliative care settings. It is associated with chronic medical illness, disability, bodily disfigurement, fear of loss of dignity, social isolation and—where there is a subjective sense of incompetence and/or powerlessness—feelings of greater dependency on others or the perception of being a burden. Because of this sense of impotence, those with the syndrome predictably progress to a desire to die or to commit suicide.

I can see how some people might be looking for a way out of what we're currently experiencing as we slide from a recession into a severe depression that will no doubt make the 1930s fiasco look like the booming 80s. However, there are quicker ways of shuffling off one's mortal coil than waiting around for a brown dwarf star to pass through so that you can drown in a tsunami or have your head rammed into your chest cavity by a large lump of falling masonry. Why don't these people form a penned-in community and, on the count of three, all drink a pint of de-icer if they're so intent on ending it all?

Because of Hope.

Another aspect of this particular theory is that Nibiru is going to cause a spiritual shift in consciousness, the 'Great Awakening'. The polar shift caused by the disturbance in earth's magnetic field in 2012 will activate the entire chain of chakras and we'll all light up like Christmas trees… or not, if you're a sinner.

Going by my inbox, people shift from despair to hope and back again, constantly battling with their deeply held beliefs, as new information—credible or otherwise—appears on YouTube.

Some of my subscribers are devout believers in the Nibiru conspiracy and appear to be almost willing it to happen. The only reference I have for that mentality is a wonderful scene in Kevin Costner's 'Waterworld', and it immediately comes to mind whenever I read an anything from the catastrophist genre:

We're nearing the end of the movie and we've established that Dennis Hopper's character has a senile old man, bobbing around in a rowing boat on a lake of oil inside his floating fortress. He is clearly there under duress, and is responsible for maintenance and reporting purposes. Kevin Costner's character has snuck aboard the oil tanker deck in order to rescue a young girl and—whilst bantering with Hopper—throws a flaming flare into a vent leading to the oil lake down below. We cut to the old guardian in the boat as he turns to see the flare land and ignite the oil. So tired of his miserable life and clearly so grateful for the release that death is about to bring, he utters, 'Oh, thank God.'

It is as funny and yet as profound a scene as you'll ever see.

I am also reminded of Revelation 9:6;

> *'And in those days shall men seek death, and shall not find it;*
> *and shall desire to die, and death shall flee from them.'*

And in those days… Those days seem to be these days, these days. The signs are certainly manifesting. Global upheaval in the forms of change, war, famine, the Middle East crisis, the faux financial crisis… Don't get me started on the prolific use of the word Crisis in the mainstream media at the moment—it appears to be the new fear-generating word to replace Terrorism.

It is, of course, the book of Revelations that my elderly female subscriber holds as her justification for Nibiru's existence. The religious Planet X advocates are the trickiest to tackle on this subject. There's just no debating with true believers where the Bible is concerned. Those who believe the Bible is the word of God will have none of it when you suggest the matter of interpretation.

Amongst the plethora of biblical references that are sent my way, this one, from Jeremiah 48:8 is the most frequent,

> *A destroyer will come to every city,*
> *So that no city will escape;*
> *The valley also will be ruined and the plateau will be destroyed,*
> *As the LORD has said.*

Who can argue with Jeremiah? He's in the Bible, for God's sake. (Forgive me my twisted sense of humour, Lord).

When those messages come in, I'm torn between engaging them in a discussion that might lead to possible enlightenment for both of us, and just leaving well enough alone.

When people are first introduced to the possibility of Planet X, they want proof, not conjecture, and they want it from a reliable source. Rightfully so. Unfortunately, there is a lot of evidence, but there is no proof whatsoever.

To get a sense of what gives this theory any weight, we first need to understand how astronomers actually discovered the outer planets in our solar system.

The search for Planet X began when early astronomers first observed agitation in the orbit of Saturn. Through mathematics, they predicted the existence of Saturn's agitator. The German-born British astronomer, William Herschel, used this mathematical prediction to discover the planet Uranus in 1781. Interestingly enough, astronomers later found agitation in the orbit of Uranus as well. Based on this agitation, and working from earlier mathematical computations, the British mathematician and astronomer John Couch Adams predicted the existence and position of a massive object in the outer solar system, one he believed to be large enough to affect Uranus. The German Astronomer Johann Galle then applied Adams' mathematical prediction to discover the planet Neptune in 1846 and—as with Uranus—astronomers would then discover agitation in the orbit of Neptune as well. Consequently, the search for Planet X was far from over.

When Clyde Thombar discovered Pluto in 1930, many jumped to the conclusion that it was the mysterious Planet X that everyone had been searching for. However, when the mathematicians began running the numbers it became obvious very quickly that Pluto had nowhere near the mass to be Neptune's agitator. When you compare Pluto with the Earth, it becomes self-evident; we see that Pluto is tiny—roughly 60% the size of our own moon. This is the reason Pluto was recently demoted to the status of a dwarf planet.

In 1976, Zecharia Sitchin wrote a controversial book titled *The Twelfth Planet.* He had interpreted a batch of ancient Sumerian texts in cuneiform—the earliest known form of writing—as a literal translation of the origin of humankind. According to theories of Sumerian cosmology, Nibiru is the twelfth member of our own solar system family of planets and its catastrophic collision with Tiamat, a planet that was once situated between Mars and Jupiter, would have formed the planet Earth, the asteroid belt, and the Moon.

According to Sitchin, it was the technologically advanced human-like alien race, the Anunnaki, who survived the collision and later came to Earth in search of gold—desired for its reflective properties—to place in their atmosphere.

On discovering our relatively primitive species, they set about creating a worker who could communicate and learn from them and, after a slew of failed prototypes, an Annunaki Goddess engineered a perfect specimen, the Adam. This was apparently achieved using eighty percent of an inferior human specimen and twenty percent of a superior Anunnaki specimen. The Sumerians depicted their goddess creator alongside a totem made up of snakes in a double helix form, with thin bars connecting them in a spiral fashion. In design, this corresponds directly with what we understand to be the double helix structure of our own DNA.

To cut a long story short, the scientific community unanimously disregarded Sitchin's work, as many of his methods of interpretation are considered imaginative at best. While Sitchin has credibility issues, his idea of our Solar System being a binary system isn't that farfetched. Current observations of nearby star systems reveal that the majority have double stars, or more. The nearest, Proxima Centauri, is a triple star system.

So, keeping an open mind, on we go.

On 26 January 1983, the National Aeronautics and Space Administration—NASA—launched their infrared astronomical satellite, IRAS, which promptly discovered something very large at the edge of our solar system. On 10 September 1984, it was reported in the US News and World Report that NASA had detected 'an object of intense speculation'. In the spirit of Herschel, Adams, Galle and Thombar, NASA continued the search for Planet X, and in 1992 they issued a landmark press release claiming that unexplained deviations in the orbits of Uranus and Neptune point to a larger outer solar system body of four to eight Earth masses, on a highly tilted orbit, more than 7 billion miles from the sun. After this announcement, the whole topic of Planet X mysteriously disappeared from the media spotlight, fuelling intense speculation of a cover-up amongst believers who insist that NASA is tracking Nibiru, but has been told to keep the information from the public in order to avoid the old-testament-wrath-of-god-fire-and-brimstone-rivers-and-seas-boiling-forty-years-of-darkness-earthquakes-volcanoes-dogs-and-cats-living-together mass-hysteria that makes people suddenly refuse to pay off their credit card statement.

In 2008, Japanese Astronomers at Kobe University lead by Dr. Mukai discovered a planet similar in size to that of earth in our solar system on a highly elliptical orbit and so—once again—this raises the Astronomical community's eye to the question of Planet X and gives energy to the believer argument.

Is there a Planet X and is it really heading this way? Is Planet X Zecharia Sitchin's Nibiru? No one knows for sure—at least, no one outside of the clique known as 'The Elite'.

As far as I can tell, it is all hearsay and conjecture. I could not find a single element of substantial proof, which is why I have never broadcast on the subject.

In my humble opinion, having researched this subject thoroughly, Planet X is merely a currently unknown, theoretically possible planet orbiting peacefully beyond the Kuiper Belt. As far as the Mayan Calendar is concerned, I can't help but feel that it is just more hyperbole from the same vein as the 'Millennium Bug' debacle of 2000, and that 2012 will pass peacefully, without incident.

If Planet X really is on the way, there may be major turmoil, in which case we're all going to be clocking off at the end of this Earthly shift whether we like it or not. Even the underground bases reported to have been built all over the globe will not be able to withstand the potential rending and tearing of the Earth's crust alluded to on the doomsday web sites, blogs, and radio talk shows. So, what is the point of worrying about it? At the risk of getting all touchy-feely-airy-fairy, surely it can only be the best reason to truly live out these days as if they are our last, love our fellow man and be thankful for the time we've had. Call me old-fashioned, if you like, but the thought of it makes me feel better.

The interesting aspect of the Nibiru story is that it is a rerun. With a couple of mouse clicks, you will find there was a major Internet concern that Nibiru would destroy the Earth in May of 2003. I am alive and well, so I'm guessing Nibiru had to make a caffeine stop at some Galactic service station on the way, possibly in order to avoid falling asleep at the wheel. Better five minutes late in this world than five minutes early in the next, that's what I always say!

Oh, and for those of you who are focussed on lizards taking over the planet, they're definitely after you—they're gonna get ya—and there's nothing I can do about that.

So, on to the stuff we *can* do something about…

ALL ABOARD THE CITIZEN SHIP

*The most terrifying words in the English language are
'I'm from the government and I'm here to help.'*
RONALD REAGAN

Over the past century, we people who were once independent, capable and able to manage our own medical, financial and legal affairs, have now been reduced to dependents. We've been made wards of powerful commercial, financial, medical and legal corporations, as well as the bureaucratic institutions of modern industrial society. We've been taught to rely upon professionals like bankers to manage our financial affairs, doctors to manage our health problems, lawyers to direct our business and legal affairs—instead of relying on our own good common sense. We've come to the point now where the Government has to do everything for us. In fact, we have been taught to go to the state or the Government every time we get a stomachache or every time we're hungry. We're no longer able to take care of ourselves. If you turned a westerner loose with a live chicken, they'd make a pet out of it and starve to death. It's unlikely they could kill that chicken, pluck it, cook it and eat it, they'd have to go out for McNuggets™ instead. The Government takes responsibility; takes good care of us—a bit like FEMA took good care of you people in New Orleans.

God bless FEMA—aren't they wonderful? They're just working their hearts out for you, aren't they? You pay your taxes and here's what you get: corruption and theft on a scale previously unimagined—until Hurricane Katrina. My friends, we Brits and Americans don't live in the Land of the Free and the Home of the Brave, we live in the land of Admiralty, where the Captain, your guardian, decides what is and isn't good for you. The Government has taken the power of the people, because we either didn't care, or didn't understand what our powers were. And the truly tragic part is that we agreed to all of it in advance.

Those who benefit from any societal mechanism rarely wish to understand that mechanism if it appears to give them power, control or authority over their fellow man. If understanding that mechanism would limit, diminish or remove that apparent power, control or authority, they simply do not want to know.
Robert-Arthur: Menard

Government isn't the servant of the people, Government is the absolute master of the people. When the Government agent comes over, you don't say to that agent, 'What are you doing here? What do you want?' You cringe.

We say, 'Yes, sir, no, sir…' We've been taught to be obedient to the Government, and we are. We, the 'voters', see ourselves as being sovereign only through the lens the government hands us; namely, we elect our representatives, they're working for us, right? We're the boss and they're our servants, right? Nonsense.

The President of the United States and the Prime Minister of the United Kingdom aren't our servants, they're our masters. We haven't elected a servant, we've elected a guardian, and as guardians, they go to Washington or Parliament and make the rules they determine are good for us. That's the way the game is played, that's the way it works. You know it as well as I do.

You can sit there and write letters to your representative all you like— until you're blue in the face—but they'll just pass whatever legislation the likes of General Motors, Microsoft and IBM tell them to. Now, if these chaps are really our servants then you've got your cleaner, your gardener and your cook making your laws for you— telling you when to get up, when to go to bed and what to do in between. They rule over us with a rigour and we complain about being in a pseudo-communist dictatorship…

Come on, people, we are the masters, yet we allow our kitchen help to make our laws for us and tell us how to live? We call this freedom? We call this liberty? Well, then, what would you call tyranny? What would you call slavery?

What greater tyranny can there be than a legislative body and a justice system working together to compel you to do what you don't want to do, against your will and over your objection? We refer to America and Britain as the free-est nations on earth. Meanwhile, we're over in Iraq trying to force that on the Iraqis and call it democracy. We're not spreading freedom and liberty to the Iraqis, we're bringing tyranny upon them; we're bringing the Admiralty upon them. The Iraqis didn't even have an income tax until we forced our way in there and imposed it upon them. They didn't have gun control either, we forced that upon them too. We foisted upon the Iraqis the same tyranny we brought upon ourselves with this process of Admiralty jurisdiction.

Unknowingly, we the people of America, Western Europe, Canada, Australia and New Zealand have been cunningly coerced out of our Common Law rights and forced into 'Admiralty'. We were enticed to volunteer into this civil jurisdiction through the benefits offered by the Social Security contract, drivers and business licences, marriage licences and other contractual entanglements with the Government. It's done with our consent. We gave up our unalienable rights under the Common Law and our constitutions for privileges under the civil law of the state.

We hear a lot about Admiralty in Patriot and freedom circles—people talk about Admiralty Courts and Admiralty process and Admiralty fringes on flags and Admiralty this and Admiralty that—so, what is it? Has anyone ever taken a real look at this animal called Admiralty, dissected it a little? It's quite a topic and I'm not sure that the average Patriot or freedom-seeker out there knows as much as he thinks he knows about it.

Admiralty is a little different from the common law—they got that right—but I doubt the average Joe or Jane knows what the Common Law is, where it came from or what its history is. Nor do they know very much about Admiralty—where it comes from or what its roots are or how and why it works the way it does.

There's a process in the US called 'The uniform code of military Justice…' I like to avoid Admiralty or military courts if it's at all possible. I would like to have justice though, and I'm here to tell you there is no justice in the world today. The theory behind justice is 'we would rather turn a guilty man loose than to lock an innocent man up,' whereas under the Admiralty, it is a case of 'if you can't prove your innocence then you must be guilty.' What kind of Justice is that?

By the same token, there's no peace either. Just take a look at the Middle East and ask yourself, what do George Bush, Tony Blair, Gordon Brown, Barack Obama know about peace? Do they understand the laws that govern peace in the land? We don't even have peace in the United States and United Kingdom, so the only conclusion I can come to is that they don't know the ways of peace; a true and accurate statement, I'm sure you'll agree. I'll go one step further and say they don't know anything about justice either. The reason there's no justice is because we don't have a justice system, we have an adversarial system. Because we have an adversarial system we have Advocates, and Advocates are not looking for justice, they're looking for an adversary.

I'm not so sure most of these people who get belligerent in court claiming to have rights actually have these rights at all. It could well be that they do have rights but they simply don't know how to claim them.

99.5% of people have no rights when they walk into court to start with, because I'm pretty sure all of them have what I like to call 'seaman's papers' or 'Admiralty enlistment papers'. This isn't a technical term, you won't find it in a legal dictionary, it's more of an affectionate term I use to describe the offending documentation. But before we get to 'enlistment papers' and we get into the nitty-gritty of why having them works against us when we try to get up off our knees, we ought to take a look at American Jurisprudence on the subject of Admiralty. Amongst other topics, it talks about Remedies, Admiralty practice and procedure, The Public Vessels Act, Suits and Admiralties Act, Tort jurisdiction, *In Personum* Jurisdiction, *In Rem* Jurisdiction, and the Saving to suitors clause.

Have you Americans ever wondered about the 'Saving to suitors' clause? People sometimes walk into an American court and demand their rights under the common law, quoting from the clause in the constitution that provides for 'saving to suitors'. It seems to me that if you walked into a traffic court and you wanted a Common Law remedy in that court, you'd first have to file a motion in order to bring up the subject matter of jurisdiction. Most of this paperwork that comes from the Patriot and freedom groups seems to be absolute nonsense. You can tell it's nonsense, because the Judges don't listen to it. After all, if the Judge is looking at a piece of paper and it doesn't have any legal merit, he dismisses it, he over-rules it, he doesn't implement it, he doesn't give you what you want. That ought to be a clue that something isn't right here. Of course, this is assuming that Judges are the bastions of integrity they're sworn to be.

Generally speaking, if you follow the rules you're most likely to succeed. In most cases you'll be walking into an Admiralty court but the Judge has three hats: an Admiralty hat, a Common Law hat and an Equity hat. Under the Common Law you're entitled to a jury trial. Having said that, if you managed to get a jury trial in an Admiralty court these days, as a rule, it would only be an 'advisory jury'.

In the 1980's, in Kansas City, there was a case dubbed the 'Ugly Anchorwoman Case'. An anchorwoman had been employed by a local TV station for a number of years and—as she got older—the station decided they needed 'younger blood'. Personally, as anchorwomen go, I'd rather see Jan Leeming than Britney Spears, but, sex sells and I guess that's what they were after. This lady had been unceremoniously dumped and took offence at that, so she sued. The jury awarded her a certain sum of money, somewhere in the realm of $500,000. However, the Judge set the judgment aside, saying it was excessive. It was later reported that the jury was only there in an advisory capacity. There may be advisory juries to ease the conscience of the court and determine certain facts, but they're not permitted to hear any arguments regarding the law. Does that sound familiar? You go into a jury trial today and the Judge makes the jurors swear an oath that they will decide the facts, and he will give them 'jury instructions'. Excuse me, friends, 'jury instructions' is nothing more or less than 'jury tampering', isn't it? Right away that tells you that we aren't dealing with Common Law; we're not dealing in justice. Now why isn't this jury verdict binding in this case? Because there's something different about this anchorwoman. I'm sure she went to public school and I'm sure she went into court and said, 'I'm an American citizen, I'm a voter and I've got rights.' All you have to do is look at the outcome and you can see she clearly didn't have the rights she thought she had.

Here's why:

If you're an American or British 'citizen' with a driver's licence and registration; you've been to college and got letters after your name; you're a 'somebody'. You've got a job making a lot of money and you probably vote. You may have privileges, you may have some immunities, you may have some permits and licences, but I'm afraid you don't have any rights. As a result of this rights issue, you don't have property because Admiralty doesn't deal with property; the Common Law deals with property. I don't know of many Americans or Britons who own property. There are a lot of Americans or Britons who claim to own property—believe they own property— but if we apply the law to it, I don't think so. I think they're practising 'the abolition of all right to property'— the first plank of the Communist manifesto—and that they have a 'chose in action', or they have an equitable right of interest, or possessory right to someone else's property.

It's a little like renting an Avis car and you say to yourself, 'I own this car.' I can see that you are in possession of it, I can see you're driving it and I can see you've got the keys to it but that's not your car, it belongs to the Avis Corporation. If we dig a little deeper and we ask ourselves, 'Does the Avis Corporation own this car?' I am sure they would say, 'Yes, this is a property right and we own that property.' I would take issue with that. I don't think the Avis Company owns that car either because on the front and the back of that vehicle there is a small oblong object called a licence plate and it will have a government identification number on there. I am pretty sure that car is 'registered'. Registered. If you look up the legal definitions of 'registration', 'property', 'ownership', 'chose in action', and 'equitable interest' in a law dictionary—Blacks or Ballantine's, for instance—I think it will become very clear to you very quickly that the Avis company doesn't own that car either.

I think you'll find that the government owns that car.

Painting in broad brush strokes here, let's take a look at why I can say that with such confidence.

The two contending systems of law in the world today that are in constant ideological conflict with one another are the Common Law and the Roman civil law.

J. Reuben Clark, a former US Under-Secretary of State and Ambassador to Mexico, clearly stated the rules and applications of these two systems of law when he wrote:

'Briefly, and stated in general terms, the basic concept of these two systems was as opposite as the poles.

In the Civil Law, the source of all law is the personal ruler, whether, Prince, king, or emperor; he is sovereign. In the Common Law, certainly as developed in America, the source of all law is the people. They, as a whole, are sovereign. During the centuries, these two systems have had an almost deadly rivalry for the control of society, the Civil Law and its fundamental concepts being the instrument through which ambitious men of genius and selfishness have set up and maintained despotisms: the Common Law, with its basic principles, being the instrument through which men of equal genius, but with love of mankind burning in their souls, have established and preserved liberty and free institutions. The Constitution of the United States embodies the loftiest concepts yet framed of this exalted concept.'

So there's a clear distinction between Common-law and Admiralty jurisdiction. There are a couple of other things we should keep in mind, like Equity; that's Judge Judy, the small claims Judge.

You may recall the story of King Solomon; two ladies came to him and demanded custody of a child. King Solomon said, 'Let's be fair about this, we'll cut the baby in half and you can both have half each.' One of the women said, 'No, that will kill the child, don't kill it, give it to her,' whereas the second woman said, 'That's a great idea, Your Magnificentness, I want my half of that child.' Solomon reviewed the evidence and came to the conclusion that the second woman didn't care about the welfare or the interest of the child; she was just motivated by jealousy and was willing to kill the child in order to stop the first woman from having it. Solomon—using a little good judgment—decided that the first woman clearly had an interest in the child's welfare and was prepared to give it up in order to save its life. In any event, even if the child is not her biological offspring, it's better to give the child to the woman who cares whether or not it lives or dies. That is what Equity is all about.

The Common Law is just that, the law of the commoners; it's the rule of the land, and the people on the land, dealing with land, labour and substance. It's the law of property and it operates directly from the 'ultimate contract' called The Ten Commandments. I don't want to go off on a whole religious thing here, but I think even an atheist would agree that the Ten Commandments provide a fairly reliable moral compass. In my humble opinion, there are certain aspects to the Ten Commandments that work well for society— thou shalt not kill, though shalt not steal, and so on. Let's go with the general agreement that all 'Law' (the prevention of harm, injury or loss) comes from someone's God or Religion. Keeping that in mind, then, in Biblical terms, when God was making the deal with his people, he wasn't thinking about Admiralty or jury trials. He was thinking about a basic law for all of us to follow so that we could all live together, because there were many different races to take into consideration, as well as gender and age. The Common Law doesn't change, it's brutal; it's not kind, it's not gentle and it's not flexible. It was brutal when it was enacted, it was brutal when it was enforced and it is as brutal today as it was back then. That's why the Common Law is about as popular as pubic lice at an office Christmas party. We don't have to deal with contracts, there's no contract involved. If we catch you committing adultery we don't give you lethal injection, we don't lock you up for five years, we don't put a big 'A' on your forehead and parade you around in public; we take you out and chuck heavy lumps of stone at you until you croak. Job done. That's what the law requires. Common Law is black and white, there's no grey area.

What is it about adultery that you fail to grasp, friend? What is it about 'Thou shalt not steal' that you're having a problem with, comrade? Theft is theft, and theft is punishable.

We've tried the Common Law and we've rejected it resoundingly. There isn't a country in the world that maintains the standards of the Common Law to the letter. I don't know of any state in the US that punishes adultery, let alone kills people for it, and we certainly don't here in the United Kingdom. Sabbath breaking is another one. If you get caught breaking the Sabbath, the penalty is death. We want God out of our Government, that's the bottom line. Apparently, we want God out of our law, period.

The Golden Rule of the Common Law is and was, 'Do not unto others as you would not have others do unto you.' Common Law controlled and ruled the land of England before the reign of William the Conqueror, who conquered the Anglo-Saxons in 1066.

After William the Conqueror, the golden rule was changed to, 'Do unto others as you would have others do unto you.' You can easily see that the former is the higher form of the rule.

There was one part of England William wasn't able to conquer, the Inner City of London. I'm not talking about the metropolitan city that you call London, I'm talking about the one square mile sitting in the heart of London. The merchants had a defensive wall around it and had a system whereby they were able to use their ships to carry food up to their facilities and unload them out of Willam's reach. William built the White Tower to look down on the city to see why his men were losing. He finally decided that he wasn't going going to be able to take the City, and that his control was slipping, so he went to the merchants and said, 'What is it that you people want?'

The merchants replied, 'We want the Maritime law, we want the Law of Merchants.'

In those days they called it *Lex Mercantoria*. William, realising it was the most expedient solution to what was becoming a costly, time-consuming headache, relented, and the merchants got their law.

To this day, the inner city of London practices the Merchant's Law and, in fact, *the Queen has no jurisdiction over that one square mile*; the Lord Mayor of the City of London has to escort her into the city. It should be noted that The Bank of England is located in the city of London. Just like the Vatican sitting in the heart of Rome, the City of London is not part of England, it's a sovereign territory of and by itself, and has been since 1066.

In 1215, at Runnymede, the Barons of England forced King John to sign the Magna Carta, which became the basic document establishing the fundamental rights of the English people to this day. Most American colonists were well-schooled in the Common Law and—because many of them were merchants and traders—they also knew the merchant's law. They knew that the King and Parliament were forcing the Admiralty jurisdiction upon them and this finally motivated them to revolt.

As English society developed over the years, situations arose for which the courts of Common Law couldn't provide relief by any process; the disputes didn't involve property—they didn't involve any substance. The only remedy was to petition the King, who appointed his first minister to solve these problems. The minister was called a Chancellor and the relief granted was called Equity. Equity basically meant 'what would be fair if the Common Law principle was extended and applied to the case at hand?' As a result, England and America developed two distinct systems of law and courts, each having a unique and specific relevance and jurisdiction. Equity jurisdiction is designated *'in personum,'* a jurisdiction in which you don't have any rights but one to which you volunteer to be subject. In other words, we can submit to binding arbitration, but it has to be with our consent.

The Roman civil law—an ancient body of law—came before the Roman Empire, but helped to build it and ultimately survived Rome's untimely demise. The Romans had their maritime law, which was part and parcel of their civil law. The earliest recorded knowledge of Maritime Admiralty Law is in the Isle of Rhodes and dates back to about 900 BC.

Admiralty Maritime jurisdiction — firmly entrenched in the civil law system—is the law of the ruler, the rule of the sea, the rule of money, the law of the nobility; it deals with profits, taxes and contracts. It's predicated upon the Ten Planks of the Communist Manifesto, and the Ten Planks are simply a reincarnation of the ancient Babylonian mystery religions that have been around for about 5000 years. You can call it communism, you can call it socialism, you can call it Admiralty, you can call it the Roman civil law, but it is the exact opposite, the diametric opposite of the Ten Commandments, 180 degree opposite to The Bill of Rights and Constitution. You don't have to be on a ship at sea to come under Admiralty jurisdiction. The jurisdiction can apply simply because the issue falls within the scope of maritime law, such as the use of bills, notes, checks (cheques) and credit.

Admiralty primarily works on ships and on the ocean up to the high tide mark, but over the past 200 years, slowly but surely, like a bad smell taking over a room, Admiralty has moved inland. We see it operating in central Eastern Europe about as far from the coast as you can get. We see it operating in Kansas City, Missouri, with an 'ugly' anchorwoman suing because she's been wrongfully discharged. Why is she in an Admiralty Court and why is the jury only an advisory one? And if Admiralty law deals with ships and water and commerce and things like that, what does it have to do with this woman's wrongful discharge?

Commerce. We Brits and Americans eat commerce for breakfast, lunch and dinner. We have little groups called Chambers of Commerce in every city to promote commerce and don't forget, the American founding fathers wove commerce right into the Constitution, and prominently so. Commerce is opposite to property and property rights. We had a choice to make between property and commerce, and we chose Commerce. We want cheques and negotiable instruments, we want adjustable rate mortgages, we want to be able to buy a house with very little money down so that we can speculate on the value of that house into the future. We want to speculate under the terms of contracts, over time, for profit and gain, which generates income, for which we pay 'income tax'. And then we want to complain about Government and taxing policies and the pseudo-communist regime we seem to be under. Friends, I'm not sure that we can blame Government for this situation we're in; we can't make a choice and then complain about the outcome. That boat's just not going to float.

People often write to me and tell me they feel like England is the worst place in the world—worse than Communist China. The difference is that Communist countries haven't had any Common Law there to start with, so they don't complain about not having it, everybody works under Admiralty or the Roman civil law.

Admiralty contains a harsh set of rules and procedures where there are no 'rights'. In fact, there are no rights under any civil law jurisdiction, only privileges granted by the Captain of the maritime venture. Obama is that Captain. Gordon Brown is that Captain on the great ship United Kingdom in a maritime adventure, practising the Ten Planks of the Communist Manifesto, under Admiralty.

In Admiralty, there is no right not to testify against yourself in a criminal matter. However, the Captain can, if he wishes, grant the privilege against self-incrimination. There's no such thing as a right to use your property on the motorways of the United Kingdom, but the Captain can grant the privilege to do so. There's no such thing as a right to operate a public business. It's only a privilege allowed so long as you perform according to the Captain's rules and regulations.

There are 2.5 million statutes in the West, and they're all done by contract, specifically by adhesion contracts. An adhesion contract—that's probably a contract you don't know anything about, and you don't have to know anything about the terms and conditions of these contracts to be bound by them. A warranty, for instance, that's an adhesion contract. Driver's licences, marriage licences, business licences, Social Security, the dole—they're all adhesion contracts.

Of course, we Brits and Americans—and Canadians and New Zealanders and Australians—we contract all the time. We contract with our Government and with corporations, and the corporations contract with the Government; it's a very incestuous relationship, a relationship based on money and power. The corporations have the money and the Government has the power. The people have neither.

Do you have a contract that would bind you to Admiralty? Most people do, they have Social Security numbers and drivers' licences and permits or marriage licences, business licences and—perhaps most ominously—birth certificates. Which brings us conveniently to the subject of 'enlistment papers'.

An 'enlisted' chap is one who has agreed to the terms and conditions in the contract of that particular area of law. Enlistment papers are what you receive when you join the contract, when you join the union. Your Social Security account number, or your national insurance number serves as your 'enlistment papers' in Admiralty jurisdiction in that subject matter called Social Security. Your driver's licence serves as your 'enlistment papers' in that regulated activity called 'driving'. When you go to a National Forest and you get a camping permit, it serves as your 'enlistment papers' in that regulated activity called 'camping'. When you get a marriage licence, that licence serves as your 'enlistment papers' for the regulated activity called 'marriage'. Business licences serve as your papers in the activity called 'business', and so on. Admiralty Jurisdiction is constantly being modified and expanded by countless enactments. Admiralty law, friends, changes like the tides.

There are thirty-seven of these regulated enterprises; activities that you may be involved in that will bring you into Admiralty jurisdiction. It's not strictly called Admiralty and you'll have great difficulty getting a Judge to admit that you're in an Admiralty

Court. The civil law was never part of the law of England and has never been declared as laws of the realm by the parliament, nor by any experts of English jurisprudence, such as Blackstone for instance.

But if it looks like a duck and it quacks like a duck...

A contract is legally defined as 'an offer with acceptance over time with consideration'.

Consideration is usually money but there has to be reciprocity. There has to be an offer, there has to be acceptance and there has to be a time frame. If any one of those elements is missing, you don't have a contract, but every one of those elements is in place with a driver's licence. Yet, when you go to the dictionary and you look up 'licence', it will imply that a licence is not a contract. And they tell you that Social Security is not a contract. Well, excuse me, Social Security makes an offer, we accept it, there's a time frame and there is consideration. Can you say, 'Quack'?

A rose by any other name; you can call it anything you like but that's a duck, right there. Just for practical purposes, when you've got an offer with acceptance over time with consideration, you've got yourself a contract, and when you've got a contract, it's going to be settled in Admiralty. See how simple that is? There might be an exception or two but that's the general rule.

These contracts have consequences. When you sign up for the driver's licence, you're inviting the traffic policemen to come into your life. When you sign up for that business licence, when you're acting in trade, commerce, business and industry, then you're asking the state to get involved in your business. When you join the army you're asking someone to run your life—they tell you when to get up in the morning, when to go to bed, and what to do in between. There's little or no freedom involved with these Admiralty contracts.

Now, all contracts are voluntary. There isn't a single obligatory contract on the entire planet. You have the right to contract and the right not to contract. You see, it's a bit like joining the army—there's a voluntary action in joining the army. But what goes on after you've joined, after you've signed the contract, is mandatory.

Let's suppose you're sitting on your bunk and the sergeant comes in and tells you he wants to inspect your footlocker. You look at him and you say, 'Sarge, have you got a search warrant?' Do you believe the sergeant needs a search warrant to search your footlocker?

Here we are complaining that we have no rights, but we

waived all of our rights when we voluntarily got a national insurance number, our social insurance number or our Social Security number. We waived our rights when we got the employment contract. We waived our rights when we got our drivers licences and marriage licences and we registered our children with the Government. You see, we can't complain about the Government trying to vaccinate our children, we can't complain about social services getting involved with our children's lives and dragging them off to foster homes. We can't complain about the social worker knocking on our doors to check on our children, because they're not our children, they belong to the state. When you registered your child you handed over title to it and you got a birth certificate, 'certificate of title' in return. Again, look up the legal definition of the word 'registration' and get a good sense of what you've actually done with your children. The social worker doesn't need a search warrant. You've got to have a marriage licence, a birth certificate and citizenship to get the social worker to pay you a visit. Let's think about that one for a minute.

Let's suppose that the French ambassador to the United Nations is living in London and he has a twelve-year-old child. The child is romping around at eleven o'clock in the morning or two o'clock in the afternoon and a social worker or a truant officer sees him playing in the street during school hours. She walks up to him and says, 'Hey you, how come you're not in school?' and the little scallywag says, 'Get lost, lady, I don't have to answer your questions.' So she grabs the little fella and hauls him off to juvenile hall, or wherever it may be. She calls his father in, who is the ambassador from the country of France but is stationed here in London. Maybe he's been here for five years, maybe he has a flat in central London. He speaks English, he looks English, acts English, eats English food but he's not English, he's French and his child is French. They're both 'registered' in France. He doesn't have his child enrolled in school and social worker lady is a little upset at that because he is worth £30 a day in school. On the street he's not worth anything. Now, how do you think that case is going to work out? Do you think that the father is going to plead 'not guilty' and cry in front of Judge Judy, or do you think he's going to raise a jurisdictional challenge based on citizenship and tell her to mind her own business? He'll probably say, 'I've got diplomatic immunity. I might look like an enlisted British seaman, I might act like an enlisted British seaman, but I'm not one of yours.'

You have to have a contract in place before the court can haul you in for a traffic infringement, before the court can have jurisdiction over you, you have to have a driver's licence. Before the divorce court can have jurisdiction over you, you have to have a marriage licence. Same deal with business licences and court. Now, don't go jumping in at the deep end here and open a store on Oxford Street without a business licence—remember you're also a party to the social contract. Abraham Lincoln made the observation that Government is done by the will of the people; done by the people, for the people and he was referring to the contract, the social contract that we citizens have with the countries that we live in. I'm living here in Great Britain and I have a social contract under a number of documents and laws and rules and regulations that I've never even read, but they are binding upon me all the same.

If you're going to deal in trade, commerce, business and industry, you come under what's called the 'commerce clause'. 'Private' business is a different animal entirely. I'm aware of one or two businesses that operate solely in the private, they don't affect trade, commerce, business or industry and don't affect any 'public' interest. How do you like that? I know some will be reading this and thinking, 'You doofus, AT, how do they get any clients without operating in the public?' Believe me, they have no shortage of clients; they're all 'private' clients. They don't come under Admiralty Law, and they're very careful not to get a business licence. They have nothing to do with VAT (purchase tax) and they have to be very careful about the way they conduct their business so that they don't infringe upon Admiralty, so that they don't infringe upon the Roman Civil Law. The trick here is to obey all the laws all of the time, which is tricky but not impossible. You might say, 'You can't practice all the laws, all the time'. Sure you can; they do. If they can do it, with a minimal, very basic state-funded, comprehensive education, I'm sure that you can. After all, you're smarter than they are, as evidenced by the fact you've got letters after your name, you could do it at least as well as they do, and probably exceed their efforts.

If you don't have a Social Security number, or a national insurance number, you won't have any contact with the Inland Revenue or the IRS—unless, of course, you're out there operating in trade, commerce, business and industry, depositing your Bank of England notes or Federal Reserve notes into a bank. But if you're working in private business and trading your labour, which is property, for gold and silver, which is property, in a property-for-property transaction, you're never going to hear from the IRS or the Inland

Revenue. If you buy a house and pay for it in gold coin and work on that house and fix it up then sell the house for gold coin, you'll never hear from the Government. Now, don't write me an e-mail and say that's impossible, it's done every day in certain circles. It's just that most of us don't know how to do it.

Admiralty law covers all issues that come from acts done on or relating to the sea and questions of 'prize'. Prize is that law dealing with war and the spoils of war, such as the capture of ships, goods, materials and property, both real and personal. Every once in a while a traffic policy enforcement officer will stop a car on the M1 motorway and they'll find a few hundred thousand pounds in the boot, or they'll find that it's full of drugs. They seize the person, they seize the car, they seize the money and they seize the drugs. These are called 'Admiralty prizes'. And the M1 is a long way from the ocean.

Admiralty prizes come under the fourth plank of the Communist manifesto, which calls for the 'seizure of the property of immigrants and rebels'. Many years ago, the Queen of England said 'I'm going to offer a prize to my sea captains that go out and capture Spanish and French ships. You go out there with one of my navy ships and capture any one of those French or Spanish ships, bring it in here and I'll give you some land, or some gold. I'll pay you.' So the captains went out on a pirating spree, motivated by the prize. Inevitably, various nations came to the conclusion, 'If the English are going to steal our ships, then we're going to steal their ships.' All's fair in love and war, after all.

A chap goes down to the airport with £5000 in cash in his pocket. He buys a ticket with the cash and, because the ticket agent has to report transactions of £5000 and over, she informs the relevant authorities. The police detain him, take his £5000 cash and he then has to prove that he's paid his taxes and that it isn't drug money. That's an Admiralty prize right there.

A young lad of about 25 years old is in court, with a barrister, an undercover police officer, the Judge and the usher. There are just five people in this play; the court is otherwise empty.

The barrister puts the undercover police officer on the stand.

'Officer, on June 13 where you at the 'Skittles' bowling and pool hall?

'Yes, yes I was.'

'And while you were in the Skittles bowling and pool hall, did you see Stephen Perkins there?'

'Yes, I did.'

'And is Stephen Perkins in court here today?'

'Yes, he is'

'Could you point him out, please?'

(Pointing). 'Yes, there he is, right there at the defence table.'

'Did you know of Mr Perkins before you saw him at the pool hall?'

'Yes, I did.'

'Did you know that Mr Perkins was a convicted drug dealer and user?'

'Yes'

'Did you know that he was on parole?'

'Yes, I did'

'Did you go over and search him?'

'Yes, I did'

'And when you searched him, did you find anything?'

'Yes, I found £1500 in cash on him.'

'Did you seize the £1500?'

'Yes, I did.'

'Did you submit that £1500 to a laboratory examination.'

'Yes, I did'

'And what did they find?'

'They found that 80% of the money had cocaine residue on it.'

The Judge turns to the defendant and says, 'Do you have anything you want to say? Do you have any witnesses or evidence to support your case? Do you want to take the stand in your own defence?'

'No, I don't.'

Turning back to the Barrister. 'Do you have any closing arguments?'

'Well, Mr Perkins is a convicted drug dealer. We tested the £1500 in cash that he had on his person and 80% it was found to have cocaine residue on it, so therefore we think it is drug money and it ought to be forfeited to the Crown.'

'Thank you very much.' The Judge then turns back to the Defendant. 'Do you have a closing statement, Mr Perkins?'

'You had better believe I do, Judge. 80% of all money in circulation has cocaine residue on it. I am an employee of a contractor and that was my paycheck. On Friday I got £1500 and I went to the bank and Jackie the clerk cashed my cheque for me. I went down to the pool hall and was buying a few rounds of beers and having a good time, minding my own business. I haven't touched drugs for a long time and I'm as clean as you can be. You should give me back my £1500 because that's my money, earned lawfully and legally in the contracting business.'

'Thank you very much.'

So, the Judge renders his verdict.

'Based upon all of the witnesses, evidence and testimony that has been presented here today, the court finds that the state has proved its case. The case is now closed.'

If Perkins wanted to win his case, it would be fairly easy. He needed to subpoena his boss and subpoena Barbara the bank clerk. Barbara would have said, 'Yes, he came in about five o'clock and I cashed his £1500 cheque for him.'

He could have subpoenaed in the cheque. He could have brought his boss in under subpoena and said, 'Hey Boss, do I work for you? Did you pay me £1500 for the month?'

He could have proven his case, he just didn't know how. He's in Admiralty, there is no jury, and the £1500 is an Admiralty prize.

There shouldn't be Admiralty prizes and the Government shouldn't be taking people's property away from them, but you also have to bear in mind that Stephen Perkins has a parole agreement; that's a contract. He decided he wanted to get out of prison early, so he gave up his rights and signed a parole contract, which he was probably in breach of.

The pertinent question might be, how can we defend ourselves against something we don't even understand?

The answer—we are not meant to understand it. We live in tyranny and we don't even know it. How can we collectively oppose it if most people don't even know there is a problem?

What you really have going on here is just organized theft—it's just Mafioso-type theft that goes on in national circles with Governments. The United States and the United Kingdom goes over to Iraq to steal their oil in a corporate takeover. What's happening here in reality is just business. We're just dealing in trade, commerce, business and industry. Governments and corporations do it all the time but when you and I do it, we're breaking some law or other. That's what these statutes are all about; they are designed to keep you out of the monopolies.

We go to the Government and we get a driver's licence application and we sign the little document that goes in our wallet. Your signature is your agreement to the terms and conditions of the contract, but the terms and conditions are written in the statutes, not in the document you just signed. Most of us have never read those thousands of statutes. I'll bet any money you like right now there isn't a police officer in the United Kingdom or the United States, or Canada, New Zealand, or anywhere else for that matter, who has read all of those statutes. I'll go so far as to say there isn't a politician, prime minister, or member of the House of Lords who has actually read all of those statutes, either. Judges certainly don't read them. The only time a Judge is ever interested in a particular traffic statute is when some policy enforcement officer drags you into court. Only then will the Judge get the book out, look at the statute while listening to you lie about doing whatever it was you were doing. That's the way this aspect of what they like to call 'law' works. These Judges don't have time to memorise all of the thousands of statutes, rules and regulations, not while the sun is out anyway; not while there is golf to be played and mistresses to be serviced.

We have to have rules and regulations, and the Common Law doesn't fit in very well with those rules and regulations as they relate to property. So back in 1932/33 our Governments came up with a plan. In the United States, for instance, they said, 'Our Constitution is in the way of the happiness and success of the American people so—rather than amend our constitution—what we'll do is we'll create more contracts; drivers licences, marriage licences, and so on—we'll enlist all of the citizens of America as merchant seamen in various aspects of Admiralty jurisdiction'. In Admiralty, you're an enlisted seaman on their ship. By contracting with them, you agreed that you will follow the orders of the Captain and if you don't follow those orders, as I will explain shortly, if necessary, that Captain can kill you. Need I remind you that Captain is a military term?

Let's suppose you're on a plane and the Captain flips on the no-smoking sign, and you sit back and light up a Benson & Hedges. A stewardess comes over and she says, 'Sir, would you please put out that cigarette, this is a no smoking flight and the no smoking sign is clearly on.'

So, you give her the finger and say, 'Get lost, lady, I'm going to enjoy this cigarette while I sip my Jack Daniels.' So she goes up to the cockpit and she tells the Captain that you won't put it out. The

Captain comes back and tells you the same. You tell the Captain exactly where he can get off.

See, unbeknownst to you, because you're not in the cockpit and you can't see all the instruments, maybe there's a leak in the gas tank somewhere. Maybe there's a very good reason why the captain insists you put out your cigarette, other than just trying to spoil your fun and wreck your flight. Maybe there is a real hazard involved here, maybe there is a threat to the health and safety and welfare of this maritime adventure, flying from London to New York. So the Captain has a duty to protect the plane—for the stockholders of British Airways, for himself and for the other three hundred passengers. Someone has to be in charge here; there have to be rules and they have to be enforced. The Captain can't just dial 999 and call for the local police, 'We've got this idiot here who won't put a cigarette out and he's threatening the safety of my passengers.' You're 35,000 feet up in the air. So the Captain then has to use some sort of force.

You've got the Captain, the co-pilot and the flight engineer, and then you've got a few stewards and stewardesses; maybe eight to ten crew members in total and their job is to keep order on the plane. The Captain grabs you by the arm, he takes the cigarette out of your mouth and he stomps it out on the floor. You get belligerent with him and you start giving him lip, and he tries to restrain you, but maybe you're a little stronger than he is. He has to bring in a couple of stewards to help, but you're clearly a very strong guy. We've got three men trying to restrain you unsuccessfully, and someone forgot to recharge the batteries on the tazer. Eventually the Captain says, 'Well, no hard feelings,' and he pulls out a pistol and shoots you twice in the chest. He had to use lethal force in order to maintain order. Admiralty jurisdiction.

When you're on an plane, or on a ship, or in the army, because of the circumstances of the events that take place, and the location in which these events take place, we've developed a different form of 'law' and it has to be adapted from time to time as changing conditions might require. Ordinarily, we'd let you smoke, but sometimes—depending on what the changing conditions might require—somebody has to be in charge and we call him the Captain. This Captain has unusual, extraordinary powers. He has the power of life and death on board the plane, and when you buy a ticket to get on that plane, you agree to the terms and conditions of maritime law as it applies to airlines, or on ships, or in the army. Now this doesn't mean the Captain gets to kill passengers just because he doesn't like them, it simply means that if the circumstance gets to where something drastic has to be done to stop you from causing harm or criminal damage, then he's got to do what he's got to do.

I'm not opposed to Admiralty; I'm not trying to overthrow it. However, I don't think Admiralty is as good as the Common Law—it certainly has nothing to do with a justice system—but, as I said, it's not designed for justice, it's designed for adversarial proceedings and I think that in context it works pretty well. There has to be someone on board the Standard Oil tanker who says, 'There's no smoking on this ship,' and someone has to have the power to enforce those rules. I know it may seem harsh, I know it may seem unusual, but that's the way the game has got to be played.

Let's suppose you're in a bar in London and somebody slips a drug into your drink, you pass out and they load you on to a ship. You wake up the next morning and you're 100 miles out beyond the Thames estuary on your way to Shanghai. You've been kidnapped—Shanghaied. You've got a Common Law action against the ship, the ship's owners and the Captain. Where are you going to bring your action? You're 100 miles out to sea and you got this Captain who has the power of life and death over the crewman on the ship; if you mutiny on his ship, he can bury you at sea. You're not in a very good position here. So you shut your mouth and you go to Shanghai and eventually you return to London. Now, you've got an action, and you need to sue the Captain and the owners of the ship and you're going to bring this up as a property right. They kidnapped you—that's a violation of the Common Law—but they took you off the land and out to sea—Common Law doesn't apply because the Common Law stops at the high tide mark. As your complaint is against the Captain and the owners of the ship, this is an Admiralty jurisdiction matter. You're a Common Law citizen in an Admiralty case and you've got a tough battle ahead of you.

Let's suppose again that you're walking down the street in Manhattan and an MP (military police officer) comes up to you and says, 'Hey, you, you're under arrest, I'm taking you back to the Army Barracks.' So you're arrested right off the street, he loads you into a jeep and carts you off to a military base and you end up in the brig. They bring you into a military court and they say, 'You are charged with being 'absent without leave' from the Army Barracks. How do you plead? Guilty or not guilty?'

Now, you've been watching television—say, Ironside or Judge Judy—so you know how to plead and you plead, 'Not guilty'. From that point on, you're going to be convicted of being absent without leave from the Army Barracks and you can't win. The reason you can't win is because you're in an Admiralty Court and they have jurisdiction over you because this is where you are; they have physical possession of you, so they have *'in personum'* jurisdiction. They've got jurisdiction over soldiers who are 'AWOL' and you just admitted to being a soldier when you plead 'not guilty'. You see, only an enlisted soldier, in a military jurisdiction can 'plead guilty or not guilty'.

The correct procedure in a case like this would be to 'Demur'. A 'Demur' is a challenge to the jurisdiction of the court. Rather than plead into the 'fiction of law' that you're a soldier by pleading 'not guilty', you might plead *'non assumpsit* by way of confession and avoidance' in a Demur, with a *Subpoena Duces Tecum* to compel the prosecution to bring forward the enlistment contract that proves that you're a soldier in the army. 'Yes, it's true, I am absent without leave from the Army Barracks and I don't deny it BUT I do deny being a soldier in the army and I demand that you produce the enlistment papers that give you jurisdiction; the military enlistment contract. I'm not a soldier and I don't have any agreement with you people.'

If you plead 'not guilty', what you are saying is, 'I agree with the prosecution that the issue to be decided here is 'am I or am I not absent from the Army Barracks.' Well, friends, if you were arrested in Manhattan, the guy who arrested you is going to testify that he found you in Manhattan, so obviously you were absent from the Army Barracks, weren't you? The real issue to be argued here is 'Am I or am I not a soldier in the army?' not 'Am I or am I not absent from the Army Barracks?'

At the risk of over-articulating this point, for the sake of being really clear, picture this: you're just having a good time on board a cruise liner—as you do—playing shuffleboard, and all of a sudden the second mate comes up to you and says, 'Hey, Jimmy,' and you look at him like a dog that's just been shown a new card trick. He says, 'I'm ordering you to go down to the engine room and shovel coal,' and then he walks off.

You say, 'What the hell was that all about?' and continue to play shuffleboard with your buddy.

A little while later, the First Mate comes back and says, 'Hey, you, didn't I tell you to go shovel coal in the boiler room?'

'Yep, I heard you.'

'Did you go shovel coal?'

'No, I stayed right here, I've been playing shuffleboard all morning.'

'You're under arrest, I'm taking you down to the brig.'

He then arrests you and you end up staring at four walls below deck. Next morning at ten o'clock, they bring you up to the Captain's quarters and the Captain says, 'Is it true, the report I received about you, Jimmy, that you were ordered to go down to the boiler room and shovel coal and you didn't do it?'

Maybe you're a Christian and you cannot tell a lie and you say, 'Yeah, it's true, he ordered me to shovel coal and I didn't do it.'

'Well, how do you plead to this charge of insubordination then, Jimmy? Guilty or not guilty?'

Jimmy, if you plead 'guilty' then you admit that you have a duty to shovel coal and you didn't do it and therefore all we have to do is administer the punishment. If you plead 'not guilty' then we've got to give you a trial, we've got to bring in witnesses, evidence and testimony and let you cross-examine those witnesses and the Captain's going to ask you, 'Did the First Mate come along and address you by the name Jimmy?'

'Yep'

'Did he tell you to go shovel coal?'

'Yep'

'Did you go shovel coal?'

'Nope'

'Did you willfully refuse to shovel coal?'

'Yep'

'Did you continue to play shuffleboard?'

'Yup, I did.'

'Did you win or lose the shuffleboard game?'

'I won'

'Okay, next witness.'

When all is said and done, the only thing we need to decide in this case after you pled, 'not guilty' is did you or did you not shovel coal.

What tends to happen in some of these cases that come up in court over taxes is you walk in and plead 'not guilty'. Maybe you're being charged with tax evasion or willful failure to file. By pleading 'not guilty', friends, you have just confessed to being a 'taxpayer'. People with Social Security numbers are taxpayers. So, the next question is, did you or did you not fail to pay your taxes?

Don't you think that, maybe, if you were a non-taxpayer you'd be better off walking in there with an amendment to the pleadings, saying, 'Hang on there, Judge, Do you have any evidence that I'm even a citizen (employee) of the United States Corporation? If I am a 'citizen', what is a 'citizen', legally speaking, and how did I become one? Can you point to the contract? Was I told it was actually a contract, and was there full disclosure when I signed it? Once you've done that, you've got to prove that I had 'income'. Legally speaking, what is 'income'?'

I wouldn't plead into a 'fiction of law', but most people do. Most people don't even understand what a 'fiction of law' is, but it's pretty pervasive in Admiralty courts because they presume that everybody is 'enlisted', a seaman under contract. They presume that you've got a national insurance number, a driver's licence, a marriage licence, a business licence, and so on. It would be highly unusual for you not to have at least one of those but your job is to rebut their presumptions from the get-go.

When you walk into a court yelling and screaming, 'You can't bring me into Admiralty,' that's simply not true. Once they get you in there, they'll listen to your motion to amend, or your demurral, and see whether they want to proceed in Admiralty, or move into Common law, or into Equity. The Judge can look at commerce and bring you in, or they can look at some other aspect of the case and determine that Admiralty is the way to proceed; essentially, the Judge determines how to proceed based upon your pleadings.

The pleadings are the single most important aspect of law to learn because once the pleading section is closed by the question, 'Are you ready to move forward?' it's a dead-letter issue. If you want to raise the issue of being a passenger and not a crewman on the ship , you needed to do that at the pleading section because once this degenerates into trial, you can't raise that issue again, and you certainly can't raise it on appeal. You can't raise anything on appeal that you didn't raise in the pretrial pleadings.

I suspect that many of these people who are trying to act as *pro se* litigants are getting themselves into trouble because they just don't understand the rules of the game. And, of course, the rules are not meant to be understood by us plebs. Judges will listen to you if you have something intelligent to say but if you go in there flapping your gums and there's nothing intelligent coming out of your mouth, the Judge isn't going to give you the time of day.

Now you might decide to head out onto the motorway in your car without a driver's licence and you might say to yourself, 'I don't have a driver's licence, I don't have a contract, so therefore I can drive my car on the public road with impunity.' Well, you've got a couple of problems that are still there to overcome. Number one, whose car is that? Number two, whose road is that?

When you're taken to the traffic courts, it's alleged that you breached your contract—there's a duty that you have that you didn't perform.

First duty is that you didn't get a drivers licence. There is also a property dispute; the state is claiming that you're driving their vehicle on their road without their permission and you're contending that you're driving your conveyance on your road because it's a public right of way. You don't own that car and it's not a public right of way. That's what the controversy is all about.

We have an assumption that these are public rights of way and, in some cases there may well be some that are still public rights of way, but most of them are Government-owned motorways and highways. This is property owned by a corporation called the United Kingdom, or the state of Oregon, or the United States. There was a time when we had public rights of way but that is just about passed.

You're trying to operate an Avis car on the United Kingdom Corporation motorway without a licence and that isn't going to fly very far.

There's quite a difference between bringing up an issue of 'right to travel' in the usual and ordinary conveyance of the day on a public right of way, as opposed to making a claim that you've got a right to drive somebody else's registered vessel on a Corporation-owned motorway. That licence plate on the front and back of your vehicle is effectively a flag. If you didn't have the flag of the United Kingdom Corporation on your car, and if you could claim that car as property, and if you could claim that you weren't licenced and therefore you had rights, you might have a better argument, but most of the time people don't have all their dominoes in a row. They might just have four dominoes out of five in a row. Friends, you have to have all of them in a row; you have to own the car and have the title to it, you have to be unlicensed, you can't use that car on their roads, and you can't have a Social Security number.

And I don't know many people who can make that kind of a claim.

When Congress and Parliament enacts legislation like the Patriot Act or *Corpus Juris*, they're not acting in the interest of Equity or the course of the Common law, they're acting in the course of Admiralty, because that's where the money is. The state doesn't make any money from the Common law, and you can forget Judge Judy and Equity, that's a service that costs money. Traffic courts and marriage licences, that's moneymaking stuff right there, that's where Governments rake in a fortune—taxation is what it boils down to.

You know, Bush wasn't wrong about all those searches you heard about from the intellectual prostitutes on the media. There wasn't anything that Bush was going after that he needed a warrant for. The president's not in violation of any laws, that's all been adjudicated long ago. He doesn't have to bow down to the Constitution—that's why Bush said it was just a piece of paper. Now pay close attention:

The president of The United States doesn't have to worry about the constitution or your rights because they're not a part of his corporate charter. The elements of the Constitution that you hold so dear have been tolerated since the United States was incorporated all those years ago and now he is just stripping them away, simply because they're impeding his commercial progress, the progress of his corporation. The president of the United States is operating in Admiralty jurisdiction as a businessman running a corporation. He can remove any element of the constitution he wants, and he wouldn't be breaking any laws, because he is not operating in the Common Law, which the constitution is based on.

Iraq was a corporate takeover. It's nothing personal, its just business. There's oil there, and we want it. We're a rich, powerful corporation and we are going to buy you out. Or make you an offer you can't refuse.

You don't have a right to privacy—there is no contingency to privacy in Admiralty jurisdiction, none whatsoever. There's no right to have a gun in Admiralty jurisdiction, and that's why all you guys out there in the States with licensed weapons are going to lose your weapons first because you registered them; you handed over title to the Government.

The Government now owns your weapon, they have a controlling share in the contract with you and they can remove it from you anytime they like because it's more theirs than yours. You gave up your claim to property and property rights and adopted the first plank to the Communist manifesto, the abolition of all rights to property. You got what you wanted—you asked for it—what are you complaining about? However, you guys out there who have unregistered, unlicensed weapons, you're going be fine as long as you don't register them.

Except, of course, then it's just a case of the Government taking them from you using unlawful force…

Law stands mute in the midst of arms.
MARCUS TULLIUS CICERO

As far as I can see, the only people who can be involved in Social Security are people who can't count because if at any time you people learned how to count and were able to do the math concerning Social Security, you'll find that it's the poorest retirement programme that was ever devised by the mind of man. I don't know of anything that pays as poorly as Social Security; if there's anything out there that is as poor a programme as Social Security, e-mail me and let me know, would you? No insurance company in the United Kingdom or the United States can pay you back a penny less than what you paid in—only Social Security can do that. Social Security hurts the smartest people most; people with the most talent and the highest incomes get screwed the hardest by Social Security. I guess it is poetic justice, for being educated idiots. If you're a doctor, or a lawyer, or a real estate broker making £50,000-100,000 a year or more, you're up in the top 5% of income earners—95% of us chumps make less than you do—you are paying the maximum Social Security payment possible.

Let's say for argument's sake that it's £8,000 a year over 45 years, which works out at £360,000. When you retire you get approximately £800 per month, so let's work out what that means. How long are you going to live? Let's say you are going to retire at 65 and you going to live till you're 75, taking the average into consideration. So, we take £800 per month times 120 months… that's £96,000. You paid in £360,000 and you get £96,000 back. Good deal, eh? And you've got a degree with letters after your name. Could you do worse than that? Could you put £360,000 into any other insurance scheme and get a worse return than that? Insurance companies aren't allowed to do that, not in the US or the UK, as far as I'm aware. Yet, Social Security does it.

As far as you blue-collar workers are concerned—you labourers—you think your boss is paying half of that for you, don't you?

I've got news for you, friend, your boss isn't paying a single penny of it, you're paying all of it and you pay it through your labour. It's your labour that creates all of the wealth, every bloody penny of it, every cent.

You labourers out there, let me tell you, from the perspective of the boss—because I'm the employer, the CEO—let me tell you it's the hired help that produces every damn penny. And then out of that, I give you your paid holiday. Like I'm your great benefactor here, my friend. Where do you think I got the money to pay you to go on holiday? Didn't I get that from your labour? And where did you think I got the money to pay your half of the Social Security tax? Didn't I get that from your Labour? Where do you think I got the money to pay your unemployment tax? Did you think I'm just a really nice fella and I'm digging into my personal bank account to pay your unemployment tax for you?

So, you are a plumber working for 'Bob's Plumbing' on about $20 an hour—times that by 2000 hours a year is $40,000. You're paying 16% to Social Security, we'll say $6500 per year. Let's times that by 45 years: $300,000. You are going to earn $300,000, which gets paid into the Social Security fund for you. Have you worked out how much you are going to get back? Where do you think the rest of it went?

Social Security is a classic case of Admiralty and if you've got a Social Security complaint, Social Security has its own administrative Law Court. No juries, of course, you're dealing with a summary administrative process.

Back in 1848, the US Supreme Court ruled that under the Common Law, ship owners were liable for the acts of their ship Captains. In other words, if a party was to ship goods on board a ship and something happened to the goods—being destroyed or damaged by the perils of the sea—the ship owner was responsible to the owner of the goods. If the ship owner didn't pay the debt, the owner of the goods could sue the ship owner and collect. If the ship owner failed to pay, the creditor could then file a lien on the ship, called a maritime lien, which doesn't require possession of the object.

Ship owners decided they didn't want to be responsible for the goods they were transporting on their ships, so they went to Congress and conspired to bring about the Limited Liability Act of 1851, which was followed up in 1855 in the United Kingdom. The Act protected the ship owners from their carelessness or their liability to their customers. As a result of these acts, persons will no longer be drawn into ownership of ships because of a liability involved. Shipping on the high seas is very risky and it was especially so at that time. Shipping then was the only means of commerce and the above acts would drastically reduce commerce in both the United States and the United Kingdom, and commerce is where Government makes all of its money.

In those days, our countries made their money by import and export taxes, so when countries wanted to come into the United States or the United Kingdom to sell their goods, they had to pay tax, which financed our Governments. The purpose of this act—amended many times since—was to limit the liability for the payment of debts of persons who were ship owners involved in maritime commerce. Seamen, enlisted. That's you.

Limited Liability is insurance—it's the exact opposite of strict liability. We want to practise limited Liability because we don't want to be responsible for our actions.

Let's suppose you're driving down the road, you have an accident and it's your fault and there's about £30,000 worth of damage. You don't want to pay that £30,000, you'd rather pay £500 a year in premium to the insurance company. Right? If you have an accident you become the winner in a bet. You bet, in effect, that you were going to have an accident and it was going to cost £30,000. The insurance company, by contrast, has bet that you are not going to have an accident costing £30,000, but if you do, they will pay for the accident plus the costs of litigation. So you go out there and, sure enough, you have an accident and you get to collect on the bet.

How many of those accidents occur? The insurance companies aren't stupid; they are masters at figuring out the odds. They've done the calculations, and here in the UK every driver—statistically—has one accident every 32 years, which costs on average £2000 to repair, and they price their premiums accordingly. Now you figure out, friends, how many accidents you've had in the past, how much is your insurance bill today and whether or not you've paid more in premiums than you've collected in benefits. I don't know anyone who's collected more in benefits than they've paid in insurance premiums, do you? We people have been propagandised into believing that we wouldn't dare live a day of our lives without insurance.

Just take a look at your house. Have you got fire insurance on your house? £100-£200 per year? When was the last time your house burned to the ground? When was the last time the fire department had to put the fire out in your house? Never? That's about right. I woke up to the insurance scam a while back. I used to have insurance; I've not always been awake. I bought insurance because I was told to. On the very few occasions I've tried to make a claim on my insurance policy, they fought like angry badgers not to pay me. I thought that was a little odd. I thought these chaps were a little like Las Vegas, when you win on the slot machine and they turn on all the bells and whistles and get all excited and take your picture, but they're not. I came to the realization that if you have a claim you almost have to sue them to get them to pay out, unless it's something quite minor and it's to their advantage to pay off so that you don't sue them for more.

On a £200,000 house, the insurance companies require £200,000 worth of coverage. The average fire only costs around £20,000, usually a kitchen grease fire. So common sense would say insure your place for £20,000 but if you do, there is a clause in the contract that says if the house isn't fully insured, the insurance company will only pay the pro rated amount of the insurance purchased. So if you've got a £200,000 house and you're buying £20,000 worth of insurance and you have a kitchen grease fire and it costs £20,000, the insurance company won't pay you £20,000, they'll only pay you £2000, because you only insured your house for about 10% of its value.

The insurance company works with the banks and your Government. In the case of Government, they require that all drivers have insurance. Of course they give you freedom here; we've got to have freedom, this is England, after all. You can buy this insurance, which is mandated by law, from any insurance company you want. Isn't that just fantastic? Insurance, by the way, is *prima facie* evidence of 'income'. You might want to look up 'income' in Black's Law Dictionary and see if it applies to you.

If the Government and the insurance companies can get together and compel you to buy car insurance, they can compel you to buy television sets and carpet, or anything they want, can't they? Think about it—if the Government can compel you to buy car insurance why can't they compel you to buy health insurance, life insurance, toothbrushes, furniture or bowling balls? Friends, you agreed to it in advance. Remember, joining Social Security and getting a national insurance number was voluntary, what goes after that voluntary action is mandatory.

So, you good folks down in New Orleans bought hurricane insurance, remember? And then you had a hurricane, called Katrina, remember that? Then this tidal surge came in, destroyed the levee and washed your houses away. You didn't buy flood insurance, did you? The insurance company told you they weren't paying. 'We collected your premiums for 20 years but we aren't paying because you didn't have flood insurance and you had a flood. That is what destroyed your house.'

Friends, you said you'd rather play the game of limited liability with an insurance company, than practice strict liability under the Common Law. So you got your limited liability—you paid your premiums but they won't pay you out. How is it working out for you? That's Admiralty. You can go and sue them if you want but you'll probably lose. Isn't that just wonderful?

Now of course, we make our choices in life, there are choices that simply have to be made. When you make those choices, there are consequences or results that come from them. You're driving down the motorway, tootling along at 80 or 90 mph, and you approach a sign that says 'slow to 50 mph' and it has an arrow that shows a 90 degree turn and you have to make a decision. Shall I slow to 50, or should I carry on at the same speed? If you make the wrong choice, there are laws called gravity and inertia, and force and so on that's going to affect the outcome of your decision.

Limited liability is another of those choices you have to make. I have to choose whether or not I want life insurance. Maybe you haven't been paying your yearly health insurance, maybe your employer has. In truth, your employer hasn't paid a penny towards your health insurance, you can rest assured on that score. Bill Gates may be a wonderful chap but he isn't paying your health insurance. You're paying it yourself out of your productivity, your labour. He might send the cheque off, he might negotiate the policy but he isn't paying a penny of it. At the end of the twenty years, you're going to be down £'s or $'s. If you were to practice strict liability, and at the same time practiced healthy living, you wouldn't get ill and you'd have enough money to buy a decent property outright. Go figure.

Governments—in collusion with the insurance companies—are always going to be telling us all that we need health insurance. 'You could be walking down the street and inhale polio virus and get polio, or you could have an accident and you could get hurt and have all of these expenses to pay. You better have insurance.'

Let's say I lived outside the city, middle of absolute nowhere and I was out with the boys having a good old time getting mashed up on Jack Daniels. It comes to home-time and one of my buddies says to me, 'You're a mess, you ought to get a taxi.' I think about it for a second and say, 'Well, you know, I only live three miles from here down a country lane. I have a fully comprehensive insurance policy; I'm covered for hundreds of thousands of pounds. I don't think I can cause that much damage in 3 miles of open road.' So I get in my car and I drive home, and I was right; I drove all the way home and I didn't cause any damage at all. No worries at all because I was fully insured, I had insurance coming out of my backside. Would that have been responsible behaviour? I don't think so; it's the insurance company that would have carried the can. I paid my £400 premium, my conscience is clear... right?

Or could it be that because I know I'm not ultimately responsible for the damage I may cause, I'm prepared to do something as profoundly irresponsible as driving under the influence of alcohol?

Let's say I'm driving down the road today and I'm approaching a school and I see a sign that says 'slow to 30 mph.' I slow to 25 because I want to have a little margin of safety and because the Ritilin-guzzling children are darting back and forth across the road trying to cause me to cash in on my insurance. But let's say I don't have any insurance and that I'm prepared to pay for any child I kill, I would drive far more carefully than you do, I can assure you of that. Instead of insurance I might consider a recognizance Bond, where you put up your own collateral, and risk losing what is yours in favour of being 'responsible' but that's a subject for another book.

I think that if you were to practice strict liability, with your own collateral at stake, you'd have fewer accidents, if any. This is what individual responsibility is all about. Limited liability insurance means you don't have to be responsible. If you want a responsible society, you lay the responsibility on the shoulders of the people themselves. Of course, some people are never going to be responsible and those people need the option of limited liability, but the blanket, scattergun effect of Admiralty means we've all got to get insurance. Which is why I advocate learning the rules of the game—once you wake up to it—so you can exercise the choice. If you're not going to be responsible, then your guardian will have to be responsible for you.

Insurance is a pretty good racket. If the insurance company is prepared to bet you're not going to have an accident, why should you believe you're going to have one? If the insurance company is prepared to bet your house is not going to burn down, why should you believe it might?

Take a look at your land, your property. Who owns it? Don't you have a mortgage? The mortgage is *prima facie* evidence that you don't own that property, but you do have an equitable right of possession. You have the highest and best title, as long as you perform under the terms of the contract.

There are only two types of land on this planet; allodial and feudal. Feudal land is owned by the King/State and the state collects a fee from its tenants and requires all tenants to specifically perform. Allodial land is held without subjection to any superior. The possessor of allodial land exercises 'an unqualified dominion over the land'. Do you pay a property tax on your property? Is your property feudal or allodial? If you're paying a property tax you've got feudal land, which is owned by the state and you're a mere renter; a tenant in possession. As long as you pay your rent, you can stay there. How does that grab you?

How many of you hold your land in allodial title? I would venture a guess and say none. Zero. What happened to our allodial tenure and title? We sold it! How did we sell it? We mortgaged it. The Government came in and said, 'Wouldn't you like to have a school down the street?' and we said, 'Oh, yes, please,' and we voted in the school. So we got these bonds as notes with our land as collateral. They would come to us every so often and say, 'Wouldn't you like to have paved streets and gutters, lights and hospitals?' And we fell for it.

What do you think you're paying this property tax for? You know, every acre of land in the United Kingdom and in the United States is now, in some way, under some kind of a bond. We've become the State's men. Welcome to Feudal Serfdom, Mark II.

You should be living on your land without any property tax, you should be practicing allodial tenure and title. You should be living your life preparing for your own old age on your own land with your own money, without the state or Social Security or anybody else promising you anything. Because, after all, they can't give you any more than they took from you, and then they've got to administer it so its going to cost you something more than what you gave them. You're going to get back something less than what you paid in. How much less? Well, in the case of Social Security, you'll get around 25% of what you pay in if you're rich. If you're middle-class, for every three dollars you pay in, you'll get a dollar back. For every dollar you pay in you get 68 cents back if you're poor. Are you getting a sense of it?

Oh, and seriously, that's the state's child you've got there. They let you raise him, they let you put braces on his teeth, they let you wipe his backside, they let you take care of him until he's old enough to go to war, and then they ship him off to Iraq as cannon fodder. I didn't join the army, the navy or the air force. You won't catch me signing an enlistment contract to go to Iraq. I understand the law and how that law applies to me, what the consequences might be, and I've decided that's a contract I don't want any part of. And all you good folk who joined the army, navy and the air force can sit down, zip it, and do as you're told. When you buy an airline ticket, bend over and lube up. When you're on that ship and the Captain says, 'Swab the deck, Sailor,' you just salute sharply, say 'Aye, aye, Captain,' get your mop out and shut your mouth. Fulfil your part of the contract you volunteered into. Don't talk to the Captain about having rights. Crewmen on a ship in a maritime adventure don't have rights. Rights don't come from Barack Obama, they don't come from Gordon Brown, rights don't come from Congress or Parliament—they don't come from FEMA, rights don't come from General Motors either, or IBM or Microsoft...

If you need a guardian, if you need the Government to look after you, change your nappy for you, fine, no one's going to force you to change your lifestyle. Some people like rules and control, it makes them feel safe. But if you're complaining about this 'prison without bars' we're in right now—if you're complaining about the tyranny we're facing at the moment, you're complaining about the contracts that you have volunteered into, even if unknowingly so.

You can complain about being under a pseudo-communist dictatorship until hell freezes over, and if you think Government's going to solve your problems, knock yourselves out—go and vote three times in the next election—but you'll be wasting your time. The solution to your problem is not more government, it's less government; you need to investigate and take control of the adhesion contracts. Look into your Social Security contract, your driver's contracts and your marriage licences. Any contract created without full disclosure is a fraud. Were you made aware you were giving up your rights when you signed these contracts?

It's time we stood on our own two feet again and behaved like responsible, able men and women. Come on people, it's time to wake up.

Take Responsibility... look it up for yourself. Search engine paths regarding topics addressed in this chapter:

Saving to Suitors Clause
Admiralty
City of London
Civil Law
Common Law
Hurricane Katrina
Limited Liability Insurance
Social Security.

DUMBOCRACY

In every society where there is a ruling class there is one kind of education for rulers and another for the ruled. Vocational training, which confines itself to teaching skills, tends to limit the individual's interest in general social problems and to discourage intelligent participation in political life. As such, it is the ideal education for the servants of the ruling class. It is sharply distinguished from a vital program of liberal education such as that which provides a broad general training for rulers... The real issue is a political rather than an academic one: how widely available should liberal education be? There is no more radical and democratic idea afloat in educational circles today than that of providing liberal education for everyone.

MEDFORD EVANS AND GEORGE R. CLARK
HARPER'S MAGAZINE 1944

It takes a long time to recover from the institutionalisation called public school. I'm still recovering from it, and I'm pushing forty. Every year our public (Government-run) schools turn out millions of young adults who are totally unprepared for the task of living responsibly in a free society, and the most alarming news is that it was planned that way.

When discussing the nefarious nature of Government involvement in education, some people might suggest that I've a personal agenda. Absolutely. Of course I've got an agenda. However, the idea that the Government doesn't have agendas is absolute nonsense. Those people have at least one agenda that gets them out of bed in the morning: to continue forcing me to pay for their Government public school twaddle.

So why is it that most people get upset at the view that public schools have an agenda? Why is it that people who recognise their own agendas can't recognise that the folks running the school system have agendas too, that those who fought for Government-run

schools had a malevolent agenda, or that Government schools today are used for nefarious purposes?

The first reason is that the main goal of Government-run education is to produce graduates who support 'the system', and it's
very, very effective. This isn't some hidden agenda; it's right out in
the open. The prize is called citizenship, and a good citizen always
sings the praises of Government education. When the schools say,
'Our aim is to educate citizens,' you can be sure that they don't
mean citizens who question the Government or its bureaucracies
and unions. Good citizens believe that teachers and administrators, as Government employees, know best. A good citizen trusts
the schools. And, should a parent begin to question the schools,
the collective consisting of neighbours, friends, and so on, applies
increasing pressure to bring the disobedient back in line, back to
being a good citizen, all of which brings a whole new meaning to
the term *Neighbourhood Watch.*

My definition of a free society is a society where it is safe to be unpopular.
ADLAI E. STEVENSON

The second reason is that anyone looking to influence and program children couldn't find a better way to do that than a system of compulsory education, whether the point is to expand and
improve the forceful power of Government or to poison young
minds with perverse nonsense, or for any other goal—no matter
how nefarious or seemingly benign. Public schools are the agent of
change. It's completely obvious to me why the majority of people
support Government schools.

If your goal is to create citizens who support the collective, and
you're not willing to do it by force, you slowly destroy the institutions of free association: of freedom. You subtly attack the family
and the church, and indoctrinate the children. By doing that, you
break the parent/child bond. You just use the classroom to define
the pecking order, and then you sit back and allow the following
Government-educated generations to chip away at the foundations
over time. Sure, you have the odd battle in the front garden, but
these are only distractions, while you send the rest of your troops
to kick in the back door and take over the kitchen.

It isn't about the individual versus the collective any more, it's
who has the most control and power to educate and indoctrinate.

A man can use any method that doesn't violate the property
rights of others. He can't march into your property to deliver his

message. He can't use force to make you pay for his message either. Other than those two rules, all's fair in love and war, as they say. The public schools violate both of those rules. Government has first claim to your children, even if you home school, and will invade your property to deliver its message in the form of a Government-authorised syllabus and exams. Government and its schools have first claim to your income, your property.

> *Their means is one of evil,*
> *as it is a means backed by Government —*
> *the social apparatus of coercion and compulsion.*
> Ludwig von Mises

Yes, I have an agenda, and so does Government, its schools, and associated minions. Mine is an agenda of competence, freedom and peace, while theirs is one of violence, indoctrination and control. Considering we don't want to resort to their methods to achieve our agenda, we have to waken and educate the sleepers. There's a lot to do, but at the very least, the Governments are getting more and more careless and their mistakes are becoming more obvious, even to those with their heads in the sand.

Get your pen and paper out, friends. What we have coming up shortly is an eighth-grade final exam from 1895. Maybe you have a college degree, but if you're like me, you couldn't pass this test. That's right, I couldn't pass the test, but I've only had a very basic, Government-funded, 'comprehensive' public school education.

What I would like to see is you good folks out there with college and University educations take a stab at it. Let's see if we've been short-changed by our educational system here in 2009.

Today in the UK and the US, we graduate 1-2 million students a year who are functionally illiterate. It isn't that there are 2 million students in the US and UK who are functionally illiterate but are turned out anyway, that's not what I'm suggesting. It's that these students actually have a piece of paper in their hand that says they have completed an education, and they take that piece of paper and place it on the desk of a prospective employer and say, 'I'm educated, I'm skilled, I'm trained, I want you to give me a job.' The truth of the matter is that these people are not only uneducated, but they are perpetrating a fraud upon everyone who believes they are educated. And a fraud has been perpetrated upon these students who believe that they themselves have been educated.

Only forty or fifty years ago, as a trainee, you went out on the job and your first hurdle was to persuade the new boss to give you an opportunity. After working on the job for a couple of weeks, the boss would come to you and tell you if he thinks you're going to make a good mechanic, or typist, or lathe operator, or whatever it may be. Or he would probably give you a little fatherly advice and tell you that you don't have a knack, the skill, the talent to learn how to do this particular job.

In this day and age we no longer practise that particular element of apprenticeship, we send people to school and they can go through the whole curriculum without really having any talent in that particular field. Just because someone has been to law school, it doesn't mean they have a talent or ability in law. By the same token, just because we send people to medical school, it doesn't mean they're going to turn out to be good doctors. They are going to have a piece of paper that says they've done all the things that doctors are supposed to qualify, or that lawyers are supposed to do to qualify, but in the final analysis, how many cases do you win? How many bodies do you bury? That's the bottom line.

Education is a system whereby we set choices before you, and you make choices. Knowledge of and by itself isn't education; having choices and choosing is education. Current education isn't education at all, it's indoctrination into socialism and communism—a political ideology, a new-age religion.

Back in the late 1800s, early 1900s, people had an education; they had choices. You weren't compelled to go to school; you went to school because you wanted to go to school, because you wanted to learn something. Many people in those days weren't 'educated', not everybody wanted to go to school, and it was a choice they made. One day someone woke up and decided, 'We don't think people should have that choice. We believe that everybody should be educated, indoctrinated into a standard of knowledge, *a standard of information.*'

When you go to public school, you don't get the luxury of choice; you're going to be indoctrinated. That's the last word on the subject and if you refuse, you will be punished. That's how this game is played. Public schools not only have a crappy curriculum, they actually oppress their students by forcing them to participate in it. It's one thing to offer a density of shallow assignments, and quite another to make students do them.

I noticed a while back that my grandmother's handwriting was unusually good. She could write a straight line from one side of the page to the other, from the top to the bottom of the page—and there were no lines on the paper. I couldn't write a straight line if my life depended on it, I have to have lines to follow. Besides that aspect, my handwriting looks like I've dipped a spider in ink and let it walk across the page—and I'm willing to bet that yours is as poor as mine is.

Now, if you have your pen and paper ready, and you've got your college degree sitting in front of you, and you've got the courage to put yourself through it, and if your brain hasn't already switched off at the prospect of a test, let's take a look at the 1895 exam for 14-year-olds and see how we do.

First of all, we'll deal with Grammar. There are ten questions and you have one hour; that's 6 minutes per question.

1. Give nine rules for the use of Capital Letters.
2. Name the Parts of Speech and define those that have no modifications.
3. Define Verse, Stanza and Paragraph.
4. What are the Principal Parts of a verb? Give the Principal Parts of do, lie, play and run.
5. Define Case, Illustrate each Case.
6. What is Punctuation? Give rules for principal marks of Punctuation.
7. Write a composition of about 150 words and show therein that you understand the practical use of the rules of grammar.

I can see already, just having looked at the first part of this test, that my grandparents and their parents were better-educated at the age of sixteen than I am now, at forty. I was educated under a system that professes to be one of the best in the world and I found it incredibly difficult. I certainly won't embarrass myself by telling you how poorly I did.

Charlotte Thomson Iserbyt, the former Senior Policy Advisor in the US Department of Education, wrote an excellent book called *The Deliberate Dumbing Down of America*. Now, if you've been 'dumbed down', I guess it's up to you to re-educate yourself, and by taking this test, you're going to see just how ignorant you are today, one hundred or so years after this test was given to 14 year-olds in Kansas. You couldn't get out of the eighth grade until you answered 70% of each section correctly.

Arithmetic, and you have one hour and 15 minutes. That's about seven and a half minutes per question.

1. Name and define the Fundamental Rules of Arithmetic.
2. A wagon box is 2 feet deep, 10 feet long, and 3 feet wide. How many bushels of wheat will it hold?

3. If a load of wheat weighs 3942 lbs., what is it worth at 50cents per bushel, deducting 1050 lbs. for tare?
4. District No. 33 has a valuation of $35,000. What is the necessary levy to carry on a school seven months at $50 per month, and have $104 for incidentals?
5. Find cost of 6720 lbs. coal at $6.00 per ton.
6. Find the interest of $512.60 for 8 months and 18 days at 7 percent.
7. What is the cost of 40 boards 12 inches wide and 16 feet long at $.20 per inch?
8. Find bank discount on $300 for 90 days (no grace) at 10 percent.
9. What is the cost of a square farm at $15 per acre, the distance around which is 640 rods?
10. Write a Bank Check, a Promissory Note, and a Receipt.

US History (Time, 45 minutes)

1. Give the epochs into which US History is divided.
2. Give an account of the discovery of America by Columbus.
3. Relate the causes and results of the Revolutionary War.
4. Show the territorial growth of the United States.
5. Tell what you can of the history of Kansas.
6. Describe three of the most prominent battles of the Rebellion.
7. Who were the following: Morse, Whitney, Fulton, Bell, Lincoln, Penn, and Howe?
8. Name events connected with the following dates: 1607, 1620, 1800, 1849, and 1865?

Orthography—the correct way of using a specific writing system to write the language. (Time, one hour)

1. What is meant by the following: Alphabet, phonetic orthography, etymology, syllabication?
2. What are elementary sounds? How classified?
3. What are the following, and give examples of each: Trigraph, subvocals, diphthong, cognate letters, linguals?
4. Give four substitutes for caret (the letter) 'u.'
5. Give two rules for spelling words with final 'e.' Name two exceptions under each rule.
6. Give two uses of silent letters in spelling. Illustrate each.
7. Define the following prefixes and use in connection with a word: Bi, dis, mis, pre, semi, post, non, inter, mono, super.
8. Mark diacritically and divide into syllables the following, and

name the sign that indicates the sound: Card, ball, mercy, sir, odd, cell, rise, blood, fare, last.
9. Use the following correctly in sentences, Cite, site, sight, fane, fain, feign, vane, vain, vein, raze, raise, rays.
10. Write 10 words frequently mispronounced and indicate pronunciation by use of diacritical marks and by syllabication.

Geography (Time, one hour)

1. What is climate? Upon what does climate depend?
2. How do you account for the extremes of climate in Kansas?
3. Of what use are rivers? Of what use is the ocean?
4. Describe the mountains of N.A.
5. Name and describe the following: Monrovia, Odessa, Denver, Manitoba, Hecla, Yukon, St. Helena, Juan Fermandez, Aspinwall and Orinoco.
6. Name and locate the principal trade centers of the US
7. Name all the republics of Europe and give capital of each.
8. Why is the Atlantic Coast colder than the Pacific in the same latitude?
9. Describe the process by which the water of the ocean returns to the sources of rivers.
10. Describe the movements of the earth. Give inclination of the earth.

Obviously, the History section is the only section that pertains solely to the US, but just in case you Brits think you're off the hook because it's a US test, here are a couple from a British exam from around the same time, for 12-year-old-children:

1. Find the value of 2,037½ hundredweight of sugar at £1 19s 8½d per hundredweight.
2. Does a globe or a map give a more correct view of the world? Give reasons for your answers.
3. Give the dates of the building of Hadrian's Wall and the departure of the Romans from England.

So, how did you do? Intimidated at all?

Notice there were no 'true or false or 'multiple-choice' questions. Today, we give true or false tests. Whether you know the answer to the question or not is irrelevant, you've got a fifty-fifty chance of getting the question right. In fact, I discovered that when I went to public school, teachers would not make it fifty-fifty, they would invariably make about 67%, two out of every three questions, 'true'. If you went through the test and answered all of the questions that you knew the answers to, 'true' or 'false', then went back through the rest of the test dealing with all the questions you didn't know the answers to by answering 'true', you simply could not fail the test.

The second fallacy of testing is multiple-choice. It's a fallacy because we ask you a question, and then give you four answers; we actually tell you what the answer is. So, if you know the answer but you just can't call it to mind, as soon as you read the answer, you recall it. The only way that you can miss in a multiple- choice test is if you absolutely don't know the answer.

In a real test like the one above, you're asked a question and you're expected to know the answer.

I passed my GCSE tests and I have the certificates to prove it, and the UK Government says 'Timothy AntiTerrorist is educated,' but compared to these children of 1895, I am the village idiot.

The heartbreak, as I see it, is that they're taking children who would probably be very intelligent, productive members of society and teaching them nothing but how to pass tests. They get out into the world and find they don't know anything and aren't good for anything and can't succeed. What happened? How did Great Britain and America change from nations of free people, entrepreneurs and small freeholders with their own judgment, into nations of 'employees'?

Current schooling performs the function it was created to perform, and it does it brilliantly; it creates the consciousness that's crucial for a mass production economy. In big cities, it's very useful to be able to turn out children who are good for this or that purpose. At the same time they can be institutionalised to be producers, followers and consumers of corporate business. Public education is a gigantic public works project, probably the largest public works project in the history of mankind. The education system is the largest employer in all western nations. Most dedicate more than 40% of their annual budget to education, never mind the fact that the need for education and education funding is still used today as a reason to set up lotteries.

The end of slavery or servitude predictably causes a problem; too many workers, not enough work. Then—because capital is so much stronger than labour—employers will always bid wages down to a starvation level and the starving will underbid each other for any work which, in turn, marginalises large numbers of people to starvation's edge, creating an underclass that continually threatens revolution. The welfare state was created to contain and control this potential revolution and a host of automatic stabilisers built in to control the economy.

It was Plato who first justified the idea of a ruling Elite, compassionately controlling the idiotic underclass. As the most respectable figure to voice their principles, it's only logical that the Elite keep referring back to him, isn't it?

Whenever a period of uncontrolled history opens up, like the War Between the States, for instance, it produces evidence that challenges the upperclass/underclass relationship, which raises a real problem for the social engineers to solve. If the underclasses are determined to show that they don't belong in the category where fate and the Elite have put them, then something has to be done to make them get into the box and stay there. That something is public school. Of course, a healthy share of the private schools follow the public school model too, and they use the same textbooks. They operate more cosmetically because they're smaller and drawn from a more gentile class of customer. I'm not talking about the Elite class of private boarding schools here, only the ones that fall outside of the two or three inner circles.

It's odd that the last three Presidential elections in the US should have caused an inquiry from the American journalist fraternity; George Bush came from a Top Ten boarding school, as did John Kerry. Al Gore was from a Top Ten Elite boarding school and a number of the secondary candidates like John McCain also attended a Top Ten Elite boarding school; in McCain's case, a boarding school so elite that most people have never even heard of it. A large number of these Elite school graduates show up in the national leadership, like Franklin Roosevelt from Groton and JFK, from Choate.

There are approximately 20 Elite schools in the inner circles and perhaps another 250-300 that imitate these schools in the outer darkness for everyone else. What do these Elite schools specialise in?

Apparently, these schools aim at endowing certain 'qualities'. There's a clear distinction between the best private schools and these Elite boarding schools in how they train managerial personnel; they're given a particular outlook and certain skills that aren't made available to the rest of the *hoi polloi*. One of the qualities that's given great importance at these schools is 'public speaking', a fuzzy term that makes us think of someone making a wedding speech but, basically, it's the ability to swim in any 'citizen pool'; the ability to put together a compelling argument and to deliver that argument without biting your fingernails, sweating or throwing up.

If your English class specialised in public speaking, in a relatively short time, say, three or four months, you'd at least get competency out of virtually every one in the class, including children who had never eaten with a table cloth in their entire lives.

Now, I can only imagine what would happen if the curriculum emphasised it for twelve years, and all the children of Great Britain and America were aware of why public speaking was so important. Can you imagine what would happen if the system made public speaking a priority? Minorities and suppressed races who could read, write and speak; there would be a revolution. Certainly we'd have a radically different social and economic system.

There are introverts and extroverts; the extroverts are the leaders and the introverts are the followers. Public speaking and writing are called 'the active literacies'; they allow an individual to enlist followers, and that's dangerous. You can't be allowed too many public speakers. You can't have too many leaders.

The other main difference between the Elite private schools and the public schools is writing. Public speaking and writing skills are not taught in public schools as a rule. Even relative idiots can learn how to do short pieces of coherent, rational writing. Practice over and over again and it just happens, and once it happens, it never goes away. Education is dangerous and it must be kept away from public school students at all costs. They could learn to be leaders instead of followers. We certainly can't have that in a corporate society.

The easiest way for a 'nobody' to move quickly into business success is through 'sales'. Obviously, if you can't put yourself in the other fella's mind—which drama teaches—and stroke his fears or ambitions, which literature and some other studies teach, you can't sell very well, can you? So, our standard school curriculum deliberately excludes a huge number of people from learning these easily achievable skills called public speaking and writing. Here's why: they were meant to be the tillers of fields and operators of Walmart checkout tills; corporate slaves, not leaders of society.

In my opinion, there's a clear lack of imagination in terms of what kind of economy we could have if everyone in our society was capable.

In the late 1800s, big businessmen began to see the possibilities of a mass production/mass consumption society and began the co-operation of business and Government in education, with business very much the senior partner. They also needed education to prevent potential competitors and therefore 'overproduction'. As John D. Rockefeller put it, 'Competition is a sin.' Since every child born might bring some new industry with him to replace what already exists, someone must get to that child before he affects the economic equation. The easiest way to do that is to make sure that the overwhelming number can't rock any boat, by never awakening their mind to the fact that their mind is there.

People have so much latent ability that it would erupt if schooling didn't suppress it; what would Society look like if all of these people were freed from regulations, social stratification and schooling classifications—freed from these anchors that Government, big business and public education tie around their necks?

Why is it that the British and American economies have accelerated and thrived to the degree that it would take other countries decades to catch up? Because American and British workingmen took such careful, thoughtful and intensive architecting; he now has such unusual characteristics that it would take decades to replicate him elsewhere. What are those unusual characteristics?

He defines himself by what he buys.

So, when he has nothing, you extend credit to him. He'll then mortgage himself and his children forever, just to keep consuming. He also lives in constant fear of losing his job. Since he knows that he doesn't know how to do anything at all, he lives in constant fear, and that goes right up the line of management. He knows there are twenty, thirty or eighty people waiting to take his job, and that keeps him totally obedient and docile. If he loses his job he may never get a job again. It's this fear that motivates him, and the older he gets, the less chance he has of freeing himself from the trap.

The Elite, however, are clever enough not to allow conditions to get so bad that the underclass starve to death. That's why we must have the welfare apparatus and the other built-in stabilisers installed; they prevent the system from destroying itself. Terror keeps the workmen in line, terror of losing his job, literally losing his place in the world, losing his ability to do meaningful work, even though the work isn't very meaningful, as we all well know. He's terrified that he will be cast into limbo. For a man, it's the fear of being castrated.

On some family farms, teenagers get to do everything; city-bred people could never approach the level of competence and responsibility of the country-raised. If you live on such a farm, you have to be able to make every mechanical repair yourself, and if you're not responsible for everything around you, no one else will be. So these youngsters are not ruined—far from it—they become great, competent human beings. One interesting secret that public education doesn't mention is that about 20% of the highest incomes in the country belong to 'operatives'; people who run heavy machinery or repair computers.

There's no money in employment, because the corporations control the employment. Now, if business controls the employment, they also control the wages. The corporations control the wages through the labour unions, who preach that they represent the working man—but they don't. The exporting of British and American manufacturing jobs to countries around the world is resounding proof that corporations control the Unions. The Unions should be striking or voting for someone else, but they're not. The unions are in bed with the corporations and corporations are in bed with the Government and the Government is in bed with the unions and operations; it's an orgy of corruption, money and power.

If you want ignorant children, you can't get a more ignorant child than one who's been educated in public school; a child who can't think, an automaton—a brainwashed robot—who works for a Corporation and is terrified of losing his job. The public school system is a system designed to train workers for 'the system'. Anyone with two brain cells to rub together would call that brainwashing.

Think about what is going on here: it doesn't take very long for an education system like this to take effect; a couple of generations of this nonsense and you've got the whole society in your hands. And that's where America and Great Britain are today.

I get a lot of messages from people who say, 'When the American and the British people finally wake up to what's being done to them, they'll rise up in righteous indignation!'

No, they won't, they'll sit down and do as they're told, because their brains aren't big enough to figure out what to do next.

Public schools have problems, but public educators' problems are not all their fault. One of the difficulties with public policymakers is that they insist on making public policy, and nowhere is this more of a problem than in public education. A recent study of laws and regulations affecting a typical New York high school is a good example. The study found that more than sixty sources of law and regulations including thousands of provisions applying to a New York City high school. These include New York state's eight hundred-plus pages of school law, seven hundred twenty pages of regulations from the state commissioner of education, more than fifteen thousand decisions in forty-three volumes of the Commissioner's Office, a two hundred and four page teacher union contract with the district, close to seven hundred pages in the 'No Child Left Behind' act and more than two hundred pages of regulations just concerning 'student discipline'. If you add up all of the regulations, from all of the sources, it takes more pages of material to run a New York City High School than there are in the Encyclopaedia Britannica.

If you had a disruptive student in your class, and you wanted to expel the student from school, you'd have to go through sixty-five steps to achieve it. If you were a principal in a public school and found you had an incompetent teacher, you'd have to jump through eighty-three hoops in order to fire him. There are thirty-eight hurdles to leap just to employ a teacher. Some of these procedures can take years to resolve and—even then—an attempt at firing a teacher could cost more than $100,000 and still not be successful. A typical school Principal faces 470,000 Federal, State and local regulations, an administrative impossibility; no one could possibly even be aware of so many obligations.

Policy makers incessantly making policy means that many—perhaps thousands—of these regulations are in the process of being amended, deleted, added to or changed completely. As someone once said about Government in general, there are so many laws and regulations that all of us are continually breaking some without being aware that we're doing so, or that they even exist. This is also the case with public school boards. All of this policy nonsense would be well and good if it had a positive effect but, so far, there isn't any educational policy or strategy to be found that guarantees student accomplishment.

In their 1988 book, *Winning the Brain Race*, Denis Doyle and David T. Kearns assert, 'Prescriptive rules and regulations are necessary only if there are no measurable performance objectives. Once there are performance standards, schools can be encouraged to do it their own way. The priority should be educating children, not compliance. Let them use their own best judgement and be held accountable for the results.'

In schooling, Government is not the solution to the problem, it is the problem.
RONALD REAGAN

In May of 1973, Medford Evans, former Chief of Security Training for the Atomic Energy Commission, stated in an article published in American Opinion, that 'Government schools make it a matter of policy to spend as much money as possible, and impart as little knowledge as possible—since spending demonstrates power—while keeping the scholars ignorant monopolizes power into the hands of the Government insiders. The American people had better wake up and start investigating their school systems. Every American citizen should IMMEDIATELY pull their children out of every public school and either teach them at home or start private schools that are closely managed and maintained by themselves. If they don't, we will very soon find ourselves in a Soviet America.'

In 1903, Fred T. Gates wrote an 'occasional letter' to the General Education Board, of which he was a member. This board was the predecessor to the Rockefeller Foundation, organized by John D. Rockefeller. The following is a direct quotation from that letter:

'In our dreams, we have limitless resources and the people yield themselves with perfect docility to our moulding hands. The present educational conventions fade from our minds, and unhampered by tradition, we work our own good will upon a grateful and responsive rural folk. We shall not try to make these people or any of their children into philosophers or men of learning, or of science. We have not to raise up from among them authors, editors, poets or men of letters. We shall not search for great artists, painters, musicians nor lawyers, doctors, preachers, statesmen, of whom we have an ample supply. The task we set before ourselves is a very simple as well as a very beautiful one, to train these people as we find them to a perfectly ideal life just where they are. So we will organize our children and teach them to do in a perfect way the things their fathers and mothers are doing in an imperfect way, in the homes, in the shops, and on the farm.'

In 1919, the United States Communist Party slogan was *'Give us one generation of small children to train to manhood and womanhood and we will set up a Bolshevist form of the Soviet Government in the United States.'*

And in 1979, the National Education Association released a report entitled *Education for the '70s*. The following is a direct quote from that report:

Schools will become clinics whose purpose is to provide individualized, psycho-social treatment for the student, and teachers must become psycho-

*social therapists. This will include biochemical and psychological media-
tion of learning, as drugs are introduced experimentally to improve in the
learner such qualities as personality, concentration, and memory.*

Do you still wonder why drugs like Ritalin are being administered to school-aged children? Now you know why.

*Learn: To gain knowledge of; to acquire knowledge or ideas of something
before unknown. We learn the use of letters, the meaning of words and
the principles of science. We learn things by instruction, by study, and by
experience and observation. It is much easier to learn what is right, than
to unlearn what is wrong. To acquire skill in any thing; to gain by practice
a faculty of performing; as, to learn to play on a flute or an organ.*
To teach; to communicate the knowledge of something before unknown.
AMERICAN DICTIONARY OF THE ENGLISH LANGUAGE, NOAH WEBSTER, 1828.

*Learning: 1. Knowledge acquired by systematic study in any field or
scholarly application. 2. the act or process of acquiring knowledge or skill.
3. Psychology. the modification of behaviour through practice, training, or
experience.*
RANDOM HOUSE WEBSTER'S COLLEGE DICTIONARY, 1990

Notice the change in definition since 1828: In the latter definition
of the word 'learning', we can see that learning, or training, is often
'the modification of behaviour through practice, training, or experience.' We can see that they didn't intend to pass on knowledge
or the ability to reason based on solid empirical fact, but rather to
'control behaviour' through practice, or training, as revealed by the
statement 'to train these people as we find them to a perfectly ideal
life just where they are.' Their aim is to train us just where we are.
This statement quite clearly reveals their intention to downgrade
us to a life of mediocrity lacking any real ambition, while keeping
us in the homes, in the shops, and on the farm. This statement is
close to many statements made by famous communists and socialists right through history.

If you're one of those sitting on the sidelines saying, 'I know
all of this is true and I really hate the public school system but I
don't have any other choice,' let me tell you, there are three choices
in education, or at least there are in Great Britain and the United
States of America. Obviously, choice number one is 'public school',
private school being your second choice. There's a third choice you
have called 'homeschooling'. Your child can be educated at home
and doesn't need to be subjected to the debilitating processes that
the public schools offer. So keep that in mind, there are three choic-

es and when you send your child to public school, you've made your choice. Even if you send your child to public school because you're ignorant and you don't know about the other choices available to you, you've still made your choice.

Compulsory education for children was first established in Prussia, in 1819. Society in Prussia was segmented into children who would become policy makers; children who would become assistants to policy makers (the engineers, architects, lawyers and doctors); and the children who would be the labour force. Prussia set up a three-tier school system in which one half of one percent of the population was taught to think, and attended a school called *Academie*.

5.5% of the population attended *Realschulen,* where they were only partially taught to think, as Prussia believed they were defeated by Napoleon because people were thinking for themselves under stress on the battlefield. Prussia intended to see to it *scientifically* that this couldn't happen again.

Harmony, obedience and freedom from stressful thinking—how to follow orders, essentially—was the curriculum for the remaining 94%, who went to *Volkschulen.*

The public school is primarily a social institution, education being a social process, school is simply that form of community life in which all those agencies are concentrated that will be most effective in bringing the child to share the inherited resources of the race, and to use his own powers for social ends. Education, therefore, is a process of living and not a preparation for future living. There is no God, and there is no soul. There are no needs for the props of traditional religion. With dogma and creed excluded, then immutable truth is also dead and buried. There is no room for fixed natural law or permanent moral absolutes.
JOHN DEWEY

In 1887, James McKeen Cattell, then a lecturer at Cambridge, was responsible for replacing the very effective method of using phonics for teaching reading with the 'Look-Say' method—a technique used for teaching the deaf—invented by Thomas Hopkins Gallaudet. Cattell decided that the direct memorising of words would increase normal students literacy levels. Our experience over time has proven this isn't the case—obviously— as, right now—in the 21st century—millions of British and American adults can't read or write at all.

We wonder: why don't our schools work for so many of our students? Why doesn't one-size education fit all? Our public education system was originally designed to produce controlled voters, to train a workforce for labour that didn't need much thought. Schools originally stressed order, timeliness, uniformity; essential for an industrial workforce. You needed to get to work on time, be able to stand in the line, do a repetitive job, take your break when the bell sounded, return when the bell sounded, and leave when the bell sounded. School prepared workers for that environment. Students/workers sat in rows. Teachers/bosses were not to be questioned.

Spending large sums of money on public education isn't guaranteed to produce the results Government promises to deliver, or the results you might expect. In fact, it seems that the opposite is true. With the growing awareness of poor student performance, attention has begun to focus not only on the educational system in general but on teachers in particular.

Twenty States have acted to stem the flow of teachers who cannot spell, cannot add up or cannot punctuate, by requiring competency testing for teachers. When the test was given to 1269 juniors in the Texas Teacher education programme, 38% failed the exam that tests basic skills taught to the 12th grade, such as calculating percentages, capitalising words and comprehending a 200-word passage.
DALLAS TIMES HERALD, NOVEMBER 11, 2007

So these 1,269 students in their third year of college are looking for a teaching credential and thirty-eight percent of them can't pass the test. We're not talking about rocket science here, we're talking about the fact they can't work percentages, a very simple, very basic thing that you probably learned back when you were ten or eleven years old.

How about punctuating a paragraph? You know, you've got a paragraph, you read the paragraph and you have to put in the full stops, commas, colons, semicolons, exclamation marks and question marks. Thirty-eight percent of these junior teachers in college couldn't do what their elders had to learn how to do in the fourth or fifth grades. And these are the people who graduate from college with a teaching credential. They went to college and they got a BS degree, then they go to 'teacher school' to get a teaching certificate and well over a third of them fail the competency test. Not because it's advanced math or calculus they had to go to Cambridge to learn how to do, but because they can't do simple percentages or punctuate a paragraph. How do you like that?

Now, if as a truck driver or a housewife, you happen to be sitting there and saying, 'I can't punctuate a paragraph either,' well, then, you're a victim of the public school system.

If you've got a diploma—the piece of paper that says you've successfully completed high school—I can assure you that piece of paper means less than nothing to employers. When many of the big corporations like BT, AT&T, IBM, Vauxhall Motors and General Electric employ basic workers to work on assembly lines or to work on components, they often have to put them through a remedial programme to teach them how to read, teach them how to recognize and understand instructions, and to do basic arithmetic.

Ponder this: if you can learn to read, write and count when you're twenty-five years old, working for General Electric, why couldn't you read, write and count when you were twelve, thirteen or fourteen? Is it because it's designed that way? Could it be to make you depend on the major corporations?

You're paying billions a year for this public education system, and this system turns out thousands of students a year who can't even read their own diplomas. What's worse, you're turning out the teachers who are going to teach the next generation.

The competency test was also given to 3,300 new teachers in the Houston School District. Because of cheating and other irregularities on the part of these candidates, scores for only 2,400 of the teachers were reported. Almost two thirds, *sixty-two percent*, failed the exam.

You have 3,300 new teachers and nine hundred have to be excluded for cheating and then sixty-two percent of 2,400—1,488—failed the test.

Cheating. These are the people who are supposed to be teaching your child about morality.

What would you think if your plumber came to fix the pipes and you said, 'Let me give you a simple plumbing test to make sure you're up to the job,' and your plumber failed the test? He doesn't know what sort of solder to use, or he doesn't know what size threader to thread the pipe with, or what type of compound to put on the joints. Come on, friends, out in the real world you are either a plumber or you're not. You either know how to do the job or you don't.

Now, these are people who have degrees from college and are taking a test that can qualify them to work as a teacher in a public school. What they do when these teachers fail the tests is substitute a new test with lower standards, so that they can pass it—that's why your children are getting A's and B's in school, getting higher grades on their report card, but they're getting more and more ignorant. What we're doing is reducing the requirements of the test.

You wonder why your child can't read; the bloody teacher can't read! And yet they're still employed because there isn't anyone else to fill the position.

Dallas school officials reported that on the same test, 1,223 of the 2,280 teachers hired by the Dallas School district since 1979, fifty-four percent could not answer sixty-seven percent of the questions correctly.

I'll put that in plainer English. Lets suppose there are ten of us; half of us couldn't answer two-thirds of the questions. Half of the teachers could not answer two questions out of three! And you're going to entrust your child's future to these people?

The Houston School board later lowered the passing score so that only forty-four percent of the teachers failed the test.

Sixty-two percent fail the test, so we lower the standards so that only forty-four percent fail. It beggars belief, doesn't it? If that didn't make you laugh out loud, you're not getting the joke. Read it again. What kind of stupidity are we dealing with here?

As you research this topic for yourself, you'll discover that this isn't stupid at all; it's all working to plan. You're not supposed to be educated, we're going to call you educated and we're going to call the process 'education' but that's not what it really is. If you want your child to come out as an incompetent, who can't read, can't write, and can't think, and who is an academic dimwit, public school is the place to send them. On the other hand, if you want your child to able to walk and talk and chew gum—maybe even all at the same time—perhaps you ought to send your child to the local Catholic school.

I don't want you to send me an e-mail saying, 'What the hell is the matter with you, AT, you've turned into a Catholic?' No, not at all, it is just that you can't turn a child out of the Catholic school that can't read his diploma; they just don't allow it. So, while I'm not a fan of Catholic religious philosophy, if they could just teach your child to read and write properly, it would be a step in the right direction, wouldn't it? If you want to go one step further than that, why don't you take your child out of public school, forget the private school and educate him at home? It will cost you around £500 a year, which is a fraction of the cost of educating them in a public school, and which in 2008 worked out around £9,000 a year—which, by the way, you're paying by way of taxation. Over twelve years, that's £108,000. You'd be better off taking that £108,000 and treating the family to a round-the-world cruise. Call it a field trip.

Your child doesn't need to go to public school. You don't need to spend that much money to teach a child how to be illiterate, just leave him alone and he can grow up to be illiterate all by himself, free of charge, he doesn't need the policy-makers' help. Your child isn't stupid—your child is ignorant. And he's ignorant because he's been taught in a public school by teachers who are, themselves, products of the deeply flawed, corrupt public school system. It's a classic case of the blind leading the blind.

The weakening academic abilities of students has resulted in a seventy-two percent increase in the numbers of colleges and universities adding remedial courses to accommodate the lower skill-levels of their new entrants. Such a lowering of the course content produces weaker degree programmes, which results in weaker college graduates, many of whom will re-enter the educational arena as teachers. This process is in fact what's happening. Since 1973, the SAT scores of potential teachers have fallen fifty-five points and the Department of Education reports half of the newly qualified Mathematics, Science end English teachers aren't qualified to teach those subjects.

Did you get that? *Did you get that?* If you take a look at the Mathematics, Science and English teachers in your public school, half of them aren't qualified to teach those subjects—but they're in there teaching them anyway, and they're teaching them to your children. So your children will come out with the same deficiencies the teacher has, which in turn will call for the public school your child attends to lower its standards, so that your children can get in, so that your children can get a teaching qualification and go out to teach the next generation of children. Friends, is that *survival of the fittest*?

For years, the standards for behaviour—you know, cheating or not cheating, lying or not lying, right and wrong—came from religious teachings. When those teachings were disallowed in 1962, they were replaced with a value-free teaching program allowing students to discover and then set their own standards for right and wrong, and today the results speak for themselves. Lack of discipline and school violence are now two of the more worrying problems facing modern schools. Fourteen of the fifteen Gallup polls on schools during 1968-83 listed lack of discipline as the primary problem. Before the ban on religious teachings in education, the top public school offences were listed as:

1. Talking
2. Chewing gum
3. Making noise
4. Running in the halls
5. Getting out of turn in line
6. Wearing improper clothing
7. Littering.

Polls now list the top public school offences as:

1. Rape
2. Robbery
3. Assault
4. Burglary
5. Arson
6. Bombings
7. Murder
8. Suicide
9. Absenteeism
10. Vandalism
11. Extortion
12. Drug abuse
13. Alcohol abuse
14. Gang warfare
15. Unwanted pregnancies
16. Abortion
17. Venereal diseases.

Chewing gum and making noise in class doesn't quite compare to rape, robbery and assault, does it?

From the December 12, 2006 issue of *The Los Angeles Times*:

'At most of the Oakland Unified School district's 92 schools, the fight against crime and violence is unending. An Uzi semiautomatic rifle with 15 hollow point bullets was one of the weapons confiscated by district officials within the last year. Franklin elementary school, trying to ensure that students know to hit the ground when bullets fly, carries out shooting drills twice a year...'

My God, let's think about that for a minute. You send your child to public school and they have a what? Not a fire drill, No. Not a nuclear bomb drill, No sir. They have a gun drill, a shooting drill, twice a year. What the hell is going on here? You're going to send your child to a school that needs shooting drills? Seriously? I haven't heard of any homeschool or private school shootings, have you? It's always going on in the public schools and it's always the public schools that have the students on Prozac or Ritalin or some other mind-altering poison where the shootings occur, have you noticed that? Why would you send your child into an environment like that? Your child would be safer locked up in Guantanamo Bay than he would in a modern day public school.

I don't subscribe to Christianity for the same reasons I'm not a practicing Catholic, but I would assert that having prayer, God and the Ten Commandments taught in Public schools actually had a positive influence on your children. I've always wondered when people complain about the schools, the textbooks, drugs, the teaching of evolutionary theory as fact and whatnot, why they continue to send their child there. The answer is invariably, 'It's the law, I have to.' Well, it isn't the law, and you don't have to.

It is true we have compulsory education; it is true that it's against the law. It's against the law of man and it's against the law of God; you cannot have a child that you don't educate. But you're not obliged to educate him in public school!

To educate a man in mind and not in morals is to educate a menace to society.
THEODORE ROOSEVELT

You know, if history is written a thousand years from now about this period of time, I suspect that 'insanity' is going to be the watchword. That the people of the world in general—but particularly the people of America and Great Britain—were suffering from mass hallucinations or mass insanity.

We've replaced the traditional educational system, the system of teaching people how to think and to be responsible for themselves, with a system that teaches people how to work for corporations. You're taught to follow the manual, to go-along-to get-along.

Science teachers have a job to do. If you tell a science teacher that what he's teaching is pure fantasy, lies, half-truths, some truth, and that the vast majority of it is just BS, he's not going to go into the class and say, 'Look, boys and girls, let me tell you the truth—we just don't know!' He'd lose his job if he did that. He's not going to say, 'The evolutionary hypothesis doesn't stand up to the math.' That would be career suicide. He goes to college to learn how to make a living and when he gets out into the business world—in this case, teaching—he's going to teach just exactly what the book says and he's going to follow his instructions.

Our education system is the laughingstock of the whole world and the sad fact is you're never going to change it; it's too well-entrenched and there is a lot of money and power behind it. The thing to do is to abandon it. If you want your child to know something, then you teach him something. He's not going to learn it in public school, and he is certainly not going to learn it from a science teacher who is more concerned about his pay cheque than he is about whether or not he is telling your child the truth.

Honesty doesn't go hand-in-hand with academics, it doesn't today and it probably never has.

Studies by Cornell University Professor Urie Bronfenbrenner suggest that at least until age ten or twelve, students who spend more time with other children their age than with their parents tend to rely on other children for their values. The result? They tend to have a lower sense of self-worth, of optimism, of respect for their parents, and—ironically—even of trust in their peers. If Bronfenbrenner is correct, this is one of the major, and unrecognised, reasons for the growing dysfunction of much adolescent behaviour.

A 1960 study for the Smithsonian Institution by Harold McCurdy concluded that genius is more likely to develop among children who spend more time with their parents and other adults, spend less time with their peers, and have freedom to work out their fantasies. McCurdy also suggested the public school system tends to do the reverse and restrict the development of geniuses.
DAVID W. KIRKPATRICK, HEARTLAND INSTITUTE

When you send your child to public school, ninety-nine percent of all of the people your child comes into contact with are other children. That's not the way normal society works. The greater part of their life experience from the ages of five to eighteen is with their peers and is artificial. Then, when they come home from the artificial environment of school, they sit down in front of the artificial society on television, where the drama is heightened and the sitcom families are surreal. Your children are learning their values from other children, when they should be learning them from adults at home. Home-school is where reality is at. Reality is where your child is going to meet three or four adults on a regular basis, adults who can pass on their experience-based values.

Considering public education is so bad, what can working parents with children in public schools do to redress the balance? Firstly, that family relationship has to be very active. The intellectual and character-building part of it can't be, 'What did you do in school today and let me help you with your homework…' Even if your child goes to a local public school, you have to 'homeschool' and show your child that education is something that you *take*, since no one *gives* education to anyone.

Homeschooling starts with buying a program; obviously you can't teach what you don't know yourself. You buy the materials and you teach your child from the materials that you've purchased, using the step-by-step guides. No degrees or diplomas required. You can get religious or nonreligious materials, and two plus two equals four at home just as it does in public school.

What's being taught in public school is random, useless, and meaningless. Too much time is wasted on useless topics. Quality of education has been sacrificed for quantity and, as a result, the depreciation of information has turned educational ambition into apathy and bright minds into dull, grey mush. There's no profit for the supplier in quality. When consumers of education have been 'dumbed down' to primal levels, judgment and appreciation of quality disappears.

In trying to be multicultural and diverse, class programs have become shallow and inept in their effort to teach children a global point of view. Topics are taught bit by bit, and teachers never spend time to help students assimilate the pieces into a logical picture that can be used or built on. And even if the ideas are put together within a class, between classes the big picture is left fractured. The experience in the public education system becomes a vague memory of random, meaningless, and useless facts; in the same way a dismantled engine is just a pile of random metal parts.

Most school subjects themselves aren't even real knowledge. History books are full of intentional inaccuracies and distortions for the sake of corporate gain and political correctness. The true function of education is—supposedly—to make you an independent, competent thinker, someone who can make a difference in the world for the better, and someone who has the best chance for survival and success.

Despite the obvious problems that come with public schooling, almost everyone is happy. Parents are happy. Mums get to watch Coronation Street and Dad gets to go to the local pub while their children are being babysat. They don't have to worry about teaching morality or ethics to their children because it's supposedly being done for them in school.

Teachers are happy; they've got a steady job from 9-to-5, and the more they work, the more they get paid. The more school programs there are with Government funding, the more money they get. The more schools have the programs, the more funding and bonuses they get from their Government benefactors. Everyone is happy, that is, except for the students. But who cares? Who are they to complain? He who has the gold makes the rules.

In school, you spend more time learning how to obey and what to think, instead of how to think, and think for yourself. You're forcefully occupied with nonsense to prevent you from learning something useful. Almost everything important you've learned, you learned on your own time outside school. But as you progressed through school, you were given increasingly useless homework, which taught you nothing, but occupied your time nevertheless. You wish you had more time to research things that inspire you, to learn true physics and history, to make a difference. But this time is eroded by the wasteful components of the school curriculum.

What was being taught to you was compartmentalised, full of holes and errors, shallow, and politically correct to the point of nonsense. Was it your job to assimilate the parts and learn the material well enough so that you could apply it? Of course it was, but the huge amount of homework prevented you from finding time to do just that. Now you're in college, and it's no different. The repression continues, except now you're getting wiser and have caught onto their devious scheme to produce robots instead of competent men and women.

It's not your fault you're lacking in critical thinking skills. You're not being held back by your own laziness, but by direct oppression from a system with the power to punish you or put a bad mark on your paperwork if you don't give up your individual quest for knowledge in favour of hollow school course-work. There are many consequences to this program of quantity over quality. You're under a lot of stress nowadays due to this, and—as a result—you shift into a survival mode.

Survival mode consists of taking shortcuts and getting by with the least amount of effort possible, but even this small amount of effort feels like too much and doesn't seem to have any purpose. Studying becomes a means to an end and the true goal of education is disconnected from day to day life. Studying is only applied to taking the test and long-term retention of the information seems pointless. Escapism takes hold and you watch television, take drugs, engage in delinquent behaviour and over socialise, which distracts you even further from learning what's really important.

Under stress, you reach a crossroads and you either play the game or you fail.

You conform and learn the rules of the game, no matter how illogical they are and you play the game to the satisfaction of the teaching staff. You become detached from reality, from what really matters, and you're as hampered in your potential as you are stripped of your inspiration, creativity, and originality. Quantity over quality matters as part of the survival mode, and there is no profit in overdoing quality when you might not receive the benefits of that effort for decades. Because you're in survival mode, you give up thinking that far into the future. You become 'robotised' and you're respected for how well you fit the mould. The natural curiosity to discover the world has turned into irrational efforts to escape punishment.

You decide not to play ball and fall behind, unless you're clever enough to find another source of education that suits you. Your grades are average because you're disillusioned with the system and don't care about pleasing it any more. Your chances of graduation and following on with higher education are minimal, and you either drop out, or graduate at once and get a low-paying job. The price you've paid by refusing to conform is rejection into second-rate wage earning.

Either way, by entering public education, you leave either as a robot or a peasant.

Your teachers aren't to blame. They're like soldiers in the trenches fighting a war to educate you, taking orders from their bosses who are out of touch with what is happening on the front lines. They're over-stressed, underpaid, and limited in their ability to deal with what they see in the classroom. Due to political correctness, threat of legal action by parents, and apologetic school boards scared of reproach by a vocal minority with big political whack, they're limited to the strict syllabus they're forced to follow. They're told to teach some things, and they're not allowed to teach others, regulations set by a panel of nodding puppets who wouldn't know truth if it bit them on the arse, not to mention the wherewithal to spread it, if they actually recognised it. Despite once being teachers themselves, these puppets—who design the school curriculum—are detached from the classroom feedback system. Because of a tight budget, they worry about saving paper, staples, or pens, but when your school receives thousands of pounds of funding from the

Government, it uses that money to buy more computers that aren't even needed, just to keep up with the politically correct trend for schools to be technologically up-to-date. They spend more of class time teaching you how to shut up and sit still than to pay attention and think. Troublesome students are put in the same class with you, creating a form of educational socialism in which equality is maintained by dragging up the idiots at the expense of the smart ones. Separating you from your peers based on the wrong criteria leads to inconsistencies and a breakdown of the system and its components. Putting you into a grade based on your age, when you should be in a class with other students who have a similar level of knowledge and skill, results in the smart becoming dumb, and the dumb learning how to waste others' time. Because they aren't allowed to discipline you beyond telling you you're a bad influence and keeping you behind after school, everyone suffers as the idiotic and the mindless few run amok.

Conflict within the system through the poor management of resources invariably causes contempt within its ranks, as each department suffers and blames each other instead of blaming the system itself. The system is set up so that the individual elements feed off one another in a long-term downward spiral.

Here's a word for students: teachers have contempt for you. They often make an effort to take out their aggression on you, seeing you as the enemy and cause of their own stress. You see authority as something to be defied, unless your spirit is already broken by it. Teachers make up illogical rules to test how well you obey, like making you walk a certain way through the canteen, or not use certain exits at certain times, and other trivial things which annoy you and allow teaching staff to feel good when they wield their powers. This tension between you and the teacher undermines trust, and any teaching and learning between you and the teacher enters the realm of negative reinforcement. Instead of respecting one another, you despise each other, but do what you're supposed to, to avoid punishment if you don't.

As a student, you're low on ambition and initiative, but you're desperate for recognition and self-esteem; a characteristic of a system that's anti-life, anti-independence, and anti-spirit. The quest for knowledge, having become the source of your suffering, is put at the bottom of your list of priorities, as you have to do whatever is possible to regain your self-esteem, recognition, and peace of mind. However, you have to do that within the limits of the system. As a coping mechanism, you to start wearing unusual clothes, having funny hair, and seeking attention through odd behaviour for either fame or notoriety, instead of thinking for yourself and looking for your own truth and sense of morality. Your true human spirit, however, is suppressed.

You're broken and follow the teacher's illogical rules and learn to trust authority over your own instincts. You become a cog in the wheel. Breaking orders is taboo to you, something you get very nervous about when it happens, and you certainly don't do it willingly. You become a neurotic and unstable perfectionist, standing high on shaky foundations. Once your individuality is broken, you become a robot and very good at your tasks. You go on to college, absorb what's fed to you well, and find a wonderful little niche and a nice income in your field of research. However, as wonderful as that sounds, you're a drone and nothing more. You're a cow, common stock. You don't know that being the best cow still doesn't make you a farmer.

You hear stories of those who go from rags to riches, entrepreneurs who strike it rich after dropping out of college and pursuing their dreams, those who defied convention and revolutionised the world. But what did you hear in school? You heard that these people are the exception, not the rule. That's certainly true, but what the system is implying is that you're the rule, not the exception, so don't even try to stray from the production line.

The workers on the production line tell you, 'You need to do your assignment to get good results. When you get good results, employers and colleges will favour your CV. You might even get a scholarship to go to a good college. If you're good in college, you'll get a degree and have a good chance of getting a good job. And with a good job you'll have a good wife, good children, and a good life.'

What they're actually saying is this,

'Don't worry about making a difference, just concentrate on getting decent results because that's the only thing that counts in the eyes of those you'll serve. Go to college and find your quiet niche in the world, where your job will be safe because you're so specialised, there's no one else in the world that can take your place. You'll be working to maintain the system as you're seen fit. Focus all of your energy into this specialised area and don't worry about making an impact on the world because as long as you stay specialised and compartmentalised, we'll clothe you, feed you, give you a good family, and then bury you in a good plot of our land.'

Deviating from the production line is detested by the system.

If you show initiative and take risks, you become a threat to the system because you're a seed with the potential to draw back the curtain and reveal the reality behind this silent war.

You can't fulfil your true human and spiritual potential unless you defy the system.

If you only do what you're told, you'll be no better than average. The system has been designed by the biggest corporation of all; the Government. Public schools either turn out mindless drones who serve the system and the covetous corporations that operate within it, or they turn out dole spongers who are the perfect excuse for the Government to justify its massive parasitic size and an idiotic consumer base to buy the corporations' useless trinkets and toxins.

You're under an illusion, the illusion being that you either stay on the production line, try to be the best cow in the herd to maintain financial and social security, or else defy the system, fail miserably, and end up living in a cardboard box on the street. You're seen as a social failure if you defy the system. If you measure your success by what the system considers successful, then you're inevitably afraid of getting off the production line because that's a sure sign of failure.

You must work at becoming 'dis-illusioned'.

You have to redesign your standards for success. Would dropping out of a Government-run college make you a failure? In the eyes of the rest of the herd, maybe, but getting a better, independent education somewhere else, or having some real world experience would more than make up for it.

How many famous people do you know who did everything they were told and nothing more, who never took risks for fear of challenging the status quo? Very, very few. Not only are you obliged to take risks and make the most of your innate initiative, you also have to get over your fear of defying the system and do so to get ahead of the herd. If you so choose, you have the power to be the exception, not the rule.

Now, the drones in the system are definitely needed. We still need employees, soldiers, and scientists who are specialised in what they do, but there is an excess of these right now, so it's essential that we produce more individualists and entrepreneurs.

And the only way for them to increase in numbers is for people like you to break out of the mould and fulfil your destiny as a living, breathing, sentient and potent soul, not to live a shallow, empty life as a corporate robot.

Take Responsibility... look it up for yourself. Search engine paths regarding topics addressed in this chapter:

Crime in school
GCSE
Homeschooling
Look-Say Method
National Education Association
No Child Left Behind
Public school system
Ritalin
Standardized testing
Teacher qualification standards
The Deliberate Dumbing Down of America
Thomas Hopkins Gallaudet
Top Ten School
Winning the Brain Race.

BEST LAID PLANS

We are on the verge of a global transformation. All we need is the right major crisis and the nations will accept the new world order.
DAVID ROCKEFELLER
MEMOIRS, 2002

Thesis + antithesis = synthesis
HEGELIAN DIALECTIC

We're told that we are using up the earth's precious, finite resources at a brisk rate. We have the technology to see a car licence plate from a satellite orbiting our planet, and our governments have computers that can tune in to any telephone conversation they care to. We've created an implantable computer chip, smaller than a grain of rice, which can store and transmit megabytes, if not gigabytes, of data. Are we seriously expected to believe that we don't have the ability and technology to utilise and recycle the earth's immense natural resources expediently enough to feed and clothe everyone on the planet on an ongoing basis? Our governments actually pay farmers to not grow food. Meanwhile, food being delivered to third world countries is stored in buildings and left to rot. It all beggars belief.

To feed a starving child is to exacerbate the world population problem.
DR. LAMONT COLE, PROFESSOR OF ECOLOGY, CORNELL UNIVERSITY
QUOTED BY ELIZABETH WHELAN IN HER BOOK TOXIC TERROR

The first I heard of the New World Order and Global 2000 was from former president George Bush Sr back in the 1990s, when he began to crowbar it into his speeches from time to time. Many underground press writers have covered the subject but I don't think anyone has had the same insight and inside information that Dr. John Coleman has. Back in 1992 he wrote a small booklet called

Global 2000 — A Blueprint for Global Genocide: The Reduction of the Earth's Population by 90%.

Coleman has very impressive credentials; he's a former MI6 undercover intelligence officer and has lectured on the subject all over the world. According to Coleman, MI6 is the most powerful and the oldest of all the world's intelligence agencies; they reportedly taught the likes of the CIA, Vatican Intelligence, French Intelligence and the Mossad. On being questioned regarding the possibility that he may be revealing state secrets, he asserted that everything that he's published he's had clearance to publish. It appears that, once you sign on as her Majesty's servant in MI6, it isn't that you spent 30 years speaking in hushed tones then retire and go about your business; once you join, you're in the organisation until you pop your clogs. Everything he writes has to be approved by MI6, period. He went on to say there's nothing that he has ever written on the agenda that hasn't already been revealed. If only 10% of what Coleman has written about is true, the world really is up crap creek without a paddle. Having said all that, I'm not one to hang my hat on the disclosures of ex-intelligence officers, especially since David Shayler, a once-credible MI5 whistleblower, revealed himself to be the Christ reborn not so long ago. That particular revelation colours all of his previous information a hazy shade of 'hmmmm' in my opinion. For the sake of a good argument though, let's assume that Coleman is still as sharp as the tack MI6 employed all those years ago and is telling us the gospel truth.

In 1979, Coleman received a copy of a massive document commissioned by the Committee of 300, via the Club of Rome, three days after President James Earl Carter accepted it as official US Policy. The Global 2000 report was unknown outside the Committee of 300 and carefully chosen officials inside US Government circles and was based on the musings of 19th century writers such as Lord Bertrand Russell and H. G. Wells, who asserted that the world is populated with too many redundant people and that, by 2050, the planet would become overpopulated and would lack the natural resources to sustain its inhabitants. Apparently, we 'useless eaters', a term first heard during Hitler's reign of terror, must be controlled and shouldn't be allowed to procreate and consume scarce natural resources, and thus becoming a drain on the privileged rulers.

Mankind's problems can no longer be solved by national governments.
What is needed is a world government.
UNITED NATIONS 'HUMAN DEVELOPMENT, 1994 (PAGE 88)

First established in 1727 by the British Aristocracy, the Committee of 300 is a supranational body that knows no boundaries and respects the laws of no country. The Committee's primary goal is to create a world system of financial control, in private hands, able to dominate the political system of each country, and the economy of the world as a whole. The first time they were publicly announced was by a German socialist by the name of Walther Rathenau, who was the financial adviser to the Kaiser of Germany and the French contingent of the Rothschild family.

Writing in the Wiener Press on the 24th December 1921, he stated, 'Only 300 men, each of whom knows all others govern the fate of Europe, select their successors from their own entourage. These men have the means in their hands of putting an end to the form of State which they find unreasonable.'

Exactly six months after publication, Rathenau was assassinated.

Allegedly, when former head of State Mikhail Gorbachev visited the United States to open his Gorbachev foundation, whilst flanked by George Bush senior and Dan Quayle, he let the cat out of the bag by inadvertently proclaiming his actions had been approved by the Committee of 300; the CNN cameras trained on him at the time, immediately switched focus and the comment was swiftly glossed over.

By all accounts, the Committee is more than capable of achieving their plan, not only by virtue of their own incredible wealth but by funding from the so-called Black Nobility, and the fact that they control thousands of the top banking institutions, the political organisations, insurance companies, mining conglomerates and corporations. It doesn't matter who is in the White House or 10 Downing Street, the Committee of 300, through the Royal Institute for International Affairs (RIIA) and the Council on Foreign Relations (CFR), exercises complete control. For instance, given the more subtle methods that are well known in intelligence circles for getting rid of bothersome people, it would have been a very simple matter to make it look as though JFK had died of a heart attack or some other natural cause but instead of doing that and in order to warn every president that would follow in his wake, as well as every powerful person in the country, every one 'in the know', essentially, Kennedy was publicly and brutally executed. The inarguable message stated clearly as, 'You will obey, or you suffer the same fate.'

Kennedy's famous address before the American Newspaper

Publishers Association on April 27th, 1961 has often been cited as the reason for his assassination, but he was killed more than two years later, on November 22nd, 1963, making it appear as though the two events are unrelated—or that the PTB have the patience of saints. If this Global 2000/Protocols of Zion conspiracy has any credence, I'm inclined to believe the latter. Kennedy's speech is profoundly relevant and I highly recommend taking the time to read it in full. Insert the following phrase, 'The very word 'secrecy' is repugnant in a free and open society' into a search engine and look for the entire text.

As with Gorbachev's *faux-pas*, I can only imagine the wailing and gnashing of teeth in the Elites' fortress of solitude as they heard Kennedy uttering these words—assuming they didn't write the speech themselves, in the hope of getting caught. After all, you know what they say about psychopaths having a subconscious desire to be found out, so they can finally receive public recognition and bask in the glow of their achievements.

The strongest arm of the Committee of 300 is an Elite 'think tank' called the Club of Rome, one of the most insidious, baneful organisations in existence today. It was created in April 1968 by Aurelio Peccai and Alexander King at the Rockefeller's private estate in Bellagio, Italy and was created solely to serve the interests of the Committee of 300. The Club of Rome was responsible for the birth of the modern day environmental movement in the late 60s. In 1972, COR released an alarmist publication entitled *Limits to Growth,* warning of worldwide overpopulation and the need for sustainable development and population control. In 1976, the US subsidiary of the Club of Rome, also known as USACOR, was established. Their main purpose was to bring down the industries, stall the agricultural development of the United States and formulate global crisis by which the world can be united under a world government.

The COR is allegedly a marriage between Anglo-American financiers and the Black Nobility families of Europe, particularly the so-called nobilities of London, Venice and Genoa. The Black Nobility families got their name because of the very dark nature of their deeds; they make Lucrezia Borgia look like a Sunday school teacher.

These families—the Habsburgs, the Liechtensteins and the Guelphs—date back to the 11th century and as a result of drug trading, and investing in and controlling the natural resources of the world, have accumulated enough wealth to make even King

Midas envious. The Black Guelphs were the worst of them. Interestingly enough, Queen Elizabeth II is a Guelph, not a Windsor. In a rebranding move to separate the royal family from their Germanic roots, Saxe-Coburg-Gotha was changed to the House of Windsor by her grandfather in 1917, to put researchers off the scent. It's important to keep this in mind as every time there is a financial crisis, it follows a meeting of the Black Guelphs with the world's elite banksters on the Britannia yacht, anchored off the coast of Venice.

In 1991 the Club of Rome published *The First Global Revolution*, authored by Alexander King and Bertrand Schneider. On pages 104-105, we find the following statement, *'In searching for an enemy to unite us, we came up with the idea that pollution, the threat of global warming, water shortages, famine and the like would fit the bill... all these dangers are caused by human intervention. The real enemy then, is humanity itself.'*

If you're having difficulty believing that the Committee of 300 considers man to be an enemy of the planet then you ought to read what Club of Rome member and founder Aurelio Peccei wrote on the subject, *'For the first time since the millennium was approached in Christendom, large masses of people are really in suspense about the impending advent of something unknown which could change their collective fate entirely. Animals know how to be animals but only man is vile. Now they (animals) are in danger because their deadliest enemy, the enemy tyrant of most forms of life, man, moves evermore against them. Man invented the story of the 'bad dragon' but if there ever was a bad dragon on earth is man himself, since man opened the Pandora's box of new technologies he has suffered uncontrollable human proliferation, the mania for growth, energy crisis, actual or potential resource scarcity, degradation of the environment, nuclear folly and countless other afflictions.'*

I need to ask you at this point, friends, who are the dangerous enemies? Isn't it our professions and professionals? You know it wasn't bin lorry drivers in London who created AIDS in a laboratory and unleashed it upon the Africans. It wasn't the carpenters, plumbers and electricians who discovered nuclear energy; it's the governments and the politicians and the scientists and the intelligentsia that unleashed that genie of nuclear technology upon the world. It's the scientists, the politicians that are the problem, not the electricians in London or the plumbers in New York, or the boat people of Vietnam or anywhere else. The common people on planet Earth are happy to go out and catch fish, collect the rubbish, build houses and live out their lives peacefully and quietly. That's the reality of the matter. And we've got this chap, Aurelio Peccei,

blaming all of us commoners for the consequences of their desire
to have more wealth and power.

Peccei goes on to say, *'Surely this dangerous enemy (man) must be
held in check.'*

Lets take a look at who is killing whom over in Iraq. Is it the
common people of Iraq that are the dangerous enemies, or is it
'the powers that be'? You can decide for yourself, but remember,
I didn't invent nuclear weapons, or mustard gas or some other
means of mass destruction.

Another of Peccei's now infamous quotes is as follows:

> *Damaged by conflicting policies of three major countries and blocs,
> roughly patched up here and there, the existing international economic
> order is visibly coming apart at the seams. The prospect of the necessity
> of the recourse to triage deciding who must be saved is a very grim one
> indeed. But, if lamentably, events should come to such a pass, the right to
> make such decisions cannot be left to just a few nations because it would
> lend themselves to ominous power over life of the world's hungry.*

What Global 2000 says must be done here is to give a central
organisation—a one world government, New World Order—omi-
nous powers over the lives of the world's hungry. In other words,
the right to play God. We've seen just how this works in Soma-
lia, Eritrea and Ethiopia, and we're going to see in the future how
Global 2000 powers unfold in the other areas of Africa, especially
South Africa.

Once the African National Congress (ANC) gains control with
the connivance, knavery and treason of Washington, we'll have an
opportunity to witness starvation stalk the land alongside AIDS,
both of which will carry away millions upon millions of blacks in
South Africa where famine and plague has never been experienced
before. The puppet government of Africa will have no qualms in
obeying the Committee of 300 orders to implement mass genocide
of the black 'useless eaters'. Bear in mind that it's a white man's
plan, which is not to say that all the white people in the world are
seeking to dominate all Blacks and Chinese. It means that the cadre
of oligarchs, the Committee of 300, are white Anglo-Saxons and
they simply aim to rule world. Who are the real racist people in the
world though? Isn't it the oligarchs? Isn't it the snobs at the top of
the feeding chain?

The 1976 Global 2000 forerunner, *Resource Shaping and International Order,* also published by the Club of Rome, carried an article
under the title *Mankind at the turning point,* Mihajlo Mesarovic and

Edward Pestel, who wrote it, called it *'A master plan to lead to the creation of a new mankind.'* The work started with these words, *'The world has cancer and that cancer is man,'* and Global 2000 was written strictly with this premise as the basis of its conclusion; billions of human beings must be ruthless ruthlessly culled out by the end of the year 2050.

Global 2000 used 'Mankind at the turning point' to claim that a new strategy to redistribute natural resources was utterly essential. It also attacked the consumerism in America and called Americans 'greedy and unwilling to make sacrifices of any kind.' The report recommended that 'out of theatre' NATO forces be used to bring Third World countries into line with its new economic policies. Global 2000 borrowed heavily from Holland Cleveland's Atlantic Council report, which mandated a world body taking control of the natural resources of all the nations, and to advise Third World nations to decide democratically among themselves which populations would be eliminated. Isn't that just wonderful? You can just about bet that the people who are voting are going to be voting to eliminate those who are not voting, and what we see going on in Iraq at the moment is part and parcel of the programme. The United States needs oil and will take it from the Iraqis, who just won't lay down and die, it seems. They've apparently decided that they may as well go down fighting because they're going to be killed and pillaged anyway, which is what the game plan calls for.

Can you think of a better example of 'useless eaters' than a bunch of 'rag-heads' running around in the desert? They're all just out there consuming natural resources—of what value are they? The people of Africa, millions of people—useless eaters—what do we need them for? They're not making us any profit, they're costing us money, let's get rid of them; let's give them AIDS. What about the teeming millions in India and China? Get rid of them.

These people see themselves as gods and they are treating us as pawns in some sick chess game.

The anti-Semitic forgery created in or around 1884, entitled *The Protocols of the Learned Elders of Zion,* has caused a great deal of controversy, not to mention suffering. Some people believe its veracity to this day, but you need to ask yourself, would the Elite really leave the minutes of such a crucial meeting lying around? Or would they be more likely to plant false minutes to further their own ends? Do the research and make up your own mind.

Perhaps the most interesting thing about the *Protocols* is that there was truth wrapped up in the lie: the document is chillingly prophetic of the unfolding aims and methods being brought to fruition right now. Somehow, whoever created it had inside information on how things were going to turn out over the following century and more.

The 9th protocol states in part:

'By all these means we shall so wear down the gentiles that they will be compelled to offer us international power of a nature that by its position will enable us without any violence gradually to absorb all the state forces of the world and to form a super government… We have in our service persons of all opinions, of all doctrines, monarchists, demagogues, socialists, communists, and utopian dreamers of every kind. We have harnessed them all to the task: each one of them on his own account is boring away at the last remnants of authority, is striving to overthrow all established form of order. By these acts all States are in torture; they exhort to tranquility, are ready to sacrifice everything for peace: but we will not give them peace until they openly acknowledge our international Super-Government, and with submissiveness.'

A world government is coming into play, friends. Fifty or a hundred years ago when we talked about world government it was a fantasy, it was 100% Buck Rogers. We're just about there right now though, aren't we?

From the 6th protocol:

'We shall soon begin to establish huge monopolies, colossal reservoirs of wealth, upon which even the big gentile properties will be dependant to such an extent that they will all fall together with the government credit on the day following the political catastrophe.'

The collapse of the world's economic system will usher in the new world order. Gigantic, 'colossal reservoirs of wealth' like General Motors, Microsoft and Walmart, Citicorp, Bank of America, the credit card companies. Of course, today we call ourselves 'employees' but back in the day we'd all be called debt feudal serfs, which is closer to the truth.

From the Protocols:

'The aristocracy of the gentiles as a political force, is dead—we no longer need to take it into account, but as landed proprietors they can still be harmful to us by the fact that they are self-sufficing in the resources upon which they live. It is essential therefore for us at whatever cost to deprive them of their land.'

Brits and Americans are now landless serfs. How many of you people reading this chapter own your homes free and clear? How many of you own land free and clear? Alan Greenspan, as part of this NWO program, lowered interest rates in the US to 1%. Mortgages that carried 7,8, or 9% interest rates were all refinanced. Many of us went out into the mortgage marketplace and re-mortgaged our properties, instead of paying them off and ridding ourselves of the shackles. We've buried ourselves under a mountain of debt.

From the Protocols:

> 'This object will be best attained by increasing the burdens upon landed property — in loading lands with debts. These measures will check land holding and keep it in a state of humble and unconditional submission. The aristocrats of the gentiles, being hereditarily incapable of contenting themselves with little, will rapidly burn up and fizzle out.'

Most of the people of the west are living in a fool's dreamland. Go ahead, go back to sleep and dream on, but you should know there are forces abroad that are planning to destroy you and take your property away from you, and not necessarily in that order. Most Westerners have been eager to follow that plan, we have indebted ourselves up over our heads and we'll never see daylight again. Meanwhile, Congress and Parliament is about to shut the gate behind us so that we can't declare bankruptcy. This gate is not quite closed yet, but it won't be long now. Banks and credit card companies are not going to let you bankrupt out of this mess, they're going to hang onto you as surety for your debt.

From the Protocols:

> 'At the same time we must intensively patronize trade and industry, but, first and foremost, speculation, the part played by which is to provide a counterpoise to industry: the absence of speculative industry will multiply capital in private hands and will serve to restore agriculture by freeing the land from indebtedness to the land banks. It is necessary for industry to deplete the land, both of labourers and capital, and through speculations, transfer all of the money of the world into our hands, thereby throwing the gentiles into the ranks of the proletariat. The gentiles will then bow before us to obtain the right to existence.'

Did you see what happened in 2000, with the stock market collapse? $7 trillion of your money was wiped out. Speculation, that's what stocks and bonds are all about, folks. That's what buying houses at the top of the real estate market is all about. Squander your money, and we'll take it away from you.

From the Protocols:

> 'We shall raise the rate of wages which, however, will not bring any

advantage to the workers, for, at the same time, we shall produce a rise in prices of the first necessaries of life, alleging that it arises from the decline of agriculture and cattle-breeding: we shall further undermine artfully and deeply sources of production, by accustoming the workers to anarchy and to drunkenness and side by side therewith taking all measure to extirpate from the face of the earth all the educated forces of the gentiles.'

Drugs and alcohol, summer holidays, lets have another party. More bread and circuses all round.

In Edward Gibbons' book, *The Decline and Fall of the Roman Empire,* he points out that one of the primary causes of the decimation of the Roman Empire was the debasing of their monetary system. Isn't that what we're doing right now? In truth we been doing it for about seventy years but we're really going after it now; we're going to destroy it. He also said that another prime cause of the decline and fall was the moral lapse, or the debasing of morality in the Empire. Americans and Brits are turning into nations of perverts. America, whilst being one of the most puritanical societies in the world, is also the largest producers of hard-core pornography, and while the Lewinski/Clinton scandal was going on, 73% of the American public approved of Bill Clinton. Well, birds of a feather flock together, don't they?

From Protocol 10:

'… to utterly exhaust humanity with dissension, hatred, struggle, envy and even by the use of torture, by starvation, by the inoculation of diseases, by want, so that the gentiles see no other issue than to take refuge in our complete sovereignty in money and in all else.'

In the States, it's recommended that we give our children up to thirty-five vaccinations before the age of five. British and American societies are weak from these vaccinations. One third of all babies are born by Caesarean section; we've got to cut the baby out because natural childbirth isn't a safe option? The majority of our populations are addicted to drugs. I'm not talking about the illegal drugs, not the stuff that you can buy from some sleazebag on the street corner; I mean the legitimate stuff from the likes of Pfizer, Merck & Co, and all of the other pharmaceutical companies. They're killing around a quarter of a million of us every year through iatrogenic disease. This isn't a healthy society we're talking about here. In 1918, sixty percent of us were healthy, forty percent of us had symptoms or some kind of disease. Today ninety-nine percent have symptoms and diseases, and only one percent of us are healthy and symptom-free.

Have you observed the de-industrialisation of America and Great Britain? The middle classes have to be destroyed because—in the coming push toward a new world order—they would be the stumbling block.

History has shown that when the peasant class revolted in the past they were easily crushed, but this new middle class of people who had long-term employment and job security, and were well-paid for their industry are the biggest threat to the NWO agenda. They realised that relocating certain industrial enterprises to foreign nations—in the name of free trade—could easily achieve their goal.

Have you observed the rampant debt? Have you noticed the decline of the US dollar and the British pound? Did you notice we're bogged down in two big wars? I say 'big wars' in terms of the scale of our means or our ability to finance them. Notice the death that is coming from the laboratory-created degenerative diseases which were practically unheard of 100 years ago: AIDS, Alzheimer's disease, Lou Gehrig's disease and so on. Today they're household words that are just as common as television and pizza.

Coleman claims that AIDS was developed by British intelligence in Sierra Leone, specifically for use in germ warfare, and was deliberately released for the express purpose of accomplishing the Global 2000 agenda. If you take a look at the AIDS epidemic you'll notice that it's centred in Africa. This wasn't an accident; it's aimed at the black race. There are countries in Africa—Botswana to name only one—where thirty-seven percent of the people are infected by AIDS, and the figure is twenty-five percent in the advanced industrial nation of South Africa. It's currently increasing exponentially in Asia—aimed at the Oriental race. I wonder if those millions of Indians, Chinese, Japanese and Koreans are going to sit by while the oligarchs of the Committee of 300 destroy them? Or do you think maybe they might resist?

In 2009, we have swine flu rearing its ugly head once more, only this time it's been in the laboratory blender with the avian flu to emerge more virulent and mutagenic than ever before. As I write this, the powers that be have security set at level 5—level 6 being a potential reason for national quarantine. No doubt the forced vaccines will begin with those needing to travel as part of their business practices. Will I be getting a swine flu jab? Pigs might fly…

From the Protocols:

'… For a time perhaps we might be successfully dealt with by a coalition of the gentiles of all the world: but from this danger we are secured by the discord existing among them whose roots are so deeply seated that they can never now be plucked up. We have set one against another the personal and national reckonings of the gentiles, religious and race hatreds, which we have fostered into a huge growth in the course of the past twenty centuries. This is the reason why there is not one state which would anywhere receive support if it were to raise its arm, for every one of them must bear in mind that any agreement against us would be unprofitable to itself. We are too strong — there is no evading our power. The nations cannot come to even an inconsiderable private agreement without our secretly having a hand in it… The administrators, whom we shall choose from among the public, with strict regard to their capacities for servile obedience, will not be persons trained in the arts of government, and will therefore easily become pawns in our game in the hands of men of learning and genius who will be their advisers, specialists bred and reared from early childhood to rule the affairs of the whole world.'

The real people who govern this planet govern it from behind a curtain. The people you see out front, up on the stage, on your television, in your parliament and in Congress are mere puppets and the oligarchy pull their strings. There is no independent press in the West, the journalists dance because they are paid a lot of money.

There are various citations and direct quotations from the architects of this grand scheme that go back some two hundred years. Many books have been written, but here in the West we're more concerned about summer holidays and the sexual licentiousness that comes from it, or the money to be made from it than we are about reading arcane and archaic books about some malevolent conspiracy. Maybe it is time to take a fresh look at what's going on around us.

I'm not a theologian and I'm not at all a religious man, but I do have a tremendous amount of faith in a higher power. I'm certainly not here to get you saved or converted, or to tell you which church you should go to, or to beat you over the head with the Bible. I point this out because I feel this subject wouldn't be complete without addressing biblical prophesy and I don't want your eyes to glaze over thinking I'm about to get all evangelical. There are many quotes in the Bible that relate to what is happening here and—although there's the matter of interpretation—the relationship is fascinating.

I started my research in Matthew 24, Mark 13 and Luke 21, the three gospel accounts of 'the Great Tribulation'. All three accounts essentially cover the same thing, except that each chapter will tell you a little that the others don't, so you have to read all three of them. They are extrapolated on two prophecies that Moses spoke of in Leviticus 26 and Deuteronomy 28—the core prophesies that give us the understanding we need for Revelations 6, 7, 8, 9, 11, 12, 13, 14, 16, 17, 18 and 19. All of these chapters seem to be telling the same story we are being told in Global 2000, and by Dr. Coleman, Dr. Stanley Monteith, the Georgia Guidestones and Margaret Sanger. Could it be that these prophecies are now coming to pass right before our very eyes?

From Matthew 24:

And Jesus went out, and departed from the temple: and his disciples came to him for to show him the buildings of the temple. And Jesus said unto them, 'See ye not all these things? Verily I say unto you, there shall not be left here one stone upon another that shall not be thrown down.

I should point out that the Wailing Wall,—the foundation of Solomon's Temple—is still there. Either Jesus didn't know what he was talking about—or he exaggerated, lied, or just flat-out didn't know when he said *'Look at the stones on this wall, not one of them is going to be left standing on another.'* It hasn't happened yet, so when I hear someone say Jesus has returned, or Jesus is coming, I'll have good reason to say, 'Uhhh… not yet.'

As long as those stones are in that wall, you can rest assured that the Messiah hasn't come yet and is not coming yet, otherwise the prophecy in Matthew 24 verse two is just a good after-dinner anecdote. Time will tell.

In Matthew 24 Verse 3, as the messiah sat upon the Mount of Olives, the disciples came unto him privately and said, 'So, tell us, boss, when shall these things be, and what shall be the sign of thy coming, and of the end of the world?' And Big J answered and said unto them,

'Take heed that no man deceive you. For many shall come in my name, saying, I am Christ; and shall deceive many. And ye shall hear of wars and rumours of wars: see that ye be not troubled: for all these things must come to pass, but the end is not yet. For nation shall rise against nation, and kingdom against kingdom: and there shall be famines, and pestilences, and earthquakes, in divers places.'

'…For many shall come in my name, saying, I am Christ; and shall deceive many…' I wonder if David Shayler has read this line.

Mind you, he could assert that he said it, so he doesn't need to read it.

The 20th Century saw more people killed from war than any other century in the history of the world; we watched wars and rumours of wars kill a hundred million people. We're currently at war in Iraq and Afghanistan, and war with Syria and Iran seems to be looming on the horizon. When the whole 'peak oil issue' (fake or otherwise) begins to bubble over, we'll see the Chinese and the Indians coming into the Middle East to take their fair share of the black gold.

In the first part of the Global 2000 document we get a sense that 100 million people killed weren't enough. The wars are not keeping up with population growth. In order to reduce the population by ninety percent, it's going to take something more effective. War is very valuable to these conspirators, though, and they've used it very effectively for other purposes; namely, to destabilise governments and—by default—entire nations. What we're facing today, thanks to the Bush/Obama and Blair/Brown administrations, is 'The War on Terror', which is simply another step in the book of Revelations.

We're hearing about famines, and disease epidemics like AIDS and malaria. AIDS has grown from a disease with insignificant impact in 1980 to a worldwide pandemic affecting tens of millions today and it's growing at an exponential rate; every few years it doubles in scope.

Here we are, witnessing the progress of the destruction of one and a half billion human beings, and most of us haven't noticed, it's just a statistic; we're completely jaded to what is going on around us. Could it be that we're already in the death throes of civilisation and humanity and we just haven't been paying attention? Open your eyes and look around, friends, pay attention to what you're seeing.

Most people don't recognise the signs, and indeed most won't recognise them because they haven't read the Bible. Whether you are religious or not, you'd think people would pick up and read the book that—directly or indirectly—informs all of our lives.

These 'Elites' don't believe in God in the Biblical sense, they're Evolutionists. They have their own God, they have their own religion, they have a plan that has been in operation for 200-plus years, they're willing to die for it, and you're not in on it. Think about this for a second, my American cousins: George W. Bush was a member of the satanic 'club', Skull and Bones. His daddy was also a member, as was Prescott Bush, his granddaddy. Do you really believe the policies of the Bush family suddenly took a change when George Bush Junior declared that he was a born-again Christian in order to capture the Bible Belt vote during the 2004 election? Did you really think he was working for you and your Christian principles and philosophies? If you believe that nonsense, I've got a bridge on the Thames to sell you.

> *Those least fit to carry on race are increasing most rapidly…*
> *funds that should be used to raise the standard of our civilisation*
> *are diverted to the maintenance of those who should never have been born.*
> MARGARET SANGER
> THE PIVOT OF CIVILIZATION, 1922

The Global Economy is now well into a (pre-planned) depression and it's only now politicians are acknowledging that fact. In the 1990s, the West went through a robust period of inflation and expansion, and heartily approved the World Trade Organisation (WTO), NAFTA and GATT. We've now exported up to 4 million jobs from the US and Britain to India, and China. We've now exported our industrial base to countries all over the world, and we've adopted this concept of the information age, the information network, and the information economy. Well, let's see how this plays out.

Since 1973, Americans and Brits have not received a real increase in productivity. We're earning more and more 'money'—more and more inflated currency—but we have poorer and poorer jobs. We now have to have a man and his wife working to support the family and debt is continually growing.

The average family debt is between £7,000-12,000 just on credit cards. Of course, we are reticent to call it a depression but let's take a look at it; your real wages are going down, your standard of living is going down, your debts are going up, your jobs are being exported to other countries, your industrial base has already been exported. Thirty-three percent of Americans and Brits worked in manufacturing twenty years ago; today it's thirteen percent. Now that's a 'depression' but it's been mislabelled. We talk about full employment, with 5.2% unemployed. We don't talk about those who are no longer looking for employment, or who are no longer engaged in manufacturing. Twenty percent of Brits and Americans who were engaged in manufacturing twenty years ago must be doing something else today—namely, working at McDonald's, at Walmart, Tesco, Asda, Burger King, or some other private enterprise, or living off the government, but they are not looking for employment.

Unlike the 1930s, we are not calling this a full depression just yet, but that's exactly where we are, folks. The people who will be dealing with your income tax returns for Her Majesty's Revenue and Collection (HMRC) will not be British; they will be Indians, in India. Tens of thousands of these white-collar jobs are already being exported to India. I'm sure that's great for India's economy and I am just so happy for all those Indians, but what about our economy? We're attacking and killing the American dream and British enterprise and before it's all over, millions upon millions of Brits and Americans and Westerners in general will have become 'useless eaters' consigned to the scrap-heap to be disposed of in the most convenient manner possible. Strong words, indeed, but they're words that must be shouted from the rooftops, we can't keep silent in the face of such present danger.

> *We must help population control at home, hopefully through changes in*
> *our value system, but by compulsion if voluntary methods fail.*
> PAUL EHRLICH
> *THE POPULATION BOMB, 1968*

Decisions that you make in the year 2009 through 2012 are going to determine whether you live or die in the years 2015 and onwards—that just where reality is. People had decisions to make in 1930-40 and many of them died because of the decisions they made, and many of them lived based upon the decisions that they made. Albert Einstein left Germany in 1935 and lived, millions of others decided to stay and see what was going to happen and were snuffed out. We're facing the same life and death decision concerning Global 2000 that German Jews had to face in 1930.

A thermonuclear war is coming to a city near you, in your lifetime. We're beginning to see more and more thermonuclear war chatter in the news as the days go by, detailing the prospects of a nuclear war with China, or an attack by North Korea, or Iran. The Chinese state has not traditionally been seen as a friend to the West—far from it—and yet here we are buying goods from the Chinese just as fast as we can, impoverishing ourselves, putting ourselves into feudal serfdom and credit debt slavery. Remember, I'm not here to tell you how to live your life, I just think that you should be aware that this is a suicidal policy. It may need some re-rethinking—if not as a nation then at least you, as an individual, might devote some time and effort into considering how it may impact your life.

In 1970, the world's food supply was seventy-three days for every man, woman and child on planet Earth. Today it's less than thirty-eight days. These Global 2000 mad scientists, philosophers, preachers and politicians plan to use famine, disease, plague and pestilence to reduce the earth's population by ninety percent over the next fifty years under the Club of Rome plan.

In Revelations, Chapter 6, the Bible tells us exactly the same thing, in essentially the same words; False prophets, war, famine and disease. In 1920, nearly fifty percent of our people lived on the land as subsistence farmers producing their own food and food for the rest of the world, but today we Westerners have chosen to live in cities and now only three percent of us live on the land. That translates into ninety-seven percent of us that are no longer self-sufficient in our food production. We certainly produce food for export, though, while importing goods from France, Italy and Spain, Mexico, Chile and China. Our food supplies are in the hands of foreigners and multinational corporations who support the Global 2000 world population control programme.

According to Sir Peter Vicars, The New World Order is to be an 'information service society'—the old industry-based age is dead and is in the process of being buried. Which begs the question, what need then for the millions of people who previously earned their livings in factories and machine-based agriculture? They're now surplus to requirements and must be eliminated because they are a burden on the natural resources of the world—useless eaters. We allow them to live in the hope that employment will turn up for them some day the future, while in nature they would be allowed to die. The way the elite see it, all that Global 2000 is doing is helping nature to perform its job better.

If you've been watching the news and reading newspapers throughout the Carter, Reagan, Bush, Clinton and Bush-the-Sequel administrations, you have had a front row seat to the dismantling of the American industrial base. You've lived right through it and—until now—you missed it, didn't you?

Thirty-three percent of Americans were engaged in manufacturing during the Carter administration. Today, it's thirteen percent, and even those jobs are being exported to China just as fast as companies can up sticks and move out. Essentially all of the textile industry of the United States has been exported to China, Bangladesh, or Pakistan. One of the three basic necessities of life alongside food and shelter is clothing. Next year or the year after, America will no longer be self-sufficient in food—you'll be importing more food than you'll be exporting. Today, not only are you the world's largest debtor nation, in five more years you'll be a net food consumer nation. You may not be able to feed yourselves, clothe yourselves and the roof over your head is disappearing in greater numbers each month.

Over the past thirty-five years, America has been converted from the breadbasket of the world into a basket case.

Humans on Earth behave in some ways like a pathogenic microorganism,
or like the cells of the tumour.
SIR JAMES LOVELOCK
HEALING GAIA: PRACTICAL MEDICINE FOR THE PLANET 1991

We're being told that genetic modification is a good for the world, for society. To feed the world we need genetically modified seeds. Friends, wake-up: GM seeds are created to kill you, not to feed you. It's the same deal with vaccinations, they're not designed to protect you or to save lives, they're designed to weaken your immune system so that when the time is right and these diseases are unleashed, you'll be more susceptible to croaking, kicking the bucket, leaving this earthly plane and making room for the spawn of the Elite. If you've been vaccinated, you have already been murdered; you just haven't succumbed yet! Nearly all Americans and Brits have had many, many vaccinations. There is more than enough evidence to show that a lot of these diseases are actually spread through the vaccination programs, which reminds me of a 2007 remake of the 1956 film *Invasion of the Body Snatchers* titled *The Invasion,* starring Daniel Craig (the current James Bond) and Nicole Kidman. In what was a particularly chilling scene for me, the government, which had already been infiltrated by the alien invaders, was mandating vaccinations to deal with the rapidly spreading flu like symptoms; symptoms that were the precursor to the metamorphosis into the mindless drones/hive mentality.

It's been said that AIDS was spread all over Africa through the vaccination programs…

Have you ever noticed how the United States, Britain and the United Nations wring their hands and sound off about the problems around the world? 'Well, good lord, look at that—there's

genocide going on in Rwanda or the Sudan, we need to do something about that…' but they never intervene. Instead, the United
Nations sits back and watches as millions are killed.

As these events transpire, those of us watching these events
become more and more desensitised. We Westerners are now so
numbed to this madness that if we were to see the Book of Revelation come to pass before our very eyes on the evening news, it
would leave little or no impression.

We still hear about the Jewish holocaust—if you ask me, that
catastrophe was experiment number one. They haven't unleashed
a final revelation upon us yet, we haven't seen the massive death
as described in the Book of Revelation, but it's going to be big. We
wouldn't have any idea as to what is really going on in the world if
it weren't for insiders and whistle-blowers like Coleman, who risk
life and limb to make us aware of these agendas.

How many of us read medical journals? How many of us read
reports from the Centre for Disease Control, or intelligence reports
from the CIA, bearing in mind, of course, that most of us don't
even have access to that information. You certainly won't be seeing
accurate reports on the news regarding how many millions have
died from this or that disease, or what the actual figures relating
to the genocide in Rwanda are. Insiders have contacts from which
they can get this information and their conscience obliges them to
reveal to us.

Joseph Stalin once said, *'When one person dies it's a tragedy. When
one million people die, it's a statistic.'* He starved 16 million Ukrain-
ians to death—a mere statistic, of course. It's just a number way
back in history—the 1930s—and nobody pays attention to it. Adolf
Hitler kills millions of people in concentration camps; mind you,
Hitler was pioneering about it; he took death to a whole new level,
an industrial level, which was new and novel, if not very popular.

Now having realised that it's not popular to establish death
factories as Hitler did, the Elites have decided to create designer
diseases—then they wring their hands over the 'tragedy' of it and
the president says he'll spend $15 billion on AIDS research and
one thing and another. All the while they're spreading sickness
throughout the world using vaccinations as a carrier. We believe
their disinformation, and the vast majority clamour to get their fair
share of the vaccines. Pay attention to the numbers: in 1900, the
cancer rate was one in thirty-three; today it's one in two. What the
hell has your government done for you in one hundred years of
Cancer research? They've given you cancer, which is the objective

here. And then take a look at AIDS. We spend millions and millions of pounds and dollars to combat AIDS, which went from an epidemic to a pandemic, totally out of control worldwide. What is the government doing for you there? They vaccinate you; weaken your immune system so that one of these opportunistic diseases can take you out of the gene pool... because you are a useless eater.

The 1992 Earth Summit also gave birth to 'Agenda 21'—the blueprint for the 21st Century. Agenda 21 outlines the Globalist plan for a completely managed global society, all under the auspices of the UN. It will set new global requirements for how we must live, eat, travel, learn and communicate and will be sold to the public under the guise of saving mother Earth.

An excerpt from Agenda 21 reads:

'Effective execution (of Agenda 21) will require a profound reorientation of all human society, unlike anything the world has ever experienced... a major shift in the priorities of both governments and individuals and an unprecedented redeployment of human and financial resources. This shift will demand that a concern for the environmental consequences of every human action be integrated into individual and collective decision-making at every level.'

We're living at the end of an age. We're well into the period of chaos as we make the transition from the old age of Pisces to the 'New Age' of Aquarius, and we are beginning to see the new religion of this new age emerge to replace the old age religion of Christianity; a form of state worship coupled with Gaia (earth) worship.

The resultant ideal sustainable population is hence more than 500 million but less than one billion.
CLUB OF ROME, GOALS FOR MANKIND, 1976

Located on top of a hill in Eberton, Georgia and erected in 1979 by an anonymous 'R.C. Christian'—in reference to Christian Rosenkreuz and the Rosicrucian Order—stands the 16' tall Georgia Guide Stones, a granite 'new age' shrine. Inscribed in eight different languages, the ten guiding principles on the faces of the slabs hint at global governance, a new world religion and population reduction. The Ten Commandments for the new age are as follows:

1. Maintain humanity under 500,000,000 in perpetual balance with nature
2. Guide reproduction wisely, improving fitness and diversity

3. Unite humanity with a living new language.
4. Rule passion, faith, tradition, and all things with tempered reason
5. Protect people and nations with fair laws and just courts
6. Let all the nation's rule internally, resolving external disputes in a world court
7. Avoid petty laws and useless officials
8. Balance personal rights with social duties
9. Prize truth–beauty–love, seeking harmony with the infinite
10. Be not a cancer on earth–Leave room for nature–Leave room for nature.

Whilst most of these guides seem fairly innocuous, the main thrust of the message is to dramatically reduce the population of the world, promote environmentalism, establish a world government and promote a new spirituality.

The genocidal policy of Global 2000 and the New World order is the greatest threat to our lives, liberty and property in recorded history. At the time of writing this book, Global 2000 has been accepted by Canada, the United States, Spain, Belgium, Australia, Holland, Luxembourg, Britain, France, and South Africa. Let's not delude a ourselves into believing we are going to stop these mad scientists, preachers, philosophers and politicians in their scheme to enslave the world and impose a worldwide tyranny upon all of us, but we also don't have to participate in our own demise; we don't have to help them, finance them or stand helplessly by and do nothing.

> *The world has cancer, and that cancer is Man.*
> MERTON LAMBERT
> FORMER SPOKESMAN FOR THE ROCKEFELLER FOUNDATION

The one world government began with King George III, who had already enrolled at least 50 countries in the idea of a world dictatorship during his reign.

The Kings and Queens of the world are all high masons and subject to the Roman pontiff. Behind the scenes of the Islamic and Catholic religions are the secret societies and their agenda. What is this war with Islam about? Who are these people who are pulling the strings in either camp? From the rock stars of the world, the Bonos and the Geldofs, to the political leaders, everyone seems to be bowing down to the papal Caesar. From the east to the west, the Islamic world is currently being set up as the synthesis, pitted against the antithesis that is the Judeo-Christian culture; out of this must come a synthesis and a unification.

Rich men behind the scenes, families like the Windsors, the Rockefellers, the Bushes, the Carnegies, the Bundys and the Vanderbilts, are the movers and shakers of the Global 2000 project—The New World order. Ninety percent—that's a lot of people dying, folks, and they're working hard to make it so. In short, they haven't killed you yet, but they're working on it.

If the elites can kill two million Cambodians, don't you think they can kill two million Britons, two million Americans, or three thousand-plus New Yorkers? Have you thought about it in those terms? The oligarchs of the New World Order have in mind that they will keep alive about 500 million people of European stock. All the rest of you people can just shut up, lie down and die quietly. Question is, *will you?*

I contend that it's time for us to wise up and start listening to our instincts and stop following these crazy scientists, philosophers, pulpit parrots and politicians, and instead prepare to live through and survive this New World Order and Global 2000 insanity.

I've been telling you throughout this chapter that the intent coming from the Club of Rome, the primary political motivator around the world today, is to reduce the world's population by ninety percent. A little over five billion people have to die, and you are probably on the list. Sounds ridiculous? We've taken a brief look at a couple of sources, including Dr. Coleman's report on Global 2000, we've looked at a few of the protocols of Zion, written over a century ago. Their intent has even been engraved in granite in the form of the Georgia guide stones. They've made it pretty clear that they want to get rid of all of you Blacks, Jews, Orientals, Indians, Christians and Muslims... think about that. If that doesn't blow your mind, I don't know what will.

These globalists with a genocide agenda have a cause to die for.

I say let them die for it and—instead—let you and me live for ours.

Take Responsibility... look it up for yourself. Search engine paths regarding topics addressed in this chapter:

Al Gore
Bilderberger
Committee of 300
Council on Foreign Relations
David Rockefeller
Earth Charter
European Union
Georgia Guidestones
Global 2000
Harland Cleveland
Henry Kissinger
Javier Solana
Katherine Graham AKA Katharine Meyer
Kennedy Speech—search term: The very word 'secrecy' is repugnant in a free and open society'
Kyoto Protocol
Maurice Strong
Mikhail Gorbachev
NATO
Ted Turner
The Protocols of the Learned Elders of Zion
Trilateral Commission
United Nations Commission on Global Governance
United Nations Environment Programme
The Club of Rome.

VACCINE NATION

'A cynic may suggest the swine flu pandemic frenzy has been encouraged by governments around the world. It is a relatively mild disease, but animal-derived, so They can induce The Fear. By then throwing money at their friends in Big Pharma they can also appear to be Doing Something. Regarding mandatory vaccination, if you line up to let Her Majesty's Government inject you with whatever they say you need, you get what you deserve.'

DR. ALUN KIRBY, PH.D.
CENTRE FOR IMMUNOLOGY AND INFECTION
DEPARTMENT OF BIOLOGY AND HULL YORK MEDICAL SCHOOL

Nature is the curer of disease.
HIPPOCRATES

You might know what the word *responsibility* means on an intellectual level, and you may well have an understanding of it that empowers you to deal with people effectively as an employer or a teacher, for instance, but I believe that it is not until you have children of your own that you actually get it.

It's a little like gaining 'balance'. When your mother or father is teaching you how to ride a bicycle, they tell you that you have to keep your handlebars straight and keep the bike moving forward by pedaling. You understand the steps you need to take and you follow them as best you can but, sure enough, you take the odd painful fall every now and then. At some point, though, the penny drops and you get it—you get 'balance'. Afterward, it becomes entirely intuitive, a momentary understanding that you cannot unlearn.

In the moment you get that you are 100% accountable for another life, you understand what responsibility truly is; it moves from an abstract concept to the purely intuitive.

When my daughter was born—practically as she was being weighed—we were instructed to present her for vaccination *as soon as possible.* We then did what—in our blissful ignorance—we thought was the responsible thing to do; capitulated.

Before we did, we researched the effect of combined vaccinations. The MMR was getting a lot of attention at the time and we were becoming increasingly suspicious that the massive dose of three-in-one might be responsible for a spate of Sudden Infant Death Syndrome (SIDS). We expressed our concerns to our general practitioner, who assured us it was completely safe but—if it would ease our minds—we ought to consider administering the shots separately. It turned out to be much more expensive, but our conscience was clear that we had done the best for our child under the circumstances. Of course, knowing what I know now I can see we may have done more harm than good, as she had effectively been given three times the amount of preservative she would have received if we had stuck to the combined shot. When we get to the preservative section of this chapter, you will understand my concern and regret.

I don't recall having many vaccinations when I was a child, and my parents tell me vaccination wasn't anywhere near as prevalent as it is today. We had childhood diseases like measles and chickenpox and once we had gotten over them we had life-long immunity. These days, if you get these vaccinations, you don't have life-long immunity, you just have immunity for a few years. Most people who get measles these days have already had their measles vaccinations. I've often wondered about that. Why would the medical community, pharmaceutical companies and the Government want to get involved in the natural process of childhood diseases? The government then comes along and mandates it: '*If you want your children to go school they have to have these shots every five years to protect them.*' Why on earth would they want to do that?

I can think of a couple of good reasons: it's big money for the pharmaceutical industry and the pharmaceutical companies give a lot of money to political parties. One hand washes the other.

The germ theory of disease asserts that specific micro-organisms cause infectious diseases. In the past, doctors were left with little or no real way of treating the conditions of these diseases, other than to ease the symptoms, by replacing fluids during extreme vomiting and diarrhoea, body cooling for high fever, and/or pain relief. It seemed that the next logical step towards an effective treatment would be to try and fight the action of these micro-organisms in the body and to avoid infection by contamination. It would seem that through the progress of antibiotics and vaccines this has been achieved, to some degree.

Under normal conditions in the body, immune cells recognise alien particles such as bacteria and viruses. The purpose of the immune cells is to produce antibodies that are able to stick to the invading alien particles, effectively making them harmless. The antibodies fit on to specific sections on each particle, just like a key would fit a lock. The first response to infection would be the creation of the correct antibody for the particular alien particle present; the right key to fit the specific lock, so to speak. During this stage, you would usually experience the symptoms of that particular infection. For example, where measles is concerned, you might experience fever, depression and the appearance of red blotches. Once enough antibodies have been created, the measles virus is disabled, and you recover. These antibodies stay in the body and are able to recognise later infections of the same (or related) type and are more able to deal with their removal without manifesting all the symptoms of the disease. So, a person who has suffered from an infectious disease is less likely to surrender to a second spell of the illness and is said to be immune. This process is called 'acquired immunity'.

A vaccine is a unique concoction of bacterial or viral particles, which are similar to those thought to be responsible for the disease. However, these particles must be dissolved or weakened, to reduce their harmful properties. The vaccine is said to mimic the disease and—when injected into the blood stream—the immune cells of the body are stimulated into producing antibodies against the specific vaccine ingredients. These antibodies stay in the body and are able to recognise these or related micro-organisms if any infections happen in the future. Because of the method of vaccine preparation, the vaccine particles shouldn't have any harmful effects and shouldn't produce the symptoms of disease. For example, a measles vaccine might contain disabled (killed) measles virus, which would stimulate the immune cells into producing antibodies to the measles virus when injected into the blood stream. There are no symptoms of measles because the virus has been disabled but the antibodies stay in the body and theoretically protect the person from further infection. So we seem to have antibody production and protection from a vaccine, without having to suffer the symptoms of the disease. This is called artificial immunity.

Vaccination is sold as the only effective means of stopping potentially dangerous infectious diseases and epidemics. It's said to be responsible for the decline in infectious diseases and is supposedly harmless compared to the risk of serious disorders resulting from infectious diseases. However, the trouble with vaccine preparation is in the production of vaccine micro-organisms that are properly related to the active micro-organisms apparently responsible for the disease. If deactivation of the vaccine micro-organism changes it noticeably from its original active state, then the antibodies created don't react to active micro-organisms in the real disease situation; the key doesn't fit the lock. On the other hand, if the vaccine micro-organism isn't properly adapted (in the deactivation process), it may cause the very symptoms and problems you're trying to avoid in the real disease situation; in fact, it may be more dangerous.

Decades of studies published in the world's leading medical journals have reported vaccine failure and seriously harmful vaccine events, including death. Dozens of books written by doctors, researchers, and independent investigators reveal serious flaws in immunisation theory and practice. Yet, incredibly, most paediatricians and parents are ignorant of these results.

You may be shocked to learn there is no law or statute or professional value-system obliging paediatricians to be completely aware of the risks of vaccination, let alone to tell parents that their children risk death or lasting handicap after being vaccinated. I was just as surprised to see the frequency with which physicians who practice vaccination based their choice to do so on incomplete information (and in some cases, outright misinformation), even if with the best of intentions.

Having had another child recently, I've found paediatricians unwilling or unable to discuss this subject calmly and with an open mind. Maybe this is because they have staked their personal identities and professional reputations on the supposed safety and efficacy of vaccines, as well as the fact their profession obliges them to promote vaccination. In any case, subjective reports suggest that most doctors have great difficulty admitting evidence of harm regarding vaccines.

The first paediatrician I tried to share my findings with literally walked out of the room when I calmly brought up the subject, and refused to take my calls when I pressed the issue.

They say openly in the [medical] legal system that if you advise against vaccination the AMA will push to de-register.
DR. ROBYN COSFORD, MB, B.SC, FACNEM

When you take under-reporting into account, the vaccine may be a hundred times deadlier than the disease itself. Some claim that this is a necessary price to stop the return of a virus that would be deadlier than the vaccine. Nevertheless, when you consider that the vast majority of diseases declined this century before the prevalent use of vaccinations, and the fact that the decline rates remained unchanged after the launch of mass vaccination, vaccine casualties today can't reasonably be explained away as a necessary sacrifice for the benefit of a virus-free society.

The medical literature has a great number of studies showing vaccine failure. Measles, mumps, smallpox, whooping cough, polio and Hib outbreaks have all happened in vaccinated populations. In 1989 the CDC (Centers for Disease Control) reported:

'Among school-aged children, measles outbreaks have occurred with vaccination levels of greater than 98 percent and have occurred in all parts of the country, including areas that had not reported measles for years.'
The CDC even reported a measles outbreak in a documented 100% vaccinated population. A study examining this trend noted, *'... the apparent paradox is that as measles immunization rates rise to high levels in a population, measles becomes a disease of immunized persons.'*

A more recent report found that the measles vaccination produces immune suppression, which creates an increased sensitivity to other infections. These studies suggest that the goal of complete vaccination may actually be counterproductive, an idea emphasised by cases in which epidemics followed complete vaccination of entire countries. Japan experienced yearly increases in smallpox following the introduction of obligatory vaccines in 1872. By 1892, there were 29,979 deaths, and all had been vaccinated. In the early 1900s, the Philippines experienced their worst smallpox epidemic ever after 8 million people received 24.5 million vaccine doses (achieving a vaccination rate of 95%); the death rate quadrupled as a result. Before England's first compulsory vaccination legislation in 1853, the largest two-year smallpox death rate was about 2,000. In 1870-71, England and Wales had over 23,000 smallpox deaths. In 1989, the country of Oman experienced a widespread polio outbreak six months after achieving complete vaccination. In the USA in 1986, ninety percent of 1300 whooping cough cases in Kansas were 'adequately vaccinated'. Seventy-two percent of whooping cough cases in the 1993 Chicago outbreak were fully up-to-date with their vaccinations.

Taking flu as an example, my understanding is that the influenza virus has two main surface proteins that allow the virus to infect.

These are called the H and the N protein. When we are infected/ vaccinated with flu, we develop memory antibodies against the H and the N proteins. The antibodies produced will prevent infection if we are exposed to the same flu virus. However, as the virus travels around the world, following the local flu season, it mutates. This mutation process is called 'antigenic drift' and it leads to yearly epidemics of flu. Every year the CDC determines how the flu virus has mutated, and it then makes a new vaccine based upon the new strains. Every year we get a new flu shot. By giving me the flu shot, they are actually giving me the flu. My immune system picks up on that and it is going to give me the immunity I need to deal with this particular strain of flu.

I'll go out on a limb here and say only people who have weak immune systems can get the flu. After all, not everybody gets a flu shot and not everybody gets the flu but we all face potential exposure to it. Viruses are killed by your immune system—not by a syringe full of snake oil and rabbit droppings.

> *The only safe vaccine is one that is never used.*
> DR. JAMES R. SHANNON
> FORMER DIRECTOR, NATIONAL INSTITUTE OF HEALTH

Millions of British and Americans are going to go out and get a flu shot, and all those people who get this infection are going to be the incubation vehicle for about three weeks—and they'll be walking around infecting people like me.

It's been reported in the US that every year, 30,000 people are killed by the flu. This creates fear, and fear *creates sales.* People buy things because of their 'motivators', as discussed in a book called *The Hidden Persuaders,* written by a chap called Vance Packard back in 1958. What is it that persuades you to buy a Toyota rather than a Ford? Why is it that you buy one brand of cornflakes over another brand of cornflakes? Well, the colour on the box motivates many of us, and maybe the taste motivates some others, or maybe it's a desire you have, or a feeling that you get.

The experts, the psychologists and the psychiatrists have worked these tendencies down to five basic motivators in human nature. That's all there is—five —motivators that compel you to buy Toyota over Ford, that cause you to act in one certain way as opposed to another. Those five motivators are

VANITY

JEALOUSY

LUST

GREED
&
FEAR.

To roll up your sleeve and have someone stick a needle into your arm and shoot—for all you know—squirrel vomit and dog spit into your vein, you have to be motivated. And that motivation is fear. Fear sells vaccines. Your fear of dying from the flu is greater than the fear of the vaccine. They tell us, '30,000 people died last year because they didn't get their flu shots. Do you want to be one of them this year?' And we respond with, 'No, I don't want to be one of 30,000 corpses, I want to fight with my neighbour over the dwindling supply of shots, win, get in line and roll up my sleeve.'

Which brings us to another motivator: greed.

One of the most effective ways to sell something is to allude to a shortage. Headlines blare, 'VACCINE SHORTAGE LEADS PUBLIC CRISIS' and on-the-hour radio broadcasts bombard the public with reports that the flu epidemic is coming and there aren't enough vaccines to fight it. Eighty-nine percent of people in Britain believe in vaccination. They believe it works, they believe that it's good, they believe that it's harmless and they believe that everyone should get one. Only eleven percent of us believe that vaccinations are bad, wicked, terrible, awful and evil and ought to be avoided like AIDS, Herpes and VD.

You may have gathered by now that I'm not interested in the flu vaccine and I am going to leave my share of the vaccine for you so there won't be a shortage. No need to be greedy and fight me for it, I want to contribute to everyone in Britain having an opportunity to get his or her 'fair share' of the flu vaccine this year, and I'm doing my part *by staying away*.

Hugh Fudenberg, MD, an immunogeneticist and biologist with nearly 850 papers published in peer-review journals has reported that if an individual had five consecutive flu shots between 1970 and 1980, his or her chances of getting Alzheimer's disease is ten times higher than if they had only one or two shots during that particular decade.

Dr. Boyd Haley, a professor and chair of the chemistry department at the University of Kentucky has done extensive research in the area of mercury toxicity in the brain. His research established a likely connection between mercury toxicity and Alzheimer's disease and, in a paper published in collaboration with researchers at the university of Calgary, he stated that seven of the characteristic markers that we look for to distinguish Alzheimer's disease can be produced in normal brain tissues or cultures of neurons by the addition of extremely low levels of mercury. The connection between mercury, Alzheimer's disease and autism is becoming increasingly clear.

In California, they've banned Mercury in childhood vaccines and incidences of autism has gone down, but they didn't ban it because they wanted to, they banned it because they had to. Like Vioxx, they didn't take that off the market because they knew it was bad for you, they took it off because it got to the point where they couldn't hide it any more, and the potential for lawsuits was so great they thought they'd better cut their losses. Up until that time, Vioxx was a very profitable drug.

So I ask myself, would I rather risk flu, or would I rather risk Alzheimer's?

They recommend that babies get the flu shot at six months, and every year from then on. If we follow the CDC recommendation, if we follow the pharmaceutical companies and the doctors and all of these other paid professionals, if we follow their advice, we're going to take our babies and shoot them up with the flu shot at six months, then at eighteen months, thirty months, forty-two months, and so on. By the time the child is eighteen years old and graduates from high school, he will have had close on seventeen vaccinations in succession. Then from ages seventeen to thirty-four, he'll have another seventeen vaccinations, and then from thirty-four to forty-four to sixty-four... Do you think if we could vaccinate someone every year for forty years that—instead of just a tenfold increase in the chances of autism—we could guarantee it as an absolute certainty? Where there would be no doubt that by the time we give you forty flu vaccines laced with the neurotoxin Thimerasol, we can guarantee you, 100% of the time, that you will develop Alzheimer's disease—is that what you want? Because that's what they're offering.

I wouldn't take that program if you gave it to me free, but they want to charge me money for it. If we had a virus shop down the street that sold the HIV virus, the Polio virus, the flu virus etc, and it was $25 for the flu virus and $75 for the HIV virus and so on, and they'd shoot you up there and then, do you think that would sell? Perhaps if you put the Flu store/the virus store/the vaccine store in between two very popular stores like Tesco and Dixons, do you think anyone would go in there and buy that product? No? Then you would probably be right because *you have to have a motivator*; you have to compel people to buy this nonsense.

Despite my obvious rejection of vaccination as a viable solution to ill health, my point is not to tell anyone whether or not to vaccinate but rather, to give you some relevant reasons why everyone should be responsible and study the facts before deciding whether or not to choose the vaccination route.

I don't need a flu shot because my immune system is healthy and perfectly capable of dealing with most common viral attacks. Did it ever occur to anyone that the place to stop flu is with your immune system? Why don't we concentrate on building natural immunity? Of course, building natural immunity doesn't produce any revenue for the pharmaceutical companies and it doesn't produce campaign contributions for politicians, or for doctors who administer the shots and make a living out of all of this. Their best revenue source is to have sickness, to have flu epidemics every year and to scare us into buying their product.

According to the British Association for the Advancement of Science, *'Childhood diseases decreased ninety percent between 1850 and 1940, paralleling improved sanitation and hygienic practices, well before compulsory vaccination programs.'*

And in the US, *The Medical Sentinel* reported, *'From 1911 to 1935, the four leading causes of childhood deaths from infectious diseases in the USA were diphtheria, whooping cough, scarlet fever, and measles. However, by 1945 the combined death rates from these causes had declined by 95 percent, before the implementation of mass immunization programs.'*

So, at best, vaccinations can only be studied for their effect on the small, leftover portion of disease declines that happened after they were introduced. Even so, this point is debatable, as the decline of pre-vaccination virus-related death rates practically stayed the same after vaccines were established. Also, European countries that refused vaccination for smallpox and polio saw the outbreaks end along with those countries that had made it obligatory; vaccines were clearly not the only conclusive cause. In fact, both smallpox and polio vaccination campaigns were followed by major disease rate increases. After smallpox vaccination was made obligatory, smallpox remained a common disease with some significant increases, while other infectious diseases continued their declines at the same rate in the absence of vaccines. In England and Wales, smallpox disease and vaccination rates eventually declined at the same time over a period of several decades between the 1870's and the beginning of World War II.

As a result, it's unreasonable to say whether or not vaccinations contributed to the continuing declines in disease death rates, or if the declines continued simply due to the same forces that most likely brought about the early improvements in sanitation, hygiene and diet; better housing, transportation and infrastructure; better food preservation methods and technology and natural disease cycles. Supporting this deduction was a recent World Health Organization report which found that the disease and death rates in third world countries have no direct relationship with vaccination procedures or medical treatment, but are closely linked to the standard of hygiene and diet. In my opinion, credit given to vaccinations for our current disease rate has just been wildly exaggerated, if not totally misplaced.

Records in every country show that the so-called contagious diseases declined quite rapidly with the introduction of sanitation and nutritional reform, with the exception of smallpox and diptheria, which were kept active by virtue of the persistent use of a vaccine. In 1929, while India was still under British rule with its compulsory vaccination legislation, the League of Nations health leak referred to India as, 'The greatest centre of smallpox in the world today,' and the record shows that where vaccination enforcement was most strict, the smallpox death rate has been generally far greater than for the country as a whole, where complete enforcement wasn't possible.

The report of the League of Nations Health Division for October 1953 grudgingly admitted vaccination isn't all that it ought to be when it said *'In spite of the great efforts made by the health authorities in promoting vaccination, smallpox is not on the point of extinction and after the limited health improvement programs we find that the plagues and scourges all declined noticeably except smallpox and respiratory diseases, which is a common effect after a vaccination.'*

Here's how this game is played… a million people go out and get a flu shot and thirty-five of them keel over and kick the can, collateral damage, the price you pay for good medicine. Most of the people who get these vaccines are strong and healthy and their immune system will ward it off. The doctor gets paid, the pharmaceutical company makes money, the government gets your vote and everyone is happy. Whether or not it works is irrelevant and immaterial, it didn't hurt *you*. It's like one of those double blind tests, where half of the group gets a serum and the other half gets a placebo. The people getting the placebo will testify in court and swear to God that they feel better because of this test/trial that they're on, they can feel the difference. You can go out and get shot up and just feel a lot better believing that you're safer with the flu shot. If that makes you feel good, go out and get it by all means. After all, it doesn't kill many people, only 30,000. More than likely, the 30,000 people, if in fact that's the correct number, that pop their clogs every year are dying because of the shot and not in spite of it.

To get a sense of how these vaccinations are developed, we'll take the most widespread as an example. The flu virus is grown in specific pathogen-free eggs, which are tested for between twenty-three and thirty-one agents to confirm the absence of those particular pathogens. Laboratories limit the number of agents that are screened due to the sheer quantity of possible viruses and/or bacteria to choose from. Besides that aspect, screening for every potential agent would cost a fortune. If none of the tested pathogens are detected, the vaccine is declared to be 'pathogen-free'. There's a big difference between being 'pathogen-free' and being 'specific pathogen-free'. The advertisement says *this vaccine is safe because it's pathogen-free,'* which is simply not true. It is only 'specific pathogen-free' if they've tested it for thirty-one specific pathogens. There are thousands of pathogens out there, and they can only guarantee that it doesn't contain the thirty-one they tested for. In other words, we can guarantee that this egg does not have any polio virus in it, but we can't guarantee that it doesn't have any HIV virus in it, or some other virus, or bacteria or pathogen.

During the production process, antibiotics like Neomycin, Polymyxin B and Gentamycin are added to remove stray bacteria found in the mixture. The final solution can contain Triton X-100 (a detergent), Polysorbate 80 (a likely carcinogen), gelatin, formaldehyde (a deadly poison) and leftover egg proteins. A lot of the influenza vaccines still contain Thimerasol as a preservative. Thimerasol is mercury and is being investigated for its link to brain injury and autoimmune disease.

Everyone wants to be protected from the flu, or measles, or mumps or whatever might be the flavour of that particular season. It then follows—according to big pharma, anyway—that everyone must want to be vaccinated. At least that is the hyperbole that is put out by the mainstream media.

If we consider how the government dealt with the war in Iraq—they came to us with a story about weapons of mass destruction and the need to protect Westerners by instigating a pre-emptive strike, and then when we got fully immersed in the war with the

Iraqis we found out they didn't have any WMDs. It was a blatant lie propagated by George Bush and Tony Blair to get us into the war. And it worked. It then became a case of 'well, now we're in the war, we can't cut and run.' They succeeded in their goal—their actual agenda all along being to steal the oil from the Iraqis. That's the bottom line here. At the same time the world economy is in trouble and we need an 'infusion of liquidity' into the world's equity markets, spending two hundred billion dollars on the war in Iraq was a big shot in the arm to place that liquidity into the world economic system. If they had come to us and said, 'We need to go to war because we need a liquidity shot into the economy,' I don't think people would have been as eager to send their children over to Iraq to get killed. But to protect (or avenge) America after the 9/11 attacks, now that was the marketing tool employed. That was the sales spiel. That was the motivator. You've got to have the right spin, the right hype. You've got to have the right product to sell. And so Colin Powell went into the United Nations with maps and documents and intelligence reports and facts and figures and names, dates, times, places, witnesses and evidence and presented the case, and we all bought it.

Vaccination works the same way. What you do is you hype it up and you propagandise people.

Adolph Hitler once said, 'If you tell a big enough lie, often enough, people will believe it,' and people believe the Social Security lie, the DDT (*Dichloro-Diphenyl-Trichloroethane*) lie, the WMD lie, the vaccination lie… I could go on forever. The current big lie is man-made Global Warming. Of course, people have bought into it and one of these days we'll have legislation and that legislation is always aimed at an objective and the objective will be obtained: Taxes and money. The people who wanted to promote vaccination have achieved their objective, and that is to make a lot of money, vaccinating a lot of people. If it happens to kill a bunch of people in the process, that's just collateral damage. Tough.

I'm not here to save the world from vaccinations, I don't really care one way or the other. If people want to get shot up, or shoot their children up, that's their business. As a messenger, what I *am* interested in doing is putting the cards face up on the table and allowing you to make a play that isn't blind. My issue here is that we don't get all the facts. If we were given all of the facts concerning the war in Iraq, I doubt the average Joe would have supported the war. And if the average Jane had all the facts on vaccination, I don't think she'd go out and get her children vaccinated.

An American friend of mine told me a story recently. He sends his children to a private school, and one day the eldest boy came home with a letter from the school nurse. The letter stated that the following Wednesday vaccinations would be administered and that all children under law in California needed these vaccinations. It was mandatory. The letter closed with words to the effect of 'please sign here at the bottom of the page and we'll shoot little Tommy up next Wednesday.'

Now, normal parents who love their little children and are concerned about their health would sign that form and send it back—after all, it's the law of the State and so on. My friend, being a little smarter than your average bear, asked himself, 'If it is the law in California and it's mandatory, and every child in the State has to be shot up because he goes to school, then why are they sending me this letter asking me to sign the permission slip, giving consent? It would seem to me they don't need my consent. Seems to me they would just send a notice next Friday saying, 'Last Wednesday we vaccinated your child according to State Law. It's the law and if you don't like it, you can lump it.'

The signal was clear; they needed his consent to vaccinate.

My friend—like myself—is opposed to vaccinations, so he wrote a reply letter to send back with Tommy the next day, and it went something like this, 'Dear Nurse, thank you for your invitation regarding vaccines next Wednesday for little Tommy. Now listen, and listen well: Do not shoot my child up with chicken spit and monkey puke. If you do, rest assured, litigation will surely follow. If this is going to be a problem, I will keep Tommy home next Wednesday to make sure there's no mistake.'

The next day, my friend got a phone call from the school nurse who stated that she would like to talk to him about some facts that he was possibly unaware of.

'Lay it on me lady,' he replied, 'tell me all about these facts. Maybe there's something I don't know, since I don't claim to know everything.' So, she preached him a sermon on how vaccines had saved the world from bubonic plague and smallpox and polio and the like.

He was certain this registered nurse had gone to college, had letters after her name, was sincere, and that she believed every word she'd said. She finished her presentation, and he thanked her for taking time out of her busy schedule to inform him of these facts.

'However,' he said, 'regarding next Wednesday, I do not want my child vaccinated and, again, I will keep my child at home, if necessary.'

The nurse couldn't contain herself. 'Well, can you tell me why?'

Rather than spend his time explaining the myriad of reasons for his decision, discussing statistics, facts and figures, he simply said, 'It's enough for you to know I don't want to buy your product. I don't have to explain to the Ford salesman why it is I want to buy a Toyota. It is sufficient for me to say I don't want to buy your damn Ford.'

The nurse responded by suggesting that he hated his child and was doing him a great disservice, that he had his head up his rectum and didn't understand the consequences of his neglect.

Seeing an opportunity to educate, he asked her a few questions.

'How many of those children are going to be vaccinated next Wednesday?'

'All of them. Tommy will be the only one that isn't going to have the protection'

'... And how many children are in his class?'

'Forty'

'Let me see if I have this right. The other thirty-nine children in Tommy's class are all going to be vaccinated. So if Tommy comes to school and he has the measles, he can't give it to the other thirty-nine, because they've all been protected. How am I doing?'

'That's right.'

'And these other thirty-nine children have all been vaccinated, so they can't get the measles and they can't give it to little Tommy, can they?'

'That's right, that's right, because they're all protected they can't spread the disease to little Tommy.'

'Well, there you go then, that solves all our problems. You shoot up the other thirty nine and leave my child out of it. If my child gets measles somewhere else and comes to school, it won't affect any other public interest because they are all protected. THEY CAN'T GET THE DISEASE AND THEY CAN'T GIVE THE DISEASE BECAUSE THEY CAN'T GET IT TO GIVE IT TO HIM... so... *why does my boy need to be vaccinated?'*

A long, pregnant pause on the other end of the line. And there's always a long pregnant pause, friends, when you use reason, logic and common sense.

'Furthermore,' my friend said, 'even if he gets the measles... so what? I had the measles, I got over the measles and now I have life-long immunity, why don't you just let nature take its course?'

Without saying another word, the nurse hung up the phone and the subject was never raised again.

Some of you out there may say you don't want this vaccination, but are really afraid because you do not know how to deal with the school officials, or you don't know how to deal with the government, or you don't know how to deal with the law.

There is a form available in the US called 'Refusal of Recommended Vaccines'. Some of the grounds for refusing vaccines are; being allergic to the components; having a medical history of diabetes or some other chronic ailment, or the vaccine will exacerbate a pre-existing condition or potentially be fatal.

If you have AIDS, the vaccination could potentially kill you because you're already suffering from an immune suppression disorder. If your child has asthma, he can be exempted.

If you go to an alternative health care practitioner—that's any chiropractor, any naturopath, look them up in the yellow pages—call them and ask them if they have any information concerning vaccines and if they have a waiver form for religious exemption; they should give you a booklet giving you some idea of what you can and can't do with regards to these vaccines and the exemptions that are available to you. If not, ask them to refer you to someone who can.

In any of your contact with any of these schools, public health or legal establishments, always try and remain calm and courteous and appear humbly respectful to their position. You are only asking them that which their law-abiding duty grants you—there's no advantage to be gained by antagonizing them or giving them the finger. Most of these public officials believe the lies they have been fed regarding these vaccinations. They have no ill will towards you and in most cases simply believe that they're being completely sincere. It's up to you to bring the true facts to their attention without trying to belittle them. They more you can preserve their ego, the more likely you are going to get what you desire, which is a vaccination waiver.

You might have to get a little strong, you might have to say, 'Listen, let me explain this to you: if you want to shoot my child up then you just go right ahead and take full responsibility for any adverse reactions because I'm telling you I am opposed to it, I do not want it, do not do it. If you're going to insist that the law requires it, you take full responsibility, and if my child turns out to be autistic, I'm going to sue you. And if my child dies I'm going to sue you for wrongful death. I want you, school nurse, I want you, teacher, I want you, school principal, to take 100% liability for the adverse reactions that may come from this event. If you're willing to do that, if you want us to believe these vaccines are completely benign and there will be no adverse reactions, then you shouldn't have any problem with that.'

You are not going to get any authority figure, or teacher or nurse or pharmaceutical company to take responsibility for that vaccine, because they're not stupid. They're in business to make money, not to take responsibility for your child.

And don't even think for a minute that the school nurse has a duty to offer you the exemption—their duty is to get your child shot up, and if you don't want that child shot up, it's up to you to take a stand. If you can't take a stand, then sit down, shut up and have your child shot up. Rights are only afforded to the belligerent claimant In Person, not to those who cannot claim their rights because they don't know them. If you're ignorant of your rights you can't claim them.

If you are ignorant, you don't have any rights; you can only have the rights that you know how to claim.

The next time someone looks at you and tells you *It's The Law*, you say, 'I understand that, and I want to comply with the law. Now give me the waiver.'

If the authority comes to your door and says it's a compulsory vaccination and if you don't vaccinate, they will arrest you. You need to be smart enough to say, 'Okay. Arrest me. I'm opposed to the vaccination, I'm not going to voluntarily vaccinate, you arrest me. Go ahead. But you should be aware, if you arrest me and vaccinate me, there is a potential for a civil rights action against *you personally*, because you should have known this is a voluntary action.'

They are going to do everything they can to intimidate you, to threaten you, to make you believe that you have to do this, and if you don't do it, 'something bad is going to happen to you.'

Be smart enough to comply with the law while bearing in mind there are no compulsory vaccination laws. All vaccination laws (statutes) are voluntary.

If you volunteer for the vaccination and there are any adverse affects and you go and try to sue the authorities, you're going to lose. You did it under your own power. There's a big difference between being cunningly coerced to waive your rights and actually having your rights taken away from you, against your will and despite your objections. There's a big difference between a passive wall-flower and being an objector—a belligerent objector—and that's what the law's all about, where there's a line drawn in the sand. It empowers you to know what you can do and what you can't do. Study your rights.

When you take your child in to see the doctor and he shoots your child up, he's doing it with your consent. If your child later suffers autism, you can't sue the doctor; you can't sue the pharmaceutical company. You are responsible for the outcome. Do you know what the outcome of each vaccine is going to be? I certainly don't.

Some children suffer side-effects, some children die from the vaccinations. Only about a hundred children a year die in America, as a result of being vaccinated, which isn't very many. A hundred is statistically inconsequential; that's what they tell you. However, it's pretty damn consequential to the parents of the hundred children that died.

If we didn't have any vaccinations whatsoever, the argument goes, thousands would die from disease. Only a hundred are going to die from the vaccination and that's what makes it all worth-while…

If it's true that vaccines will prevent disease and save thousands of lives at the expense of just one hundred, it makes all the sense in the world, I don't deny that. But is it true?

I contend that it is a lie, it's false, and it is not true at all.

A 1955 survey showed that over ninety percent of the population of the United States was below par, mentally or physically, and, according to life insurance records, army reports, hospital statements, government statistics and physical examinations for marriage licences and employment, it was revealed that there was hardly one normal, healthy person in a hundred left in America.

In 1974, one out of four people in America would contract cancer in his lifetime. In 1900, it was one in thirty-three. Today it is 'one-in-two' and they tell us it will be one-in-one by 2020. Cancer is getting worse, not better, in the United States. We will have gone from 'one person in thirty three' to 'one in one' in a short span of one hundred and twenty years. That ought to tell you that the medical establishment is a poor option to whatever it was we were doing in 1899. Whatever medicine has to offer in the realm of cancer between 1900 and 2009 is a hell of a lot worse than what we had.

If we could go back to what we had in 1900, we'd all be better off; our chances of getting cancer would be one in thirty three, not one in two. Now, again, I'm not telling you not to go get your pap smear, not to go get your vaccination or whatever else you're sold on, but the cold, hard facts are that in 1918, the army, taking the eighteen to twenty-six year-old men of America into World War 1, discovered that sixty percent of all of those recruits were healthy and forty percent had something wrong with them. That wasn't good in 1918, forty percent of your population that have—statistically—some disease, some ailment. Something is physically or mentally wrong with forty percent of the population. By 1955 it was ninety percent that had something wrong with them. And you're going to sit there and tell me, 'My god, the medical establishment of America or Britain is a miracle!'

I'll say amen to that all right: it's a miracle you're still alive. It's the most ridiculous thing I've ever heard of, yet the majority of people continue to swear by it.

Let us take an accessible example. I come into your house as a contractor and you inform me that a hurricane has blown through. The roof is damaged and it leaks over the bedroom, the window in the living room was broken and a large tree fell over onto your garage. You instruct me to make repairs, so I come in and I go to work and I charge you money. I fix the roof and the window, cut the tree down and repair the garage. A week later, it rains. It not only leaks into the bedroom now but it also leaks into the kitchen and the front room. Not only has the window in the living room fallen in on itself but the surrounding windows have fallen in too. The garage has collapsed in on itself.

Now would you say that, as a contractor, I had caused you greater damage, expense and grief, or would you say I was the greatest thing since sliced bread and you would employ me again to do more work for you?

When allopathic medicine came on the scene in 1900 and they said 'What you need is vaccinations, and science in medicine and we all said, 'Hey, that makes all the sense in the world, let's do it!' Now, on hundred years later, insanity has increased by four hundred percent... we had some insanity back in 1900—no doubt about it—there were some crazy people, for sure, but now, after all of the science and after all of the medicines and after all of the antidepressants and psychiatric treatment and all the rest that goes with it, we have four times as many people who are a couple of sandwiches short of a picnic. I'm not saying that the antidepressants and the psychiatrists caused the insanity, what I'm telling you is that all of the money that we spent, all the time, effort and energy that we put into it, didn't solve our problem. It may be that the psychiatrists have increased insanity, I don't know—I'm not claiming that—but I am telling you this: all of the psychiatrists and all of the analysts and all of the sociologists haven't prevented it, they haven't reduced it and in the meantime, they have spent a lot of our money in the process.

We do this in our public schools also. We're now spending £6000 per year to educate a child in public school. In 1900 we were spending £7 to do the same job. In 1900 little Johnnie could read and write and we weren't complaining. Today Johnnie can't read, he can't add and subtract, and we're spending £6000. The increased money that you have spent on public education has not made Johnnie smarter. Spending £6000 on Johnnie, has not taught him how to read. The money that you spend on public education is irrelevant to the quality of education and the ability of the children coming up.

Now, of course, the teachers tell us, 'Well, what we need now, to get excellence in education, is to spend more money.' We've been buying into that program for a hundred years, but it seems obvious to me that we spend more money and the children get more dumbed down. We spend more money on medicine and the people get sicker. My common sense tells me we need to scrap the public education system and go back to what we were doing when Johnnie could read and Johnnie could add and subtract. By the same token, we need to get rid of the allopathic medical system and go back to doing what we were doing in 1900, when there were four times fewer insane people, three times fewer cancer patients, when epilepsy was four times less prevalent, when heart disease was less than half what it is now. Between 1900 and 2008, diabetes has increased 1800%. Modern medicine, with insulin, has not solved the diabetes problem.

After half a century of medical practice, Dr. John Tilden made the following observation regarding the inadequate medical procedures. He said: *'The ability to cure has not kept pace with diagnosis and today we behold the scientific paradox of skilled physicians sometimes knowing exactly what disease the patient is suffering with but then he is totally unable to cure the disease. The ability to diagnose but the impotence in curing is the true status of scientific medicine.'*

And in another quotation: *'Clinicians are floundering about in a sea of speculation and uncertainty concerning cause and cure and the best of them declare that autopsies prove that almost half of their diagnosis are wrong.'*

Let me run that by you this way. You go to your doctor and he puts you through a battery of tests, which you pay a lot of money for, either privately or through the NHS. The tests come back and he diagnoses you and treats you for what he says you have. Then you die. Then they put you on the slab and do an autopsy on you and they find out that your doctor's diagnosis was wrong. And fifty percent of the time, the diagnosis in every case like this is wrong. You call that science? Go look up the word—science means *knowledge!*

As a contractor, if I came out to your house and you said to me, 'It's leaking in the kitchen,' and I said to you, 'Okay, let me give you a diagnosis. Termites are eating your foundation and we need to put a new foundation under your house.' And you say, 'Oh, I didn't know that.' So, you pay me a lot of money and I put a new foundation under your house, as promised, and eliminate all of the termites. A storm comes over and it leaks in your kitchen. Would you say that my diagnosis was correct or false? If a contractor did that, wouldn't you be able to figure out that guy was a lying charlatan and that he was, in fact, deeply stupid?

We obviously haven't figured that one out with medical doctors yet. We're starting to twig to the war in Iraq though—there were no WMDs, that we were snookered and conned by the Prime Minister and the President—so, lets wake up and smell the coffee. Are these the first politicians who ever lied to us? Will they be the last politicians who ever lie to us?

It doesn't make any difference either way, as it seems we can't remember the lies as far as the next election, and the politicians know that. Besides that, you're going to vote the way you've always voted, you're not going to change just because the President lied to you. And you're not going to stop lining up to get your vaccinations or stop going to the allopathic doctors just because I said these guys have faulty diagnoses fifty percent of the time. When you go to the doctor and he says you've got cancer, you expect that you have cancer, despite the fact that half the time it will be something else.

Another American friend of mine had a boy who was diagnosed with epilepsy. They had him on epileptic medication for ten years—he spent thousands of dollars on prescriptions. After a decade, his son's seizures were worse than they had ever been. One day, he woke up and realised the medication wasn't working any more and told the doctor he was going to come off it. The doctor said, 'You can't, once a person is on it, nobody ever gets off epilepsy medication, especially after this long.'

It took him three months to detoxify his son, and—by all accounts—he was very difficult to be with during that time, like a heroin addict going 'cold turkey'. Whilst gradually easing him off the drug, he researched vitamins and minerals, and one thing and another and the more he read, the more he learned, he realized his symptoms weren't those of epilepsy at all. He didn't have epilepsy; he had a deficiency of CoQ10—a nutritional deficiency that manifested symptoms in the form of seizures.

Not all seizures are epileptic seizures.

He changed his son's diet accordingly. The seizures have disappeared completely.

Some of you might say thimerosal is an old issue, it's gone from the vaccines now and they're using other preservatives and other boosters and so on and so forth... well, you've been misinformed. Thimerosal is still very much in the vaccines, and the slightest amount of research will tell you that. However, let's say that Thimerosal is gone, just for argument's sake—they're now using aluminium sulphate, which is a well-known neurotoxin, and they might tell you, 'Well, it's a fractional amount, it's not going to do you any harm...' But you have to remember our children are having up to 35 vaccines now between the ages of 0 and 18 months, so it's a cumulative effect. It does cross the blood/brain barrier and it does cause harm. And don't even get me started on formaldehyde... there is no—zero—no safe amount for the human body where formaldehyde is concerned. It is a well-known poison.

From The Poisoned Needle by Eleanor McBean: *'After a glance at the medical records covering the past 70 years of what is boastfully called our great strides of medical science, we can hardly help wondering if those 7 league strides haven't been in reverse because there has been a very marked decline in our Nation's health and a shocking increase in the serious killer diseases during these 70 years. The acute diseases that were supposed to have been conquered by vaccination have only been masked and renamed to save face, or suppressed until the retained poisons corroded the internal organs and developed into dangerous, chronic diseases.'*

Here's a controversial point of view for you, but I stand by it and I will not retract it: Physicians who are advocating these vaccines and ignoring these independent studies—especially those who take commissions from the pharmaceutical companies for the vaccines they are administering—need to review their Hippocratic Oath, because, Doc, you have been compromised. And I would also add that if you do admit complicity or ignorance, you'll be up to your neck in lawsuits. First, Do No Harm.

Only the other day, I was watching a documentary and there was a scientist, Tobin Berger, who was looking for samples of the 1918 flu virus and he couldn't find any for love nor money. It seems that back in 1819 they didn't know too much about flu and clearly didn't know anything about saving these pathogens, so they didn't have any samples.

Anyhow, he continued to search and pretty soon he found some tissue samples in a warehouse in Maryland USA that went back to the Civil War. Sure enough, there were a couple of healthy chaps who had died suddenly, in 1918. So he examined the tissue samples and found the 1918 flu, which he cultured and now has stored in his laboratory. So he saved the 1918 flu, which is surely like saying 'Hey! We saved the 1348 pneumonic plague. We didn't want to lose that!' Madness.

I get a little suspicious when I hear people from the CFR (Council on Foreign Relations) or other International think tank organizations dedicated to the New World Order/Global 2000 project, telling us to get ready for a pandemic. Sounds to me as though if one doesn't occur naturally, they'll help it along in some way. As we saw during Hurricane Katrina when the people lined up and said, 'Yes, please save us, save us! We'll get on the bus. We don't know where we're going but we'll get on the bus and we'll go wherever you tell us to because we're so terrified, we're so needy, we are so dependent upon government.'

When a pandemic comes along, the government then charges in on a white horse and says, 'Hey, listen everyone, we've got the army here to save you, just get on this bus.' A lot like Adolph Hitler telling the Jews, 'Just get on the train and we'll take you to Auschwitz, where there's green grass and rolling lawns and plenty of food. You'll just love it there.' Ninety percent of them got on the trains but they had to point guns at the last ten percent who clearly didn't want the benefit/privilege being offered, and told them, 'Get on the train or die where you stand.'

When our babies get a sniffle or a cold, we've become so incompetent and incapable that we have to rush off to the paediatrician immediately. The paediatrician is happy to see us, of course, and gets the needle out, shoots the baby up with penicillin and/or up to 36 different vaccines by the time they're five years old, charges us for the service, then pats us on the head and tells us we're doing a great job raising our child. In the meantime, the autism rate is up 1200% over the past twenty years. Autism, that's where your child sits there rocking back and forth, totally spaced out, doesn't know whether he's here nor there, coming or going, what he's going to do next. Now, I'm not making fun of your child having autism, I can readily sympathise with you, I'm a father. I can imagine how I would feel if my child had it, but I just want you to know there's a cause and effect relationship going on here and vaccination is suspect number one. Specifically, it's the mercury in the vaccination that is the prime suspect.

Paediatricians know that—they know what causes autism—but they also know that it only causes autism in a very small percentage of children; it's less than 1%. If you take all of the millions of babies that are born every year, only a few thousand of them are going to get autism from all these vaccinations. And so they say, 'Sure, there's going to be some side effects and some people are going to die but that's the price you pay for good health.' Now if that's the risk you want to run, that's your business, you certainly have a right to do that. You have plenty of company since the majority of the population is marching in lockstep right alongside you.

Robert Mendelson, a paediatrician and medical school instructor from Illinois, America , wrote a couple of books I highly recommend called, *How to Raise a Healthy Child in Spite of Your Pediatrician* and *Confessions of a Medical Heretic*. In the former book he reported, 'Ninety percent of paediatricians do not vaccinate their children.'

Your paediatrician tells you that all of these thirty-six shots for your child between six months and five years of age are perfectly safe. Somebody woke up in California and decided to test that theory. The thirty-six shots were still given but without the Thimerasol preservative, and it was noted that the rate of autism occurrences dropped through the floor. The reason the medical community has not admitted this fact in the past is because they know they would be sued straight to hell and back, in the same way Merck was sued over the Vioxx debacle. They had to pay out billions—and they ought to pay; they caused a lot of pain, suffering, anguish and damage. They went out into the marketplace and convinced us that we should take Vioxx, and it caused a lot of heart disease and—consequently—a lot of deaths, so they should pay. The pharmaceutical industry should pay for every child that is suffering from autism but they don't and they wont because the politicians in their pockets enacted a 'statute' that shields them from any liability.

If you want to get shot up with vaccines based upon an educated guess, it's your choice. You have the right to choose. Every human being on this planet should have the right to choose whether he or she wants the vaccine or not. The eighty-nine percent of you out there who want the vaccine should exercise your right to go out and get shot up with whatever you like. What I object to is when the eighty-nine percent of you try to force your choice onto me. I too have a right to choose not to get shot up with monkey sperm and cat dribble. I know, it's a reactionary concept, a crazy idea that the minority should also have the right to choose but give it some thought. I really want you people who love it, to have it. Knock yourselves out, really. I want all of you people to have the opportunity to get a shot every year and increase your chances of getting Alzheimer's disease by a factor of ten. I also think that you ought to be informed that you run that risk. I reserve my right to doubt that they're telling you all of the facts; that you're not getting the whole story.

Autism is growing at the rate of about seventeen percent a year, which means that it doubles every 4.2 years. Before long, if it keeps doubling like that, at some point in time everyone in the country would be affected by autism, so something had to be done. In 1999 they began to phase Thimerasol out of the vaccines. Today, despite it being phased out, our children are now being exposed to more of it than they were in 1999. How is that possible? It's very simple.

Out of the thirty-six recommended vaccines you give your child over the first five years of his life, we start phasing the Thimerasol out of fifteen of them. Common sense tells you that as we were giving him thirty-six, take away the neurotoxin from fifteen of them so therefore he's getting less. That's what it looks like and that's what it is supposed to look like, but in those remaining twenty-one vaccines they have increased the amount of Thimerasol that is permitted. The hepatitis B shot, for instance, now contains 25µg (micrograms), exceeding the recommended maximum dose many times over. Why would the pharmaceutical industry want to do that? Again, it's very simple. They started using Thimerasol in 1935 as a preservative in the vaccines. It's purely a matter of economics, like pasteurizing milk. Pasteurised milk has a longer shelf life than raw milk and we want to increase the shelf life to increase our profits. Although mercury was the preservative in this case, no one thought it was a great problem.

Eight years later, we began to see a thing we called autism. It's not very likely that by 1943 we would come to the conclusion that autism was caused by Thimerasol, but by the 1980s, with autism growing in leaps and bounds, it was becoming more apparent that the increase in the total amount of mercury entering into children's' systems could be significant.

Let's suppose that you and I were given the job of protecting the pharmaceutical industry from lawsuits over a practice that's been going on for about 80 years, where would you start? They've already started, back in 1999. The process the pharmaceutical company is using, along with the FDA, the CDC, the Congress and the British Government, borders on genius. I can't knock it. Let me make a prediction right now; there will never be a connecting link between Thimerasol and autism, never. That's because if you want to put the blame somewhere else, you have to create several other possibilities, and they've already done that. They have raised the issue in a document called 'What Causes Autism?' It begins 'Scientists aren't certain what causes autism, but it's likely that both genetics and environment play a role.'

So, first thing we do is we come up with doubt. 'Scientists are uncertain as to whether Global warming is caused by this or that or the other.' You create about five or six possible alternatives but ignore the real issue. They did the same with tobacco. They said, 'You know, there are other things that cause cancer besides smoking.' Which is certainly true, but it's certainly conclusively proved after however many millions of people died from smoking over the years that it's definitely a causal factor.

Notice they tell you that genetics and environment play a role… *not* Thimerasol.

It continues, 'Researchers have identified a number of genes associated with the disorder. Studies of people with autism have found irregularities in several regions of the brain. Other studies suggest that people with autism have abnormal levels of serotonin or other neurotransmitters in the brain. These abnormalities suggest that autism could result from the disruption of normal brain development early in fetal development caused by defects in genes that control brain growth and that regulate how neurons communicate with each other. While these findings are intriguing, they are preliminary and require further study. The theory that parental practices are responsible for autism has now been disproved.'

So they've raised genetics, environment, parental practices, irregularities in the brain, abnormal levels of serotonin and abnormal neurotransmitters in the brain. No one has suggested yet, in this supposed independent study, that it might be mercury in the vaccines.

So, given that we are protecting the interests of the Pharmaceutical companies and, using a little propaganda, we've established that Thimerasol has been removed from the vaccines, whilst quietly keeping it in several of them, in greater amounts. We've also now recommended the influenza vaccine for infants, so children are now exposed to more Thimerasol than ever before. The population are under the impression that now the Thimerasol has been excluded, autism rates ought to be seen to go down, right? No, we can't afford the autism rates to go down, it would spoil our case, our defence, when we go into court. Our defence will be 'When we took the Thimerasol out of the vaccines, autism didn't go down. In fact, it went up.'

It's not only gone up, it's going up today and it's going to continue to go up, and it has to, because if we took the Thimerasol out of the vaccines and the incidents of autism went down, Thimerasol would obviously be suspect number one. The floodgates would open and we'd be drowning in lawsuits, paying out billions, maybe trillions. We can't handle numbers like that.

I don't think the Pharmaceutical industry intended to put Thimerasol into the vaccines to cause autism—I doubt that somebody would be that malevolent. There are some very malevolent people out there but I think someone woke up one day and said, 'Hey, listen, we're losing millions a year from batches of vaccines that spoil and we have to remake them and it costs us a lot of money… if we could put this Thimerasol into the vaccine and preserve it, we could extend its shelf life, and the mercury that's in it is in such small quantities it isn't going to harm anyone.'

Which is true, the amount of Thimerasol that's in one dose of vaccine doesn't amount to much at all. You'd probably get more mercury out of the fillings in your teeth, or a can of tuna. So when they gave us three or four vaccines back in the 30s and 40s, it didn't pose a problem, but as the number of vaccines increased I don't think anyone was thinking about how the level of mercury consumption was increasing or how much mercury a child can take. Especially when their systems aren't functioning at full throttle at two, three and five months old. Having said that, there may be something a little more sinister going on here that I believe you need to look into.

Research the Georgia Guidestones and look into the eugenics project. The eugenics issue is a very controversial one, and a very touchy subject. You're going to have to sort the wheat from the chaff on that one because there is a lot of information out there that deals with very esoteric ideas. On the other hand, there are some very credible sources and information that show 'the powers that be' do not have your best interests at heart when it comes to these vaccination programs and other things like it.

So TPTB are now letting the pharmaceutical industry off the hook and in order to do that they need to instigate a false flag operation like 9/11 or Pearl Harbour, the Lusitania, the Gulf of Tonkin or the Battleship Maine. They've got to get people off the central issue and onto a rabbit trail. The rabbit trail is 'genetics, environment, parental practices, irregularities in the brain, abnormal levels of serotonin and abnormal neurotransmitters in the brain,' and, 'we took the Thimerasol out of the vaccines in 1999, yet the autism rate is continually going up, which proves Thimerasol in the vaccines was not the cause of autism.' That is the objective: the Thimerasol wasn't the cause.

Regarding an article in the 24 July 2009 issue of The Guardian, *First Wave of Swine Flu May Have Peaked,* immunologist Dr. Alun Kirby offers some perspective:

> *In this article is all the evidence you need to demonstrate Her Majesty's Government complicity with media in exacerbating the size and extent of the problem. 21,000 deaths raised little public concern [during the 1999-2000 flu season] because nobody told the people! Thirty deaths from swine flu [as of August 2009] and we have a hotline manned by 2000 people, billions spent on antivirals and calls for mandatory vaccination.*

Hopefully, you can see there is a plan being implemented here with four co-conspirators working hand in hand: the CDC, the FDA, the Congress and the Pharmaceutical Industry.

Which brings me to the Global 2000 project and the Club of Rome documents.

If you read them you will be left in no doubt there is a well-formulated plan to reduce the earth's population by up to ninety percent; a cull of Biblical proportions, reminding me of the story of Noah's flood. Now you might say, 'Surely you don't think they will succeed in their plan?' I don't know if they'll succeed or not, I'm just here to report to you that these people are pretty prestigious and extremely powerful. The Rockefellers and the Rothschilds are powerful, influential, wealthy people, and they are only a couple of the many movers and shakers behind the program who have the means and motivation to get the job done.

You might also want to take a look at the Tuskegee Study, in which they took black men in the Southern US and gave them Syphilis so that they could study the effects on reproduction. Well, wasn't it just real special that they picked blacks? I mean we wouldn't want to experiment on white Anglo Saxon 'WASP's now, would we? Talk about racism in its most blatant form. I believe the race card gets played a little too often but it's not all pumping hot air, especially when you read articles by some of these New Age people who have in mind the eradication of blacks, Hispanics and American Indians. Talk about genocide.

The first line of the Georgia Guidestones—inscribed in eight different languages on four great granite pillars—reads: *Maintain humanity under 500,000,000 in perpetual balance with nature,* which is generally taken to mean the entire human race at its climax level for permanent balance with nature.

In his article entitled '*The Population Control Agenda,*' Stanley K. Monteith, M.D. writes:

> '*One of the most difficult concepts for Americans to accept is that there are human beings dedicated to coercive population control and genocide. Many readers will acknowledge that our government is helping to finance the Red Chinese program of forced abortion, forced sterilization, infanticide, and control of the numbers of live births. Most readers will accept the fact that our nation is helping to finance the United Nations' world-wide family planning program, a form of population control. Most rational men and women, however, find it impossible to believe that such programs are really part of a 'master plan' to kill off large segments of the world's population. I shall have to admit that I studied the politics of AIDS (HIV*

disease) for over a decade before I finally came to a horrifying conclusion. The real motivation behind efforts to block utilization of standard public health measures to control further spread of the HIV epidemic was 'population control.' That was not an easy concept for me to acknowledge, despite the fact that I had long recognized that the twentieth century has been the bloodiest hundred-year period in all recorded human history.

It was not until I journeyed to Elberton, Georgia, stood within the dark shadows of the great Druid-like monument built there, and read the words engraved on the massive stone pillars of that structure that I finally came to accept the truth. At that point it became obvious that just as our Lord has given mankind Ten Commandments to guide our lives, so, too, those from 'the dark side' have been given their instructions from the 'one' they worship. The ten programs of the 'guides' are inscribed in eight different languages on the four great granite pillars of the American Stonehenge. That message foretells a terrifying future for humanity, and explains why efforts to approach the AIDS epidemic from a logical point of view have been consistently thwarted.'

Having researched this topic like a man possessed, I will throw my hat over the wall here and assert that vaccination is not only an unreliable means of preventing disease but causes significant death and disability at an astounding personal and financial cost to uninformed families. It remains unclear what impact—if any— that vaccines had on the decline in infectious diseases during the 19th and 20th centuries.

Instead of allowing government and the medical establishment and the Pharmaceutical industry and all of the business interests do our thinking for us, why don't we do something really off the wall and start thinking for ourselves? It's a wild, new concept, but one which is crucial, in these times, to entertain.

Take Responsibility... look it up for yourself. Search engine paths regarding topics addressed in this chapter:

Alzheimer's
British Association for the Advancement of Science
Dr. John Tilden
Flu
H5N1
Hidden Persuaders by Vance Packard
Hugh Fudenberg, MD
MMR
NHS
SIDS
Thimerasol
Acquired immunity
Allopathy
Aluminium sulphate as a vaccine preservative
Artificial immunity
Compulsory vaccination
Mercury as vaccine preservative
Naturopathy
Pathogen-free
Polio
Smallpox
Vaccine manufacturing process.

NOR ANY DROP TO DRINK

Fluorides are general protoplasmic poisons, probably because of their capacity to modify the metabolism of cells by changing the permeability of the cell membrane and by inhibiting certain enzyme systems. The exact mechanism of such actions is obscure.
JOURNAL OF THE AMERICAN MEDICAL ASSOCIATION
SEPTEMBER 18, 1943, EDITORIAL

We'll begin this chapter with a short word-association experiment.

When you see the word *Arsenic*, what comes into your mind? Most likely, deadly poison, skull and crossbones and a terrible negative feeling comes over you. How about *Strychnine*? Here come those skull and crossbones, there's that feeling of dread again, right? Are you ready for this one? *Fluoride*, The first thing that comes into my mind when I hear that word is Colgate, the brand of toothpaste. I can't associate fluoride with a deadly toxin, poison, and skull and crossbones. I've been propagandised all of my life, fluoride to me is like bicarbonate of soda. I mean, it's something you put in your mouth, and it's something you drink in your water. What could possibly be wrong with fluoride?

Here's the problem: During the 20s and 30s, the word 'fluoride' had the same connotation as Arsenic and Strychnine. In fact, fluoride is more toxic than both arsenic and strychnine, and is a compound of fluorine, an element from the halogen group as are iodine and chlorine. It's usually added to the water supply as hydrofluosilicic acid, silicofluoride or sodium fluoride. Fluoride is also used as an additive in toothpastes and some mouthwashes, reportedly to prevent tooth decay.

No matter what side you take on the fluoride controversy, I think there's a critical misunderstanding on the part of the fluoride aficionado in thinking that the people who are opposed to fluoride are all uninformed idiots. I'm one of those idiots and I don't deny it. I avoid fluoride like I avoid arsenic, strychnine and other forms of poison that are in our environment. Surprisingly enough, there has been a lot of research done on fluoride and the dangers associated with it.

Whilst researching this topic, I came across a book called *The Fluoride Deception* by Christopher Bryson. It reads like a novel, is very accessible and covers the compelling history of this poison. Filled with all sorts of neat facts and figures, names, dates, times and places, most of the information is taken from declassified WWII Manhattan Project documents. The book doesn't set out to undermine the use of fluoride, nor does it say that fluoride is a bad, awful thing but that is certainly the impression I was left with. It tells us 'where the bodies are buried' and a little something about who these bodies are. I had no idea where the fluoride 'thing' got started, who sold us this fluoride to start with, who sold us this wonky car that is unsafe at any speed, though a man named Harold Hodge was a very serious player in the game.

Hodge was a nasty piece of work. If you think Adolph Hitler, Joseph Stalin and Genghis Kahn were homicidal maniacs, you ain't seen nuthin' till you see people who casually order potentially lethal experiments to be done on human beings. Having said that, I guess I have to concede, Hitler knew that when you put people in the gas chamber they are going to die. I'm sure that Hodge was actually surprised when their human guinea pigs died after being injected with fluoride.

Harold Hodge's reputation was detailed in the Eileen Welsome book, *The Plutonium Files*, for which she won a Pulitzer Prize. It documented chilling human experiments in which the subjects did not know they were being tested in order to ascertain the safety limits of uranium and plutonium.

An AEC memo from 1945 thanks Hodge for his planning and suggestions in the experiment in which seven victims were injected with material secretly smuggled into a hospital. Two subjects, a 24 year-old woman and a 61 year-old man were unknowingly injected with 584 micrograms of uranium and 70 micrograms of uranium respectively. Hodge also arranged for a Dr. Sweet to inject eleven terminally-ill patients with uranium for their brain tumors, though, in fairness, these subjects may have known they were being tested.

The US government settled with the victims' families, eventually paying $400,000 per family.

At the height of WWII, a severe pollution incident occurred downwind of the E.I. du Pont du Nemours Company chemical factory in Deepwater, New Jersey. The factory was then producing millions of pounds of fluoride for the Manhattan Project, the ultra-secret US military program racing to produce the world's first atomic bomb.

The farms downwind were famous for their produce, but in the summer of 1943, farmers began to report that something was 'burning up' their peach crops, and that the rest of their produce appeared to be suffering from blight, and also that farm workers who ate the produce they had picked sometimes vomited all night and into the next day.

According to once-classified documents, the attention of the Manhattan Project and the federal government was riveted on the happenings in New Jersey. In a secret Manhattan Project memo dated March 1, 1946, Hodge—who had been the project's chief of fluoride toxicology studies—wrote to his boss Colonel Stafford L. Warren—Chief of the Medical Division—about problems associated with the question of fluoride contamination in 'a certain section of New Jersey'. He mentioned four distinct problems:

1. A question of injury of the peach crop in 1944.
2. A report of extraordinary fluoride content of vegetables grown in this area.
3. A report of abnormally high fluoride content in the blood of people residing in this area.
4. A report raising the question of serious poisoning of horses and cattle in this area.

The New Jersey farmers waited until the war was over, then sued du Pont and the Manhattan Project for fluoride damage—reportedly the first lawsuits against the US atomic bomb program.

Although it was handled quietly, the lawsuits shook the government. Under the personal direction of Manhattan Project chief Major General Leslie R. Groves, secret meetings were convened in Washington, with compulsory attendance by scores of scientists and officials from the US War Department, the Manhattan Project, the Food and Drug Administration, the Agriculture and Justice Departments, the US Army's Chemical Warfare Service and Edgewood Arsenal, the Bureau of Standards, and du Pont lawyers. Declassified memos of the meetings reveal a secret mobilization of the full forces of the government to defeat the New Jersey farmers.

A nasty piece of work, indeed.

Many of the men involved were eminent professors in their colleges during the war and had worked on the Manhattan Project. There is overwhelming evidence that they knew exactly how toxic and lethal fluoride was before getting involved with the aluminium industry to sell it to the general public.

Fluoride acts in a way that lowers the I.Q. of children.
DR. PHYLLIS MULLENIX, *NEUROTOXICITY OF SODIUM FLUORIDE IN RATS,*
MULLENIX, P. NEUROTOXICOLOGY AND TERATOLOGY, 17 (2), 1995).

How did we get tricked into poisoning ourselves in the first place?

Fluoride was crucial to the H-bomb makers—it was necessary to help process uranium—tons of it was needed. During the mid-1940s the DuPont Corporation supplied the US military's Manhattan Project with the fluoride it required. There was a problem, however. The area in New Jersey surrounding the DuPont plant was being contaminated by toxic fluoride emissions. People were made ill, cattle and horses were crippled, and crops were either contaminated or completely wiped out.

In preparation for an impending court battle—and to head off any negative publicity that might negatively impact the fluoride/bomb production—the Manhattan Project authorized the military to conduct its own fluoride studies. Not only did they want information that would help defuse the farmers' anger, but they also needed to know to what extent the fluoride workers were being damaged from fluoride exposure.

Some of the lab studies were performed at Strong Memorial Hospital, the same facility that injected toxic, radioactive plutonium into unsuspecting human guinea pigs. Research from that time showed that fluoride had a negative impact on the central nervous system. This corroborates recent research showing the same thing—to the extent that the IQ levels of children in fluoridated areas are lower than normal. Other information and studies from the 1940s are apparently still classified or have 'disappeared'.

The aluminium industry was also eager to get the fluoride bandwagon rolling. They had been marketing their fluoride waste as a rat poison and insecticide and were looking for a larger market. Therefore, a ten-year test was planned to prove to the public that fluoride in water would reduce the incidence of cavities. Before the test was completed as planned, and despite the fact there was no clear evidence that fluoride was either safe or effective, water fluoridation was declared 'a triumph for public health.'

When historians come to write about this period, they will single out fluoridation as the single biggest mistake in public policy that we've ever had.

PAUL CONNETT, PH.D., BIOCHEMISTRY

Today, when fluoride's safety is questioned, people with legitimate concerns are often treated with disdain. They're told that fluoride in 'optimal' amounts is safe—the studies say so. The promoters and defenders of this toxin need to be asked: 'What studies?' When old and/or faulty research (by today's standards) is tossed out, including that from other countries like England's recent York Review of fluoridation in which important data was omitted or misinterpreted, there remain no reliable studies confirming the safety of water fluoridation. None! Zero! There are not even any double-blind studies showing fluoride's effectiveness. There are, however, more than five hundred peer-reviewed studies showing adverse effects from fluoride.

We take on board what we see in our newspapers and hear on the radio or see on television. We see ads that tell us Coco Puffs or Kellogg's cornflakes, or whatever else it may be is good for kids. We have associations with celebrities too, who claim to eat this or that. Pretty soon it becomes a case of, 'Well, if Batman eats it, it must be good, if Superman eats it, I want to be like Superman.' We go to school and the teachers tell us about fluoride and how good it is and they give us some history, telling us only part of the story. What I like to do is tell you the other side of the story and let you make up your own mind.

What could be safer than fluoride? I mean how could you be safer than in the hospital? Hospitals have to be the safest place that you can be because whenever you are ill or injured, you want to go there, don't you? Under ordinary circumstances people avoid hospitals like a dose of leprosy, but if you get ill you want to go right to the hospital where they have all of the modern medical marvels to save your life. Well that's what they're trying to do with your water supply, they're trying to save your teeth and save your life. There are lots of things they put in as additives because we need them. Because real smart people who go to college come to those conclusions and do those things for us because we're not smart enough to do them for ourselves.

The government puts fluoride in your water for the same reason they put chloride in there; because it's good for you, because you get a fluoride deficiency. I guess that's the rational basis for their contribution to our health and wellbeing. If you've got a deficiency then you have to get it somewhere or another. In milk for instance, they add a little vitamin D. Obviously mother nature didn't know what she was doing when she made milk. Mankind comes along and fixes nature's obvious error by putting vitamin D in there and solved that problem nicely. And then of course the cream kept rising to the top; nature made another mistake there, so we fixed it with homogenization. And then the evil stuff was bad for our health and filled with all kinds of disease organisms, so we had to pasteurise it; nature wasn't smart enough to figure that out either. We seem to spend most of our time, effort and energy fixing nature's mistakes, have you ever noticed that?

Fluoridation is the greatest fraud that has ever been perpetrated and it has been perpetrated on more people than any other fraud has.
ALBERT SCHATZ
PH.D. NOBEL LAUREATE FOR THE DISCOVERY OF STREPTOMYCIN

Now we have the same problem with our water supply that we had with our milk supply. Nature, evidently, for some unknown reason, not knowing how to deal with water purification and sanitation, failed to put fluoride in there in sufficient quantities. Thank God for modern technology. We came to the rescue and now we have added the fluoride to protect our teeth.

The initial key studies, conducted in Grand Rapids, MI, in Newburgh, NY , in Brantford, Ontario, and in Evanston, IL back in the 1940s, alleging proof of fluoride's effectiveness as an anti-cavity fighting compound are now being called into question.

According to Dr. Philip Sutton, author of *The Greatest Fraud: Fluoridation* (A Factual Book, Lorne, Australia, 1996) these studies are actually of dubious scientific quality. More recently, Dr. John Yiamouyiannis examined the raw data from a large study that was conducted by the National Institute for Dental Research (NIDR) and concluded that fluoride didn't appear to have any success in preventing decay. Apparently, there was little difference in the DMFT values (the mean number of decayed, missing or filled teeth) for approximately 40,000 children. It didn't matter whether they grew up in fluoridated, non-fluoridated or partially fluoridated communities.

Let's suppose I came to you and said 'Hey, listen, there's a lot of bald-headed people in London and we want to eliminate baldness, so I'm proposing that we add one part per million of motor oil into the water supply to eliminate 'slap heads' in the London population.' Then I do a media blitz and I say, 'We've got a lot of scientists here with PhDs and they've done extensive research, along with the Army, and we've concluded that when we add one part per million of motor oil into the water supply, it eliminates, alleviates, or benefits baldness.' Let's suppose you folks all believed it. So we put the motor oil in the water supply and we do this for fifty years, and we're all convinced, yet there's still some baldness around, just like there's still some tooth decay.

Then some concerned group comes along and says, 'Maybe we ought to test this scientifically, maybe we ought to take a look at some people over in Manchester or Liverpool, where they don't have any motor oil in their water supply—let's take a look at the rate of baldness in those places.'

They do the surveys and say, 'Well, sweet Lord, there isn't any difference in the rate of baldness between London, Manchester and Liverpool, whatsoever.' What would that tell you? I think it would tell you that motor oil doesn't prevent baldness. In this instance—in the case of fluoride—it demonstrates that fluoridation does absolutely nothing to prevent tooth decay in children, or anyone else for that matter. It hasn't been conclusively proven that fluoridation causes tooth decay but there is definitive proof that it doesn't prevent tooth decay

However, the addition of motor oil to the water supply might cause some other problems that hadn't been anticipated, which is what happened with fluoride. Take a look at baldness— maybe fluoride has eradicated baldness, maybe there was a side effect that was beneficial…

Water fluoridation is the single largest case of scientific fraud, promoted by the government, supported by taxpayer dollars, aided and abetted by the ADA and the AMA, in the history of the planet.
DAVID KENNEDY, D.D.S.
PRESIDENT INTERNATIONAL ACADEMY OF ORAL MEDICINE AND TOXICOLOGY

A larger study has been conducted in New Zealand. There, the New Zealand National Health Service plan examines the teeth of every child in key age groups, and have found that the teeth of children in non-fluoridated cities were slightly better than those in the fluoridated cities. (Colquhoun, J. Child Dental Health Differences in New Zealand, Community Health Services, XI 85-90, 1987).

Do you know how many teaspoons of sugar there are in a can of Coke? Nine. Do you know how much sugar your liver can process in a twenty-four hour period? Three. Every time you suck down a cola, you get nine teaspoons of sugar, that's three times more than your body can handle. Now you might say, 'Yeah but I drank three cokes yesterday and I'm still alive today.' Well, friend, you drank a load of fluoride yesterday and you're still alive today but by the time you're forty, forty-five or fifty, and your health is deteriorating and you've got heart trouble and you're taking insulin and you weigh 200kgs… is that the way you want to go out? Because if it is, you're on the right track. Knock yourself out.

I think what it could be is that we want to drink a lot of cola and then we want something that will prevent the tooth decay. You can't have both; it's just not the offer on the table. You can be a prostitute or you can be a virgin but you can't be a virgin prostitute. You can drink cola or you can have healthy teeth but you can't have both.

I'm not against Coke, if the Creator made anything better than a Coke to drink, then he must have kept it for himself, but that certainly doesn't mean that it's good for your teeth, or a good remedy for diabetes.

The consumption of cola has doubled over the past twenty years and it's just coincidental—not scientifically proven—that the cases of diabetes have also doubled over the last 20 years. How does that grab you? Leads me to conclude that if you were to cut the consumption of soda drinks in half, you'd probably cut the incidents of diabetes in half, but we don't want to do that, do we? Not if we are a pharmaceutical company, anyway.

We don't want to stop drinking Coke, we'd like to double the consumption of Coke because it's good for the national economy, it tastes great and maybe even makes us feel better until the sugar rush wears off, but we just don't want the incidents of diabetes.

You have to make choices in life and our choice is that we want to drink Coke and we want to drink fluoridated and chlorinated water but we don't want to have heart disease or diabetes.

We Brits have made our choice and I don't deny that, but I just thought I'd at least let you know what the problem is; here's what's killing you and here's why it's doing it.

Even those who aren't convinced of the toxicity of fluoride should be concerned about the level of fluoride added to the water supply. The optimum level was set in the 1940s at approximately 1 ppm (equal to 1 mg/l). This was based on assumption that the total intake of fluoride would be 1 mg per day, assuming four glasses of water were drunk in a twenty-four hour period. However, current intake of fluoride comes not just from the water supply.

A study conducted by researchers at the University of Iowa and reported in the November issue of *The Journal of The American Dental Association* found that 71% of more than three hundred soft drinks contained 0.60 ppm fluoride. Toothpaste, beverages, processed food, fresh fruits and vegetables, vitamins and mineral supplements all contribute to the intake of fluoride. It is now estimated that the total amount of fluoride ingested per day is 8 mg/day, eight times the optimum levels.

Fluoridation is the greatest case of scientific fraud of this century, if not of all time.

DR. ROBERT CARTON
SCIENTIST FOR THE UNITED STATES ENVIRONMENTAL PROTECTION AGENCY

Fluoride is so toxic that its safe dosage is set in 'parts per million'. The recommended daily dose is no more than one mg. As we've seen, many of us are receiving several times that limit from our water and elsewhere, whether we like it or not. Fluoride is pretty heavy-duty stuff, but of course we don't put a significant amount in the water, we just put in one part per million. Let's look at what that means.

You have a million parts of water and one part fluoride. I wonder how they get that one part per million. Perhaps they run a million gallons of water through the water treatment plant and then put in a gallon of fluoride. I wonder if they can get the concentration of that fluoride down to exactly one part per million throughout the 'batch' or if perhaps it's one part per billion in some of the water and maybe fifty parts per million in other parts, which means that some people might be getting a little more than their fair share of one part per million and others may not be getting what they're paying for...

I can only presume that if what they are telling us is true, we're all getting exactly the same amount of one part per million and that the amount is 'safe'. I am left wondering though, how 'safe' poison can be.

I took a look at rat poison researching this topic—Decon, in particular. Decon causes death from internal haemorrhages by interfering with the blood clotting mechanism. I noticed on the ingredients label that it only contains .050000% parts of Brodifacoum;

that's one half of one percent. The other 99.5% are called 'inert in-gredients. So it isn't that we're really upset with the rats, we're only .050000% upset with them, because that's all the poison we put in there. The rest—the other 99.95%—is all good stuff, probably filled with vitamins and minerals and other fortifying goodness. How-ever, when the rats eat a little of that compound, it kills them.

Let's hear it for fluoride. If one part per million is good, two parts per million would have to be twice as good, wouldn't it? It's my contention that if a little bit of lead would be harmless; twice as much lead couldn't hurt much more, could it? How much of a toxic, lethal poison should we be taking into our bodies?

So the health professionals tell us 'Hey, this fluoride is perfectly safe. It's a deadly poison—in the same realm as arsenic and lead—but it's perfectly safe when we only take one part per million.'

As I said earlier, fluoride used to be used as rat poison until the big manufacturers who were producing all of the fluoride realised they couldn't sell it fast enough to get rid of it. They had more of it coming out of the pipeline as waste than they could sell to the rat poison producers, so they figured, 'Well, it's good for rat poison but we're not selling enough of it and we have an excess of it, so we have to find another sales outlet. How about a small amount of fluoride compound added to the water supply? That would help us shift a bit of it, wouldn't it? We should bring the total fluoride content of the water supply to about one part per million in order to prevent tooth decay. Yeah, that's good; tooth decay prevention, let's go with that.'

You have to have a good reason for putting fluoride into the wa-ter, so someone back in around 1943 came up with a health benefit. They did the same with chlorine. They put chlorine in the water because it's cheap and it's effective. I don't deny its effectiveness, it kills the bacteria in the water and that's what we need to do so we didn't get typhoid fever, or typhus or cholera and it works a treat, but we've discovered over the years that it causes hardening of the arteries—arterial sclerosis—which contributes to heart disease.

If I came to you and said, 'I'm from the Institute of Aluminium manufacturers and we have a toxic waste product that costs us tens of millions a year to dump in toxic waste sites and we have to add that cost to the price of aluminium. Do you want us to charge you more money for this aluminium or do you want us to solve that problem in a marketplace environment? Here's what we pro-pose; we will put this toxic poison, fluoride, into your drinking water but we wont put in very much, we'll only put in one part per million. We'll then save ourselves a load of money every year disposing of it, we can turn it into a profit and lower the cost of aluminium cans, so that when you buy a product packaged in aluminium, instead of spending £1, it will only cost you 50 pence.'

You probably wouldn't buy into that, right? You probably couldn't get excited enough about that kind of proposal to suck down this deadly toxic poison, but if I come to you and I say, 'Hey, listen, this stuff is better than Viagra! I mean think of the money you're going to save on Viagra if you just drink water with our magic chemical fluoride in it. It'll improve your sex life by at least 100%… maybe 200%, depending on how impotent you are.' Wouldn't you say, 'We've got to have more fluoride in our drinking water because it improves our sex life'?

A new study shows fluoride increases absorption of aluminum from deodorants, or pots and pans by over 600%. The aluminum concentration in the brains of Alzheimer's patients is 15 times higher than in healthy individuals. The fluoride/aluminum combination spells disaster for your brain's health.

Linda Page, N.D., Ph.D
Is Flouride a Danger to Your Health and Sanity?

Now I know there is someone reading this saying, 'Lordy, AT, we have to put something in the drinking water, in order to kill the bacteria in there, otherwise we'd all be dying of cholera, or typhus, or some other infectious disease.' Well, in the likes of Moscow, Paris and a few other more sensible places around the world, they still manage to clean up the water supply but they don't use poison, they use Ozone.

Japan, with no fluoridation, has the lowest infant death rate in the world and also has the longest life expectancy. Someone needs to go to Japan and straighten those fools out over there. Who wants long life expectancy? What do those people want to do, live forever?

I'm not here to tell you how we clean up the water supply, I'm just reporting on the fluoride, trying to tell you what may be in your drinking water, maybe get you to think about it a little bit. I'm certainly not here to tell you that you shouldn't have fluoride in your drinking water, either. If you have a fluoride deficiency, I can't think of a better way to solve that deficiency by putting some in your drinking water. After all, you have to drink water, right? It's a cheap, efficient method for solving the fluoride deficiency problem in humans. However, I want to ask the question; do we really have a fluoride deficiency problem?

If you've got a vitamin D deficiency, no problem, we can put some in your milk. Maybe you've got a Vitamin B6 deficiency, in which case we can put some in your breakfast cereal. Maybe you've got some other vitamin or mineral deficiency, we can put some in your baby food. However, we're not talking about something you really need here, something that's harmless. We're talking about a heavy-duty poison, of which an insignificant amount can kill rats stone cold dead.

They have to be so careful with fluoride in order that that people don't consume more than one part per million in the supply because it may cause some kind of damage to you, or kill you. No one wants to kill you. I mean, if you're dead, who is going to help us get rid of the fluoride?

They have to have a place to get rid of this deadly toxic poison that costs so much money to get rid of. If they could put it in your water supply, they could charge you per barrel for this stuff and they'd kill two birds with one stone; get rid of this toxin that costs them money to dispose of and get paid a handsome price for doing so. I know a good business proposition when I see one. I understand the nature of the problem the aluminium industry has and I can sympathise with it, but it begs the question, 'Do I really want to drink this stuff?' I decided I didn't, so I took measures to avoid it; bought an expensive water filter that deals with fluoride very efficiently and I use it consistently.

Now you might be sitting there thinking, 'Well AT, you're not so smart, why don't you just drink bottled water? It's cheap enough and at least you know it's pure.' You might have a point there if they weren't now adding fluoride to the bottled stuff too.

Don't take my word for it, do an Internet search or take a look at the labels.

I looked through the entire section of toothpastes the other day and couldn't find a single one that didn't contain fluoride. I must have looked at fifteen or twenty brands. Some of the brands tuck the information away in microprint but others go so far as to shout about it, 'Buy our brand, we've got more fluoride than any one else,' in big bold letters. Would you buy arsenic that way? If there was arsenic in your spinach and they said in big bold letters, 'Fortified with arsenic'?

Seems to me that somewhere along the line, we've taken leave of our senses, folks.

They have to add the fluoride under the guise of health benefits. They're not going to say, 'This product contains fluoride, a deadly neurotoxin guaranteed to kill you by age thirty-eight or double your money back.' We may be ignorant, uneducated and uninformed but we're not stupid, so they're not going to put that on the label. We don't have truth in labelling going on to that extent here in the UK. However, some of us are starting to get suspicious—especially when the cancer rate went from one in thirty-three in 1900 to one in two in 2000.

Our kids are being told to brush their teeth three times a day. Right on the label, if you can be bothered to read it, it states quite clearly, *This product is not suitable for children under seven,* or, *Use only a pea-sized amount for children under six* or *Do Not Swallow.* If it's so safe and so good for you, why can't you swallow it? What does that tell you, friends? There's plenty of poison in that toothpaste. You don't need to poison your water supply; you can get all the poison you need from your local supermarket.

I recommend that you parents who want to fluoridate your children buy that stuff over the counter, take it home and poison your kids in the privacy of your own bathroom and leave my children out of this madness.

Use only a pea-sized amount for children under six. I laughed out loud when I saw that particular gem. If I were in the toothpaste business, I'd take the damn fluoride out of it and say, *Swallow this stuff! Put this on your toothbrush from the bristles, over the entire handle and halfway up your arm! Use as much toothpaste as you possibly can, so that you run out of it sooner, so that you'll come back and buy more!*

I don't know what the hell these toothpaste manufacturers are thinking about, they must be as bonkers as a bag of belligerent badgers.

Studies indicate that brushing with fluoride toothpaste may actually cause cavities.

Drinking water isn't the biggest problem, believe it or not. I have to bathe or a shower once or twice a year and—if you're a city dweller but still have a sense of smell—you'll notice the pungent smell of fluoride and chlorine as you're towelling yourself dry.

The largest elimination organ of the body is your skin, which also absorbs toxins quite efficiently. This is even more significant for children, who have a comparatively larger area of skin in relation to their body mass. I figured that while I could get rid of some fluoride poisoning by fitting a filter to the kitchen tap, the rest is going to come from bathing or taking a shower, so I fitted another expensive addition to my bathroom supply.

If you want a sure-fire way of getting a sense of how much chlorine and fluoride is in your drinking water, try this little test. Fill up a standard 2ltr plastic bottle with tap water, then bring it up to your nose and gently squeeze the bottle repeatedly to force the air just above the water up your nose. Sniff up. You like that smell? That's the pungent scent of toxic chemicals, and you're sucking them down like there's a drought coming.

Fluoride has no proven biological use inside the human body, and that includes teeth. It's a cumulative poison and only half of what we consume is excreted. You're dosed with one part per million, so let's drink one million parts, shall we? 500,000 parts are going to be excreted in your urine and out of your bowels and probably in your sweat, and the other half is going to be retained in your body. The more water you drink that contains fluoride, the more fluoride is going to be retained inside your body. What that one part per million does as it accumulates in your body is collect in your teeth and bones and makes them more brittle. The little white spots that are visible on our children's teeth are dental fluorosis, and is a sign that systemic fluoride poisoning is taking place. So all that fluoride you've been accumulating in your body over the last twenty, thirty, forty or fifty years is still there. What are you going to do about that? Most people aren't going to do anything about it and will probably say, 'You know, I've been drinking this water for forty years and I guess if it's going to kill me, it's going to kill me.'

So you turn on the kitchen tap and—even if you knew it contained fluoride and chlorine and it was poison, you knew from experience that last time you did so it didn't kill you and, probably, it isn't going to kill you when you drink a glass of water. So you drink the glass of water, you pause for five seconds, you look around furtively and you discover you didn't fall over dead and you sigh a sigh of relief and you say, 'Phew, got away with that one more time.'

Friends, if you were to ingest two or three grams of arsenic it would probably kill you in about thirty minutes or less, fluoride takes thirty years or more, but it is going to kill you nevertheless.

The primary problem with fluoride is death, premature death. I don't mind dying but I'd like to die at a hundred and ten, of old age, with my shoes off in bed, when I'm sound asleep. You aren't going to die of fluoride poisoning—to the best of my knowledge, no one has ever died from fluoride poisoning. Probably because they've not lived long enough to die from the fluoride, they probably died from atherosclerosis, or arteriosclerosis, or some other degenerative disease like cancer, muscular dystrophy or Lou Gehrig's Disease, and on the death certificate it says they died of multiple sclerosis or whatever it may be. After all, they had MS for many years and finally they died, so the conclusion is they died from MS but no one ever asks the question, what caused the Multiple Sclerosis?

The medical community says, 'We don't know what causes it and we don't know how to cure it but for £50,000 we certainly do have a treatment.' So you get ill, you go to the doctor and he spends a lot of time, effort and energy working with you for several years. He fails— as he always has in the past. You die; he signs your death certificate and says, 'Well, this poor chap died of Lou Gehrig's Disease or a heart attack.' And no one is able to connect the dots. No one has ever connected the dots at CNN, the BBC, or in Time, or Newsweek or the Guardian, or Reader's Digest but that doesn't mean that some bright young spark hasn't been researching this subject over the years. There have now been more than five hundred studies of fluoride, all of them with negative conclusions. There have only been three studies providing positive results, and the Government rejected the five hundred, and adopted the three that were pro-fluoride because they need a place to dump this stuff… and what better place to dump it than in your water supply?

Don't let me get in the way of your happiness and success, I didn't come here to spoil your day, I'm just a messenger, and what you do with this message is your own business. I'm not on any crusade, I'm not going to write any letters to Parliament and tell them to take fluoride out of the drinking water. I'm going to remove myself from the tap water and I'm not going to shower in it either. I'm not opposed to people killing themselves with fluoride. I'm not even opposed to suicide. If you want to 'top' yourself, here, use my gun. Mind you, it's only a potato gun, so it's likely to be a very slow, annoyingly painful death. I'm certainly not going to help you kill yourself either. You can use my gun but I'm not going to pull the trigger, or hold the potato while you do it.

In his tape, entitled *Dead Doctors Don't Lie*, Joel Wallach points out that medical doctors, on average, die around the age of fifty-eight. The average life span of Brits and Americans, with all of their symptoms, is about seventy-five. Now why is it that these medical practitioners are dying at such an early age if they've got all of the health answers? There's an old adage that says 'Healer, heal thyself.' I would assert that doctors have an obligation to show us the way. Dying at age fifty-eight isn't the way I want to go.

Fluoride has been in the drinking water for fifty years or so; it's certainly been with us all of my life. It's become common, and because it doesn't kill us every time we take a drink of water, and because we don't have any personal experience by which we can measure fluoride toxicity, we accept it. Besides that aspect, if I were to raise the subject at a dinner party, for instance, if I were to suggest that fluoride is bad for you and we ought to take on the authorities and get the stuff out of our water supply, I'd get looks that suggest I was a few fish short of a hat stand.

The neurotoxic nature of fluoride is also linked to motor dysfunction, IQ deficits and learning disabilities. In the year 2000, a group of Boston physicians concluded: *'Studies in animals and human populations suggest that fluoride exposure, at levels that are experienced by a significant proportion of the population whose drinking water is fluoridated, may have adverse impacts on the developing brain.'*

In other words, if you want your child to have learning difficulties, feed him lots of fluoride. Actually, if you live in an area with a fluoridated supply, you don't even have to do that—just encourage him to drink more tap water. Encourage him to stay in the bath longer, or take longer showers. That way, although he'll only ever be about as sharp as a wooden spoon, at least he'll be a particularly clean one.

Hardy Limebeck, head of the Department of Preventive Dentistry for the University of Toronto, once belonged to a group of dental professionals giving talks to promote the benefits of water fluoridation. He was one of Canada's primary promoters of public fluoridation—until he began to take a closer look at the research.

For the past 15 years, I had refused to study the toxicology information that is readily available to anyone. Poisoning our children was the furthest thing from my mind. Your well-intentioned dentist is simply following fifty years of misinformation from public health and the dental association. Unfortunately, we were wrong.
Michael Barbee

POLITICALLY INCORRECT NUTRITION
VITAL HEALTH PUBLISHING 2004

So there are only three old, flawed studies that are being relied upon by the pro-fluoride people, three studies that show it doesn't have any ill effects. Fifty years of living with fluoride in our systems prove that they're wrong.

If we need to solve the problem for the aluminium industry, why don't we do the same for the lead battery makers? I'm sure they've got extra lead they need to get rid of. Let's put one part per million of lead in our drinking water and say that it prevents your hair from falling out. Maybe the gold miners have a problem with the surplus mercury, so lets put one part per million of that in the drinking water too and claim that it prevents psoriasis. How about the arsenic manufacturers? We could say that one part per million would stop your toenails from turning yellow by killing the fungus. The possibilities are endless. I doubt it would be good for your health but it would certainly stimulate the economy.

In short:

The US Army put the reports out for the express purpose of selling the program, so that you wouldn't sue them for the adverse effects of making hydrogen bombs. And the aluminium people needed to get rid of their toxic waste and they couldn't figure out a better way of doing it than to say it prevents tooth decay and put it in your drinking water, sell it and make a profit on it.

Dr. Francis Heyroth of Kettering Institute, Cincinnati, Ohio is a proponent for fluoridation yet, when testifying under oath at Congressional Hearings to the question: 'Would you give fluoridated water to one with kidney trouble?' he answered, 'No, the advice would be that he drink fluoride-free spring water.'

Fredrick B. Exner, M.D., F.A.C.R. stated that '... *Since kidney damage can be caused by fluoride, there can be a vicious circle by which kidney damage causes more fluoride retention, which in turn causes further kidney damage.*'

You may or may not know, when you go into a hospital, having suffered a first heart attack, the first thing they do is take you off pork. It crossed my mind that maybe—just maybe—if heart patients shouldn't eat pork, then maybe they shouldn't eat pork before they become heart patients, and that if kidney patients shouldn't be drinking fluoridated water, then maybe you and I shouldn't drink fluoridated water before we become kidney patients. Has it ever occurred to us that perhaps pure water might prevent kidney failure?

If you ask a doctor if he knows what causes cancer and—if he's honest—he'll say no. Ask him if he knows how to cure it and he'll say no. Now, if you had a car that wasn't running so well and you took it to the local mechanic and you said, 'Hey Jim, do you know what's wrong with my car,' and Jim said 'Nope,' and you then asked, 'Do you know how to fix it?' and Jim said, 'No, but for £45 per hour I'll work on it until you go broke…' would you take your car to a mechanic like that? Of course not, you've got common sense, but we'll go to a doctor who doesn't know how to cure us but will work on it until our insurance policies run out or until we run out of money. And we line up at the doctor's office to buy that service.

Sodium fluoride is a very toxic chemical. It reacts with growing tooth enamel and with bones to produce irreversible damage. It may injure the nervous system, kidneys and other tissues of susceptible individuals. Fluoride isn't a necessary trace element for dental health. Consistent, uniform dosage of any drug dissolved in the water supply is obviously impossible, and some people may drink ten times as much water as others.

There are no studies today that specifically address whether the addition of fluoride affects the quality of teeth, while controlling and accounting for other factors and other sources of fluoride, but there are approximately 500 studies that show the side effects of fluoride—and the news is all bad.

The Army, Dupont and the Aluminium Association don't give out their product for independent study, they do their own studies because anyone else that does them discovers a bad result. These guys can turn out positive results by offering a morally bankrupt scientist enough money to retire to Hawaii in return for his 'expert' opinion, as long as it's in the corporation's favour. It reminds me a little of an expert witnesses in court. An expert witness is a hired gun that will come in and lie for whichever side pays them the most money. Their testimony is completely unreliable, always subjective, totally partisan, always biased, and it's always based on 'I'm an expert so you should believe me.'

This might be a nutty idea, but hear me out for a minute or two. What would happen if we eliminated fluoride altogether? What on earth would happen? Well, it would eliminate the 150 symptoms that you see associated with hypothyroidism, and you'd also see fewer incidences of Downs Syndrome, and less bone cancer. Certainly, you wouldn't see bone cancer or Downs Syndrome eradicated, but you'd see less of it. You'd see less tooth decay, you'd have fewer blotched teeth, you'd have fewer occurrences of IQ deficiency, less liver damage, less lead in the blood, less lesions to the brain, less Alzheimer's disease, less dementia, less memory loss and less sensory disorders, and so on. Less or no fluoride would do all of those things, and that sounds pretty beneficial to me. In fact, the list I've just given you here is what I want to buy, that's what I'm looking for. I would contend that if you had a product that had up to fifteen things wrong with it you'd call it a lemon, wouldn't you? If it causes or exacerbates Downs Syndrome, bone cancer, tooth decay, blotched teeth, IQ deficiency, kidney damage, lead in the blood, lesions in the brain, Alzheimer's, dementia, memory loss, sensory disorders, hypothyroidism, nervous system dysfunction... that's a lot of things wrong with the product called fluoride in your drinking water. If I went and bought a new car and it had that many problems, I'd sell it to some other poor sucker and buy something different—a bicycle, maybe.

Disease is caused by two primary functions, just two. You're either poisoning yourself—toxicity—or you're starving yourself—nutritional deficiency. So if you don't have enough iodine in your system for instance, you'll develop a thyroid problem. That's a symptom of a lack of iodine. If you don't get enough vitamin C, you'll develop scurvy. Scurvy is a symptom of a vitamin C deficiency. You don't have to have a huge brain to see the cause and-effect relationship. Carried out to its logical conclusion, if you have a symptom, be it migraines, carpal tunnel syndrome or something else, there has to be a cause to produce that effect. You're either poisoning yourself or you're starving yourself or there's a combination of the two going on in your body. If you could eliminate that you could restore optimum or good health. You're going to have a problem accomplishing that good health scenario as long as you continue to poison yourself.

Even if you aren't drinking fluoridated water, you are receiving doses of fluoride in the fruits and vegetables that you're buying from the supermarkets, because they're being irrigated with fluoridated water, or you're receiving fluoride in the form of food supplements.

Political pressure, big business and politicians keep the fluoride in your water.

Let's suppose that you live in Birmingham, or New York or some major city and your city council says, 'We're going to abandon water fluoridation, we're going to let the teeth rot out of your children's heads,' and they pass a bill that effect. Would this motivate you then to vote, or to march on Parliament? Would you get upset and excited enough and do something radical to keep fluoride in your drinking water, or would you just pass it off and not care either way? I think I'd jump up and down and shout for joy but, then again, I'm one of those uninformed idiots. I don't think the average Joe gives a rat's rectum one way or the other, concerning fluoride. I don't think they know enough about it to have an opinion. They probably believe the propaganda that asserts it's good for them, but where did they develop that opinion in the first place? They got it from the people who are very interested in fluoride, the people who really want it.

Now I would imagine that if they did pass a bill to eliminate the fluoride, you'd have professionals having an embolism, you'd have dentists and doctors and industrialists testifying in court and writing letters to the editor. You'd have a brouhaha that would never stop. I don't think the millions of city residents would give a damn either way, but the other two hundred lobbyists kicking and screaming, paying bribes or doing whatever they have to do, would make sure the fluoride stayed. The fluoride is staying in the water whether you like it or not, that's a given; if anything, fluoridation will be extended to cities and regions that are currently free of it. Whether you're going to continue drinking and bathing in that toxic concoction or not is a decision that you're going to have to make.

The UK government has been one of the key supporters of fluoridation. Why is that? Why is the government taking sides in the issue one way or the other? What are they trying to do, protect the British people again? What is Gordon Brown trying to do? Protect me from terrorists? I don't have a problem with Osama Bin Laden, I don't have a problem with terrorists, I've got a problem with my local representative putting poison in my bloody water. Bin Laden hasn't been poisoning my water.

I have to ask the question, what is it that makes my local representative want to poison me? What did I ever do to them? Turns out I haven't done anything to them and they're not opposed to me, its just that they get contributions from the aluminium manufacturers, or from the steel industry and that simply influences which way they vote when it comes time to sitting either side of the fluoride fence. It's not personal; it's just a matter of money. I suppose what they'll be proposing next is that the city or the state gives subsidies to families with children to supply them with fluoridated toothpaste at taxpayer expense.

We're all very cautious about lead. Fluoride is more toxic. In fact, lead is so toxic they took it out of paint because the children were going around chewing the skirting boards off the walls and licking their Tonka trucks—probably to cope with their mineral deficiencies. Yet we're quite happy about letting them suck on a tube of Colgate.

The fluoride story takes a darker turn here. As we've seen so far; there is absolutely no benefit whatsoever to the fluoridation of our food, water or toothpaste. And the argument they have used from day one that it benefits our teeth is just pure fantasy. So what the hell are we still doing it for? After all, it has all those side effects, remember? You can rest assured the government isn't putting fluoride in your water to benefit your teeth, so there has to be some other motivation for doing it.

As a businessman, I would want to sell as much toothpaste as I possibly could but when you put fluoride into the toothpaste it becomes so toxic that in the US, eleven thousand people a year have to call the poison control centre. We'll take lead out of the paint, which isn't a food supply, but we won't take fluoride out of the toothpaste or out of the water which is in the food supply. Folks, there has to be a reason why we're so hell-bent on keeping it in the food. It has got to be important, don't you think?

Anyone in their right mind would say, 'You've got to be dumb as a post to leave a toxin like that in your food supply, especially if you're the toothpaste company!' They're not putting the fluoride in there because they want to sell less toothpaste but they obviously want it in there for some reason. Your guess is as good as mine; I'm just giving you the facts here. Why would a company like Procter & Gamble want to restrict toothpaste sales by including a deadly poison which causes tens of thousands of calls to the centre for poison control every year? Whatever the reason is, it's something big and it's something serious and it has more to do with delivering the fluoride than it does selling the toothpaste. I would assert they're in the business of delivering fluoride to you; they needed a vehicle. The objective isn't to sell toothpaste; the objective is to sell fluoride. There has to be a reason for that.

A major clue might be provided by looking into the history of the I.G. Farben Company and their relationship with fluoride. It's a dark story that has more facts to back it up than you can shake a stick at; it's a who's who of Wall Street financiers, American banks and American multinational corporations.

What follows is but a fractional part of the 'middle' of a story that began before the turn of the century and which was provoked by a statement contained in an Address in Reply to the Government's Speech to Parliament, as recorded in Victorian Hansard of 12 August 1987, by Mr Harley Rivers Dickinson, Liberal Party Member of the Victorian Parliament for South Barwon:

'At the end of the Second World War, the United States Government sent Charles Eliot Perkins, a research worker in chemistry, biochemistry, physiology and pathology, to take charge of the vast Farben chemical plants in Germany… While there he was told by the German chemists of a scheme which had been worked out by them during the war and adopted by the German General Staff… This was to control the population in any given area through mass medication of drinking water. In this scheme, sodium fluoride occupied a prominent place… Repeated doses of infinitesimal amounts of fluoride will in time reduce an individual's power to resist domination by slowly poisoning and narcotising a certain area of the brain and will thus make him submissive to the will of those who wish to govern him… Both the Germans and the Russians added sodium fluoride to the drinking water of prisoners of war to make them stupid and docile.'

Stupid and docile… would you say that just about describes our population today? We've become a nation of people who are no longer able to make rational decisions and we're lacking common sense. When you're taking poison into your body, which causes fifteen or more problems, and you do it on a daily basis and you don't have a second thought about it, your brain is not functioning! It's the only logical conclusion you can come to.

Charlotte Thomson Iserbyt, former Senior Policy Advisor in the US Department of Education wrote a great book titled *The Deliberate Dumbing Down of America* and I recommend it highly. In it, she explains how this process works in the educational system. Now lets combine that with this 'stupid drug' called fluoride. Both the Germans and the Russians added sodium fluoride to their drinking water, especially that of their prisoners of war, to make them stupid and docile.

In a letter abstracted from *Fluoridation and Lawlessness* (published by the Committee for Mental Health and National Security) to the Lee Foundation for Nutritional Research, Milwaukee, Wisconsin, on 2nd October 1954, a Charles Eliot Perkins, scientist and author of Washington DC, and one must assume, that same Charles Eliot

Perkins of the 'Dickinson Statement' to the Victorian Parliament, said this:

'We are told by the fanatical ideologists who are advocating the fluoridation of the water supplies in this country that their purpose is to reduce the incidence of tooth decay in children, and it is the plausibility of this excuse, plus the gullibility of the public and the cupidity of public officials that is responsible for the present spread of artificial water fluoridation in this country.

However—and I want to make this very definite and positive—the real reason behind water fluoridation is not to benefit children's teeth. If this were the real reason, there are many ways in which it could be done which are much easier, cheaper and far more effective. The real purpose behind water fluoridation is to reduce the resistance of the masses to domination and control and loss of liberty...

When the Nazis, under Hitler, decided to go into Poland... the German General Staff and the Russian General Staff exchanged scientific and military ideas, plans and personnel and the scheme of mass control through water medication was seized upon by the Russian Communists because it fitted ideally into their plan to Communize the world...

I say this in all earnestness and sincerity of a scientist who has spent nearly 20 years research into the chemistry, bio-chemistry, physiology and pathology of fluorine: any person who drinks artificially fluorinated water for a period of one year or more will never again be the same person, mentally or physically.'

Friends, is this all just an accident, an accidental introduction of a poison into our food supply, with documented major side effects and mental incapacity? I don't think it can be an accident. It seems to me this is a well-thought-out plan that goes back to the Nazis in Germany and WWII; it goes back to experimentation done by the Nazis and the communists over decades, and the Americans have picked up on it and we're using it here in England to sedate the population. They're totally asleep, totally sedated. I guess the next question is, are you and I totally or partially sedated? Now I don't know how true or false that is. I've definitely been on fluoride for more than a year and I don't know whether or not I'm ever going to be the same again because I don't know what I would have been without it. I might have been smarter, I might have been savvier, I might have been less complacent, though I guess I'll never know.

Do you suppose these good folks are messing with our brains, as Charlotte Thomson Iserbyt points out in her book, because *they want to dumb us down?* You know, the smarter people are and the more informed that they are, the harder they are to control.

The good news is that 98% Of Western Europe has rejected water fluoridation. This includes Austria, Belgium, Denmark, Finland, France, Germany, Italy, Luxembourg, Netherlands, Norway, and Sweden. The main rational for Europe's rejection is the belief that public drinking water is not the appropriate means with which to distribute 'medicine' to a population. India, and Japan have also either rejected or banned the use of fluoride recently.

You might be sitting there thinking, 'There's no point in getting excited or upset because there's nothing I can do about it.' Well, yes, there is. Its called activated charcoal and it's very cheap. It absorbs 60,000 times its own weight in toxic material. Activated charcoal will absorb the fluoride and you can buy it easily enough. It would certainly be a good idea to take some time to explore that option. You can still buy activated charcoal in a capsule form from your local health shop. They haven't banned it yet, but chances are they will. You can also buy it in powder form, dissolve it in a glass of water or milk and drink it that way if you're not one for taking tablets. As a point of interest, activated charcoal is used by the Jack Daniels distillery to filter the toxic products during production, which is why it is such a damn fine, mellow whisky, in case you didn't know.

JD on the rocks—my poison of choice.

Though this chapter was originally intended to deal primarily with fluoride, its history and its hazards, I found myself increasingly inspired to include a bit about what could be an even more sinister additive.

Aspartame is yet another toxic substance we're subject to on a daily basis. It is found not only in diet drinks, but hidden in more food products than you can shake a stick at. The subject demands its own chapter, in truth, but the suspect arguments made against fluoride are practically the same with Aspartame: no human studies, selective result reporting, massive government involvement, personal financial interest, controlled media and the only research results coming from corporate payroll scientists. So for the sake of expedience, we'll just cover the basics. As with all of these subjects, I highly recommend you dig deeper and get a full understanding.

Aspartame is not a natural substance. It's an unregulated chemical food additive, and the FDA refused to approve it for over eight years because of the seizures and brain tumours it produced in lab rats. The FDA continued to refuse to approve it until President Reagan took office; it just so happened that Reagan was a friend of the pharmaceutical company Searle, which is owned by our favourite multinational corporation, Monsanto. To cut a long story short, they fired the FDA Commissioner who wouldn't approve it. That's the name of the game, if you've got a problem with your commissioner—if he won't play ball—get rid of him and get someone else who is more favourable to corporate America. Dr. Arthur Hull Hayes was appointed as commissioner but, even then, there was so much opposition to approval that a special Board of Inquiry was set up.

The special Board said: 'Do not approve Aspartame.' Dr. Hayes—not to be outdone—overruled them and approved Aspartame for use in calorie-free sodas without giving the public notice or full disclosure.

Shortly after Hayes approved the use of Aspartame, he then left for a position with Searle's public relations company. This is standard practice in London and Washington; you leave private business and work for a regulatory agency to get the regulations you want approved, and then you leave the public service and go back into private business and reap the profits that come from your brief holiday in politics.

Aspartame, like fluoride, causes slow, silent damage in those unlucky enough to not have immediate reactions. In other words, if you took a poison and it caused a harmful reaction immediately, you'd stop eating it, but what if your body can tolerate it and you don't notice any immediate ill effects? Aspartame poisoning is cumulative. As the years go by, the toxic by-products of Aspartame build up in your body and are stored in your fat because—as in the case of fluoride by products—your body can't expel them. It may take up to forty years to notice the effects in some cases, but the evidence suggests there are irreversible changes in health as well as body tissue damage with long-term use.

Methanol, also known as wood alcohol, makes up 10% of Aspartame. Methanol is a deadly poison, and is gradually released in the small intestine, and the absorption of methanol into the body is accelerated when free methanol is consumed. Free methanol is created when Aspartame is heated to above 86°F (30°C), which happens when an Aspartame-containing product isn't stored appropriately, or when it's heated, as is the case when used in jelly (JELL-O, for Americans), or in the case of diet sodas when they're left out in the sun on a hot day.

Methanol breaks down into formaldehyde in the body. Formaldehyde is a deadly poison in its own right—it's a neurotoxin who's main industrial application is to preserve cadavers in mortuaries. There's a clue for you right there.

The formaldehyde converts to formic acid, another toxin. Formic acid is used as an activator to strip epoxy and urethane coatings, so imagine what it's doing inside your body, to your body tissues. This stuff is used as a paint remover, and if you think your body is lacking in paint remover, why don't you go down to your local hardware store, buy a gallon of paint remover and start taking a teaspoon or two each day. If that doesn't seem to make any sense, then how does drinking diet soda sweetened with Aspartame make any sense to you? Remember, your body temperature is 98.6 degrees, so the minute you ingest Aspartame—even if it hasn't been heated before you got your hands on it—begins to make methanol in your body as soon as it reaches 86 degrees.

Methanol is considered a cumulative poison due to the low rate of excretion once it is absorbed. Once in the body, methanol is oxidized to formaldehyde and formic acid; both of these metabolites are toxic.
UNITED STATES ENVIRONMENTAL PROTECTION AGENCY

The recommended methanol consumption limit is 7.8 mg/day and a one-litre bottle of diet soda contains about 56 mg, so heavy users of diet soda drinks can get through as much as 250 mg of methanol a day or thirty-two times the Environmental Protection Agency limit. Diet soda drinkers are embalming themselves, effectively. At least they'll look good in an open casket.

The most well-known problems from methanol poisoning are related to vision. Formaldehyde is a known carcinogen; it causes retinal damage, it interferes with DNA replication, and it also causes birth defects. Due to the lack of a couple of key enzymes, we humans are far more sensitive to the toxic effects of methanol than animals are, so tests of Aspartame or methanol on animals don't reflect the danger for humans accurately enough to be relevant.

There are no human or mammalian studies to evaluate the possible mutagenic, teratogenic, or carcinogenic effects of chronic administration of methyl alcohol.
DR. WOODROW C. MONTE
DIRECTOR OF THE FOOD SCIENCE AND NUTRITION LABORATORY
ARIZONA STATE UNIVERSITY

No tests were ever done on primates or on people, only on rats—and rats can tolerate more methanol than we can. Yet even after realising the adverse affects on rats were so severe, they decided anyway to introduce it into our food supply.

In 1993, the FDA approved Aspartame as an ingredient in many food items that would always be heated to above 86°degrees F (30°Degrees C). On 27 June 1996, the FDA removed all limitations from Aspartame allowing it to be used in everything, including all heated and baked foods. There you have it, it's FDA approved, friends—corporation approved—so it must be safe.

The fact that fruit juices and alcoholic beverages also contain small amounts of methanol has been used as a counterpoint by advocates of Aspartame, but it's important to note that the methanol in natural products never appears alone. In every case, ethanol— an antidote for methanol toxicity in humans—is usually present in much higher amounts. The troops of Desert Storm were treated to large amounts of diet soda drinks, which had been heated to over 86 degrees Fahrenheit in the Saudi Arabian sun. Many of them returned home with various disorders similar to those seen in people who have been chemically poisoned by formaldehyde. Gulf war syndrome, anyone?

Most victims don't have a clue that Aspartame may be the cause of their many problems. Many reactions to Aspartame are very serious, since it doesn't get much more serious than death. Those reactions include:

- Abdominal Pain
- Anxiety attacks
- Arthritis
- Asthma
- Asthmatic Reactions
- Bloating,
- Edema (Fluid Retention)
- Blood Sugar Control Problems (Hypoglycaemia or Hyperglycaemia)
- Brain Cancer (Pre-approval studies in animals)
- Breathing difficulties
- Burning eyes or throat
- Burning Urination
- Inability to think straight
- Chest Pains
- Chronic cough
- Chronic Fatigue
- Confusion
- Death

- Depression
- Diarrhoea
- Dizziness
- Excessive Thirst or Hunger
- Fatigue
- Feeling 'unreal'
- Flushing of face
- Hair Loss (Baldness) or Thinning of Hair
- Headaches/Migraines Dizziness
- Hearing Loss
- Heart palpitations
- Hives
- Hypertension (High Blood Pressure)
- Impotency and Sexual Problems
- Inability to concentrate
- Infection Susceptibility
- Insomnia
- Irritability
- Itching
- Joint Pains
- Laryngitis
- Marked Personality Changes
- Memory loss
- Menstrual Problems
- Migraines and Severe Headaches
- Muscle spasms
- Nausea or Vomiting
- Numbness or tingling of extremities
- Panic Attacks
- Phobias
- Poor memory
- Rapid Heart Beat
- Rashes
- Seizures and convulsions
- Slurring of Speech
- Swallowing Pain
- Tachycardia
- Tremors
- Tinnitus
- Vertigo
- Vision Loss
- Weight gain.

Aspartame poisoning mimics a wide range of problems, such as:

- Fibromyalgia
- Arthritis
- Lupus
- Multiple Chemical Sensitivities (MCS)
- Alzheimer's disease
- Chronic Fatigue
- Syndrome
- Lymphoma
- Lyme disease
- Attention Deficit Disorder (ADD)
- Panic Disorder, depression and other psychological disorders
- Multiple Sclerosis (MS)
- Parkinson's disease
- Epilepsy
- Diabetes and diabetic complications
- Birth defects.

This is probably the longest list of side effects from anything researched over the last three years, and I've never seen anything like it. It's the only food additive that I know of that has been approved by the FDA that causes a list of symptoms like this and also mimics the diseases you see above. You may have symptoms, believing that you have Multiple Sclerosis or Parkinson's disease, for example, when really what you have is Aspartame poisoning, which may have been misdiagnosed in your case. If you detoxified your body and got off the Aspartame, the symptoms might be reversible and disappear.

Phenylalanine and aspartic acid, which make up 90% of Aspartame's formula, are also neurotoxins when certain other essential amino acids are missing. Phenylalanine breaks down into DKP—diketopiperazine—which is known to cause brain tumours. Aspartic acid is a well-known excitotoxin. An excitotoxin—simplistically put—hyper-activates the nerve receptors in your brain to such a degree that they burn out and die.

One solution to the refined sugar/chemical sweetener problem is raw honey. As well as its use as a natural sweetener, raw honey can also be applied to open wounds, scars, cuts and abrasions as a very effective antiseptic. It's also said to have anti-cancer properties. And—to top it all off—it's relatively cheap. Have you ever noticed that? These natural cures for diseases may not always be free but they're invariably easy to obtain and they're cheap, which is why the pharmaceutical companies don't like them. The majority of the population want something that's expensive and hard to obtain, something that you have to get from Searle or Pfizer, something that's patented and protected. And if they catch you with it without a prescription, they'll lock you up for five to ten years, like they do with illicit drugs. It'll be a long time before any of the big pharmaceutical companies start experimenting with honey. If it cures cancer, it's the last thing they want out there in the marketplace. Cancer is a $500-billion-a-year industry; curing cancer might destroy our economies. You could try to outlaw honey though, which is what Codex Alimentarius is all about.

You can't patent nature and therefore you can't make any money out of it, so you create legislation that makes natural therapies illegal without a licence from the very people who are attempting to stamp it out.

The moral to this story is that anything containing artificial sweetener isn't fit for human consumption. Technology can be great, but we shouldn't be eating it. You should avoid the following technology like the plague:

- Sucralose (Splenda®)
- Aspartame (NutraSweet/Equal®)
- Acesulfame-K (Sunett®)
- Neotame®
- Alitame®
- Cyclamate®

Considering the ever-increasing influx of health complaints, Big Pharma is caught between a rock and a hard place. It's a little like the situation the tobacco companies faced not so long ago. The tobacco industry realised that although their studies and their tests showed that tobacco was safe, people using their products continued to die. At the same time, the Office of the Surgeon General of the United States announced plans to include warning labels to be shown on each packet of tobacco product sold. The government wanted to go with something along the lines of, 'THIS PRODUCT CAUSES CANCER.' The powerful tobacco companies 'negotiated' to soft-pedal it to the more amorphous, 'SMOKING MAY BE HAZARDOUS TO YOUR HEALTH.' Depending on which country you're in, you'll get a mixture of soft and hard warnings.

Nevertheless, I bet you thought that warning label you see on tobacco packets was forced upon the tobacco industry, didn't you?

Afraid not—the tobacco companies realised it would serve them well in the long run because once that warning label is on there, their legal liability is terminated and you don't have a leg to stand on.

Still, though, they did get the word 'Cancer' changed to the kinder, gentler 'Hazardous'. Cancer is bad for sales, you know.

Big Pharma is now in the same position as the tobacco industry was back then, and you can bet that you'll be seeing more warning labels on these Aspartame-containing products in the very near future, which simply means they can't be sued when a member of your family kicks the bucket after drinking a litre of Coke Zero.

And you thought it was for your protection. Either wake up, or stay in a stupor. It's your choice.

Take Responsibility... look it up for yourself. Search engine paths regarding topics addressed in this chapter:

Aspartame
Dead Doctors Don't Lie, Joel Wallach
Fluoride
Harold Hodge
I.G. Farben
Manhattan Project
Politically Incorrect Nutrition, Michael Barbee.

GREAT EXPECTATIONS

Paper money eventually returns to its intrinsic value — zero.
VOLTAIRE

When engaging in conversations about the economy, the police state and the New World Order, people often say to me, 'You're really into these conspiracy theories, aren't you,' and I tell them, 'Yes, I guess 'normal' people would refer to me as a 'conspiracy theorist.' They invariably come back with, 'Well, why do you believe such nonsense?'

I believe there is a conspiracy in the international geopolitical realm because I don't believe that all of the bad things that go on in the world can happen accidentally. I think somebody out there is pulling the strings, and the reason I think they're pulling the strings is because if it was just random chance, good things would also be happening in the international geopolitical realm accidentally. If there is, send a me an e-mail and let me know what it is, I'd like to hear about it.

I, along with many others, believe that the solution to the problems that we are facing worldwide, nationally and locally, is a return to gold and silver coin, to the practice of just weights and balances instead of fiat currency. We would all be better off; we'd have a better economic system. However, when it comes to economics, the conversation is never between gold and silver and paper, it's just about paper, and different colours of paper, and then more or less paper but it's always going to be paper, and paper is the problem.

We make money the old fashioned way. We print it.
ART ROLNICK
FORMER CHIEF ECONOMIST
MINNEAPOLIS FEDERAL RESERVE BANK

Debt is a problem. We've all got credit cards, and mortgages, debts on car loans and other consumer goods and then we wonder why it is when we lose our jobs that we're in such economic trouble. Well, it's because we don't have any money. Of course, you might say, 'I've got a lot of money, what are you talking about? It's in the bank.' If you've got money in the 'bank', you don't have any money. You might have a lot of credit but you don't have any money. Now you might say, 'That's cash, I have cash in the bank, in my deposit account.' Well, let me tell you, the definition of 'cash' in the legal dictionary is 'gold and silver coin'. Those notes are just receipts for cash, promissory notes, promises to pay; in the simplest terms, we're all just using IOUs.

If you're going around calling your £20 notes and your Federal Reserve notes 'cash', you must have been to public school, friend—that's where you learn these kinds of deceptive practices. Do you know what a deposit account is? Do you know where the word deposit comes from? Do you know what the word depose means? When you put your sweat equity into a deposit account, you're 'deposing' yourself of it. You are gifting it to the bank, and they thank you for your gift with a line of 'credit'—credit they can conjure up out of thin air and deflate at will. Think about this carefully for a minute… isn't 'credit' really just another word for 'debt'? How do you like that little trick?

The number one issue being discussed at the moment is the economic collapse—we're hearing with increasing frequency the big 'D' word—deflation, deflation, deflation—closely followed by the second 'D' word—depression. Indeed, all the numbers are grim, there's no doubt about that. In fact, I would suggest the numbers are breathtaking.

What I've discovered is that the last great US depression, from the beginning, the stock market collapse in October of 1929 until the banks were closed in March 6th of 1933, took 3½ years to reach rock bottom. At the time of this book's publication, we've been engaged in the current financial debacle more than 18 months and there is no bottom in sight. It reminds me of an aeroplane that is in a nosedive, heading straight down at full power.

Paper money has had the effect in your state that it will ever have, to ruin commerce, oppress the honest, and open the door to every species of fraud and injustice.

GEORGE WASHINGTON
IN A LETTER TO J. BOWEN, RHODE ISLAND, JAN. 9, 1787

A friend who understands the economic situation we're currently in asked me recently if I intend to go on holiday this year and I
replied, 'Lord no, I'm like everyone else, I'm sitting on the sidelines
waiting and watching.' Just watching and waiting. And that's the
death knell of the economy, because that's what the economy relies
on for its very survival, buying, selling and trading. It's me going in to Thomas Cook and buying a holiday to the Maldives that
keeps those Thomas Cook chaps employed. If I don't go in and buy
a holiday, it doesn't mean the end of that company but if a lot of us
do that, it does.

The bottom line is all of us are sitting on the sidelines watching
and waiting. Did you go out and buy a holiday last week? How
about a new car? I certainly didn't. Am I going out to buy a new
car next month? Not on your life. And that's really bad news for
you car workers out there.

Everyone's getting edgy about the economy; we've all lost confidence in it. That's what the fiat money system is all about, it's
built on confidence; it's a confidence game. Some people might
even call it a Ponzi scheme. When we lose confidence, everyone
stops. The game of musical chairs is over and we only have to look
to see who is left standing. If you're not feeling edgy, you're obviously pretty happy with the status quo and you should stick with
the programme. However, reality is about to stick its foot right
up your hoo haa one of these days, and when it does I won't be
around to say 'I told you so.' I'll be somewhere quiet, tending to
my vegetable patch.

*Without the confidence factor, many believe a paper money system is liable
to collapse eventually.*
FEDERAL RESERVE BANK OF PHILADELPHIA IN *GOLD: THE ONCE AND FUTURE
MONEY* BY NATHAN LEWIS AND ADDISON WIGGIN

All of us together, acting this way, sitting back and waiting for
the fireworks, absolutely spells out the result, and there is no doubt
as to what the result is going to be; another year of dismal economic performance. We'll buy what we have to buy, but the non-
essential items will fall by the wayside. The discretionary spending has stopped and the people in those industries and businesses
who rely on discretionary spending are dead in the water. Then
the economy contracts and depression follows soon afterward. Depression is where your living standard declines. Are we in a depression now? No doubt about it. Everyone in America and Great
Britain is feeling the pinch right now.

If the American people ever allow private banks to control the issue of their currency, first by inflation and then by deflation, the banks and corporations that will grow up around them will deprive the people of all property until their children will wake up homeless on the continent their fathers conquered.

THOMAS JEFFERSON, 1802
IN A LETTER TO THEN SECRETARY OF THE TREASURY, ALBERT GALLATIN

History is a good guide to what's going to happen in the future because history tends to repeat itself. Why does this happen? Well, when you do the same thing over and over again, you can expect to get the same results over and over again. Someone particularly clever once said, 'The definition of madness is doing the same thing over and over but expecting a different result each time!' It's a little like a scientific experiment. Let's say I mix some chemicals up in the lab and there's an explosion. Someone says, 'Hmmm, that sounds like nitro-glycerine.' So we mix up the same chemicals again and it blows up again. We mix it up a third time and, sure enough, it explodes a third time. If you mix the same chemicals together time after time and each time you did it they blew up, pretty soon you'd be able to predict the result, wouldn't you? 'Okay, here's the last chemical, when I pour this one into the mix, there's going to be an explosion.' You pour the last one in and, right on cue, it blows up and you say, 'See? I'm a prophet.'

Could we do the same thing with our economy? Could we look back in history and see that when we did this in the past, here are the results we got? For instance, inflation… are we going to have inflation or deflation? That's what people are asking right now. I can assure you there's not going to be any deflation going on, just more of the same inflation. How do I know that? Because inflation is not when prices go up, it's when you print more money. Rising prices is a result of inflation; it's not the inflation itself. When prices go down, that's not depression. Deflation is when prices go down and a depression is when your living standards go down. That's what we're all suffering from right now.

About all a Federal Reserve note can legally do is wipe out one debt and replace it with itself, another debt, a note that promises nothing. If anything's been paid, the payment occurs only in the minds of the parties…

TUPPER SAUCY
AUTHOR OF *THE MIRACLE ON MAIN STREET*

Most people believe we're in a deflationary spiral, that the economic world is coming to an end and we need a 'stimulus package' but I'm here to tell you that there is no deflation, there hasn't been any genuine deflation for at least the last 2-300 years, and there'll be no deflation any time soon. However, that is what the Government is selling us right now—they're trying to sell us on the idea of massive deflation in order to push on us the idea of monetary stimulus. They came along and said that commodity prices have just collapsed, so we need to re-inflate the economy with a stimulus package.

I had a message recently advising me to look at the price of gold—it's deflating, they said—and if I was holding any gold, to get rid of it today, right now, this red-hot minute…

Let's take a look at gold.

In 2000, the price of gold was about $275 an ounce. As I write this, it's about $900 an ounce. In March 2008 it hit $1022 per ounce. It is true that the price of gold has deflated from $1022 to $900 and that's what the 'powers that be' and our Governments are telling us, 'See! Look at this deflation! We've got to have a stimulus package.'

Excuse me, but at the very bottom, gold was $275, then it climbed to $1022 and then it dropped back to $900, so if we take this info from a point of view which includes actual intelligence, the price of gold today is more than three times higher than it was in 2000. That is not deflation that's inflation. What they're telling you is that from its all-time high it has deflated—which is true—but from its all-time low it has inflated.

Take a look at the price of petrol. When Bush Jr came into power, petrol in the US was about $1 per gallon, then it went up to $4 a gallon, then dropped back down to $2 per gallon; which was when they told us we were suffering from deflation. I think you'll find that to be BS. The price of petrol in the US has effectively doubled over the last eight years; that's inflation.

The decrease in purchasing power incurred by holders of money due to inflation imparts gains to the issuers of money…
ST. LOUIS FEDERAL RESERVE BANK
IN *REVIEW*, NOV. 1975

The price of copper went from $.80 to $3.50 then back down to $1.60. The price of copper is double today what it was in 2000. The price of copper has not deflated. Take any commodity you like and look at how the prices have fluctuated in the same way over the past eight to nine years. This tells me that we should be preparing for inflation, not deflation. I can't think of a single thing that has deflated in price, and the US Government today has doubled the money supply, which means that the value of the money in your pocket has now depreciated by half. You may have noticed the consequences of that on the shelves, but there's worse coming down the line in around six to twenty-four months. The Government's trick is to double the price and then cut it down by 50%, tell us that it's deflating and that we need a monetary stimulus. Nothing has deflated, what we are dealing with is inflation and the inflation is accelerating.

Knowing that, I need to be making plans for the future, so do I want to save a lot of £50 notes under my mattress, or should I convert the £50 notes into gold and then convert the gold back into £50 notes when I want to buy something two years from now?

Deflation is a decrease in the money supply, it's not a drop in prices, although it can and usually does cause prices to drop—but then so can a lot of other things. Deflation is never a problem for central banks since they can create unlimited amounts of money at the stroke of a key.

Never forget this: the Bank of England, the Federal Reserve and the Governments have only two weapons: Inflation and Bullshit. Inflation you know; BS is the whole gamut of propaganda measures aimed at keeping the public from panicking—from promoting the Prime Minister's and the President's 'good grasp of the current situation' to assuring the TV viewers that everything is 'going to be all right.' Inflation and more inflation, BS and more BS. They'll use those two PR strategies at all times, and will cling to them till the bitter end because it's all they have.

Over the past twelve months, the British and American Governments and their respective private banks have demonstrated to the tune of 8.5 trillion dollars in new credit and bailouts that they'll use the inflation gun and the BS gun at will. The inflation has already been accomplished, it is already a done deal; it's been accomplished over the past twelve months. Now all we're waiting for is the result.

Currency Depreciation—also known as big price rises—is not merely a likelihood, it's an absolute certainty.

Forget about deflation—that's a scare tactic the Government uses so that they can manage inflation expectations. Deflation isn't bad for you and me, it's good for us. When petrol goes from four dollars a gallon to two dollars a gallon that's good for us. It's bad for the oil companies, bad for Government, tax and revenue, bad for bankers and speculators, but it's not bad for you and me. I suppose it depends on what side of the counter you're on.

Depression occurs when you have inflation. Think about that for a minute. From 1973 to today, your standard of living has decreased by 18%, which is why your spouse is out working in the market place so they can bring in that second income. That is why you're paying those people down at the local nursery school to take care of your children, so that both of you can work to pay your bills. You are making more and more money but you're able to buy less and less with it. That is not an increase in your living standards, that's called a depression. Your living standards are being depressed. So what should we be preparing for? What is it that has happened in the past that we can hang our hats on and know what results these current Government policies are going to produce?

A recent poll showed that around 62% of Americans and Brits believe Barack Obama and Gordon Brown are going to solve the current economic crisis. Well, bless them, talk about optimism. Is the Government going to solve this problem? The short answer is a resounding no.

The reason that the current Government is not going to solve the crisis is because they are following the same failed policies of the 1930s and we're going to get the same results we got in the 1930s, and that wasn't a fast, direct recession, it was a long drawn-out depression. You're mixing the same chemicals together, and I predict you'll get the same bang—and bust—you got last time.

The Government is not going to solve the problem, they're going to exacerbate it. Is it because they don't know what they are doing? The truth: they're doing it with premeditated forethought. The objective here is to collapse the world economy to make everybody desperate, and then when you're desperate, you'll follow the guidelines that are going to be set out to solve your problem.

Thesis + antithesis = synthesis
Problem + reaction = solution
HEGELIAN DIALECTIC

So for you people out there who have lost your jobs and are unemployed, that is exactly where they want you, because now when they say, 'Line up and take a chip in your right hand,' you'll do it—to save your house, to save your car, to save your family. You may not like it, you may not want to do it but you'll do it because there isn't any other solution for you.

Are we going to see more Government meddling in the economy? Gordon Brown and President Obama are activists, and they keep telling you that only Government can solve your problem for you. Friends, it was Government that caused the problem in the first place, with fraud and inept monetary policy. They're telling us that the solution is 'more of the same'; that if excessive debt and fiat paper currency has caused your problem, then the solution is more debt and more fiat paper currency. We tested that formula last time—it didn't work then and it is not going to work this time either.

By a continuing process of inflation, Governments can confiscate, secretly and unobserved, an important part of the wealth of their citizens. There is no subtler, no surer means of overturning the existing basis of society than to debauch the currency. The process engages all the hidden forces of economic law on the side of destruction, and does it in a manner which not one man in a million is able to diagnose... If, however, a Government refrains from regulations and allows matters to take their course, essential commodities soon attain a level of price out of the reach of all but the rich, the worthlessness of the money becomes apparent, and the fraud upon the public can be concealed no longer.

JOHN MAYNARD KEYNES
ECONOMIST AND AUTHOR OF *THE ECONOMIC CONSEQUENCES OF THE PEACE*
(1920)

Let me make a prediction based on the facts: In the last US depression, which kicked off in October of 1929, it took three and a half years to reach the bottom. We've been in this current contraction for about eighteen months and we still don't know where the bottom is going to be. In 1929, the US reached bottom, levelled off, then came back out of it in 1930. There was a massive gain, a rebounding of 64% before it levelled off and plateaued for a short time, and then went into the cellar. The total overall loss in stock market value from 1929 to 1933 was 89%. So far we haven't lost 89%, but my prediction would be that we're definitely going to lose 89%, or something in that neighbourhood. Will it ever lose 100%? No, not ever—the PTB are far too clever to let that happen.

If you look around the world at the history of stock market investing, there hasn't been one yet that has lost 100% of its value. At the time of writing this chapter, the stock market is down around 40% so far. Is it going to go lower? No doubt. Why? All of the fundamentals are in place, all the things that you did the last time compared to all the things we're doing this time tell us that that's what's going to happen. Is there going to be a rebounding in the stock market? Yes, absolutely. Could the stock market rebound to 10,000? Yes, it could, that's what happened in 1930 and 31. Then will it go into the pit? Yep. How do I know that? It's what happened last time.

When we look at the economic collapses of the past, they have a pattern that goes along with them. There's a result that comes from the printing of paper money, then there's a reaction to that result, and then that reaction has a result, and when we look at the reaction to the reactions and the results of the results and we put it all together, it tells us a pretty comprehensive story. This is not something brand-new, it's is not something developed by the Obama, Clinton, Bush, Blair, Brown administrations; it's happened many times before.

Are we going to have hyperinflation? You can bet your life on it. Hyperinflation, they tell us, is where prices go up 10% a month. We're not there yet but we're speeding in that direction. The inflation has already taken place, its already been accomplished. Remember, inflation is an increase in the money supply. Hyperinflation is the worst catastrophe that a monetary system and a nation can experience. We're witnessing this right now in Zimbabwe, a country that used to be a first world industrial nation in 1980. The Zimbabwean dollar was equal in value to the US dollar back then. Today it's a failed state.

> *What keeps me bright and looking forward to every day*
> *is that it can't be any worse.*
> GIDEON GONO
> GOVERNOR, RESERVE BANK ZIMBABWE, JAN 24 2009
> QUOTED IN THE *AUSTRIAN ECONOMISTS*, 2 FEBRUARY 2009

Zimbabwe elected a Marxist, who has been president now for 30 years, and they've been practising Communism in a serious way. As a result of that they've had a predictable end result, hyperinflation. Last time I looked, petrol was $237,000 per gallon, and that was the good news; if you had $237,000 you could supposedly buy a gallon of petrol. The bad news is there isn't any petrol to buy, at any price.

If you want to talk about misery, if you want to talk about heartache, hopelessness, want and despair, then hyperinflation is where it's at. If there's any way you folks could go for deflation, depression, any alternative to hyperinflation, you want to take it.

I'm sorry to say, friends, we're not going to avoid hyperinflation and that's because it's exactly what the powers that be want to bring to town, its exactly what all of the policies they're following is guaranteed to produce.

Have you ever watched the launching of a ship? The lady swings the bottle of champagne up against the hull and then somebody pulls the pin and the ship starts off down the chute. Once they pull the pin and the ship starts moving, there's no stopping that juggernaut; it's a done deal. The hyperinflation ship is well on its way, picking up speed, and Obama and Brown are saying they're going to stop it dead.

Fat chance.

Hyperinflation almost always ends with the death of a currency and its replacement by a new one. Over there in the US you'll probably be calling it the Amero. What does it mean for all of you over there who have a couple of hundred thousand dollars sitting in the bank? You've been working your backside off for years and years and you've been saving your money; it's all going to be swept away, gone. Isn't that just special?

And you wage-earners out there who think your wages are going to rise alongside inflation, think again.

Forget about the official rate of inflation. The people who are causing this inflation are lying sociopathic criminals; you can't believe the numbers that came out of the relevant Government departments. Your Government consists of pathological liars, except they don't lie to you all of the time, they tell you the truth once in a while to keep you confused, bemused and deceived.

Let's just ponder briefly what prices rising 10% a month actually means. What costs £100 today, when the year begins, costs £285 when the year ends. Did you get that? 10% per month compound inflation means petrol costing four dollars per gallon in January becomes $12.55 per gallon in December; a loaf of bread that costs £1 costs £2.85 in 12 month's time. That's just at 10%. Do you think hyperinflation stayed at 10% in Zimbabwe? Try 89.7 sextillion percent, with prices doubling every 24.7 hours.

What tends to happen during hyperinflation is that the prices will actually rise faster than the real rate of inflation because, once it gets started and were all geared to the fact that money is becoming increasingly worthless every month, we start raising prices faster and faster than the money is actually depreciating. This causes the goods to disappear from the shelves because everyone is buying everything in sight based upon the expectation of the next month's needs, and—simultaneously—getting rid of their money.

There's no shortage of money during hyperinflation, there's lots of money out there. Paper money, that is. Hyperinflation drives the goods off the shelves because there's not a corresponding production of goods and services. We're printing money faster than the goods and services can be produced, goods and services disappear off the shelves and now you have shortages. This is made worse in the United States and Great Britain by the fact that we rely on imports, and we haven't paid our suppliers. When you don't pay your suppliers they get nasty and vindictive; they put you on COD and cut off your credit. Friends, how many of you can live without credit? For those of us who want to do something constructive—immediately—we have to work towards where we are self-sustaining. We have to bring our consumption into line with our production. You can't consume more than you produce.

You may say hyperinflation is not very likely, it's not in anyone's best interest, but who has ever told you the 'Illuminati' was ever doing anything in anyone's best interest? These people are sociopaths, they're criminals, and the destruction of the dollar by virtue of hyperinflation is in their best interests.

The destruction of a nation's currency usually results in a violent political revolution. The French revolutionary hyperinflation ended with Napoleon, and the German hyperinflation eventually brought Hitler to power. And that's exactly what I think they're working for here, friends. I think they're going to promote violent revolution for the express purpose of bringing in martial law and locking up all the dissenters.

Are we going to have an economic recovery? No. Why? Because everything that is being done equals no recovery. None. Zero. If you think Roosevelt engineered recovery from 1933-37, forget about it. In 1937, unemployment was higher than it was in 1933. Unemployment is bad now and getting worse, and the policies that we're following are going to create more unemployment. Is that an accident? No way in hell. And the policymakers all know that. Can the President or the Prime Minister come out and say, 'Look, I'm working for the New World Order, and I am here to put all of you people out of work, so that we can give you a chip in your hand and rule over you with a rod of iron?' Would you vote for that?

I don't care who it is that's running for public office, he simply has to come out and say, 'I'm for the little guy, I'm from the Government and I'm here to help. We're going to get this economy going again but what we need is a stimulus package.' I would disagree. What we need is a substance-backed currency; 'just' weights and balances, and the abolition of the central banking system. Is that what we're going to get? There's more chance of a chap with two wooden legs getting out of a forest fire unscathed, and the 'powers that be' know that. The 'powers that be' make their money from inflation; they make their money from banking and insurance, from big business, from Government. And it's at your expense. Of course you're going to have more of the same.

Are we going to have shortages, wage and price controls and rationing? Absolutely. No doubt about it. What you're going to see coming out of this faux economic crisis are shortages of everything, wage and price controls and rationing in the extreme. Are we going to have more unemployment? Yep. Will it hit 25%? Without a shadow of a doubt. In Argentina, it hit 62% at the peak of their collapse. I believe we'll see 60% unemployment in the United States, probably less in Great Britain. You good people are going to be so prostrate before your masters that when they suggest to you that you should get a chip in your right hand and accept the cashless society, not only are you going to line up for it, you'll fight for positions in line. Will there be a new monetary system? You'd better believe it. How's that for a prophecy?

Will there be civil unrest and disorder? There always has been in the past. And why? Because morality in the West is at an all-time low—we've been taught and trained, shaped and bent to be amoral.

Martial law? You can count on it—it's the way they'll take power, more law and order, more control.

What about a new Constitutional Convention in the US, is there a new constitution in the wings? Sure there is, they've had it ready for many years, they're just two states short of the two-thirds they need to call a constitutional convention. Will it be anything like your old constitution? Not even close.

Are you going to have communism embedded in your new constitution? Is a pig pork? Not that it's going to change anything for the average Joe, he's been practising communism all of his life. The Ten Planks of the Communist Manifesto call for a heavy, progressive income tax, a central bank with fiat currency, social security and public school. You might want to look into that. And if you cannot be bothered, here it is again:

The Ten Planks of the Communist Manifesto

1. Abolition of private property and the application of all rents of land to public purposes.
2. A heavy progressive or graduated income tax.
3. Abolition of all rights of inheritance.

4. Confiscation of the property of all emigrants and rebels.
5. Centralization of credit in the hands of the state, by means of a national bank with State capital and an exclusive monopoly.
6. Centralization of the means of communications and transportation in the hands of the State.
7. Extension of factories and instruments of production owned by the state, the bringing into cultivation of waste lands, and the improvement of the soil generally in accordance with a common plan.
8. Equal liability of all to labour. Establishment of industrial armies, especially for agriculture.
9. Combination of agriculture with manufacturing industries, gradual abolition of the distinction between town and country, by a more equitable distribution of population over the country.
10. Free education for all children in public schools. Abolition of children's factory labour in its present form. Combination of education with industrial production.

We can't expect the American people to jump from capitalism to Communism but we can assist their leaders by giving them small amounts of Socialism until they awaken one day to find out they have Communism.
NIKITA KHRUSHCHEV
3-1/2 MONTHS BEFORE HIS VISIT TO THE UNITED STATES.
REF: CONGRESSIONAL RECORD 7/28/61 P.12622

Since the end of World War Two, we Westerners have been radical, vehement anti-Communists. We have always seen ourselves as the good guys in white hats and the Communists as bad guys in black hats. We're the defenders of freedom and democracy around the world. The Communists represent tyranny and everything we loathe and despise. Surely we Westerners can't be practising what we loathe and despise? We spend trillions on National defence to protect ourselves from a Communist takeover, and Communism is reported to be dead, but have the forces of democracy and freedom in the West really defeated it? Or embraced it?

All Ten Planks have been embraced by Democrats and Conservatives, by the Labourites, the Republicans and the Liberals alike.

The Ten Commandments are the exact opposite to the Ten Planks of the Communist Manifesto. Amongst the Ten Commandments is one that states thou shalt not steal—the basis, the very foundation, of property rights. If you want to own property, you have to have a law that says thou shalt not steal. I've often wondered if that's the reason we took the Ten Commandments out of our public schools. The first Plank of the Communist Manifesto calls for the abolition of property and land and the application of all rents of land for public purposes. You don't own any land—you're renting it from the State in the form of a property tax, are you not? Try not paying and you will see who the owner is, sharpish.

The Government claims to own much of the land here in the west, and if you want to use it, you have to go to the Department of Agriculture or some other Government department, sign a contract with them and pay them rent so you can put your property on it, or farm it, or whatever it may be. There was a time when we had private property in Britain and America; you owned the property. Today we don't have allodial tenure and title.

The second Plank to the Communist Manifesto calls for a heavy progressive or graduated income tax. There was a time in our countries when we didn't pay income tax. I suspect you already recognise the fact you're practising an aspect of communism here, so I won't harp on with this one.

The third Plank calls for the abolition of all right of inheritance. Here in the west, the inheritance tax represents approximately one third of the estate. Most of us go out and get a marriage licence and create a three-party limited general partnership with the State. Time goes on and the boy and girl, working together, accumulate some wealth; usually houses and cars and whatnot. Then, one day, old Bob dies, and Doreen says, 'Oh good, now I get all of the toys.' However, the State comes in and says, 'Whoah, hold your horses, Doreen, we have a marriage agreement here and an inheritance tax, which runs at about 28-35%. Doreen, we want you to buy us out.'

The fourth plank calls for the confiscation of the property of all immigrants and rebels. There is a process going on called 'regional government', with absolute government control over all property, public and private. This confiscation of the property of all immigrants and rebels was part and parcel of the IRS/Inland Revenue program of seizing and distraining people's property, and selling it if they don't pay their income tax, or social security taxes and the like. We have a whole host and plethora of government agencies that have the power to seize our bank accounts, take our businesses, our homes and property.

The fifth Plank calls for the centralisation of credit in the hands of the state, by means of a national bank with state capital and an exclusive monopoly. We have the Bank of England and the Federal Reserve Banks in Britain and America, and we have fiat currencies in the form of the Federal Reserve note and the British pound circulating in our stores and businesses. We use these central banks to clear our cheques, and we use credit cards and other unjust weights and balances.

The sixth Plank calls for the centralisation of the means of communication and transportation in the hands of the state. In the US we have the FCC, the Federal Communications Commission, and the UK has OFCOM, the Office of Communications. You can't transmit your beliefs over the airwaves without a licence from the government, and they regulate what you can say. Even as I write this, there are limitations on my free speech; there are certain things I can't say to you, certain things that are prohibited by the government. So, even though you have a right to free speech, you can't necessarily practise 100% of it. Yes, there is free speech in Communist China, and there's free speech in Russia; there is free speech in totalitarian regimes all around the world but there are limitations on that free speech. For instance, we have prohibitions against hate speech. Did you know that, in Canada, if you were to say, 'I don't believe in the Holocaust, I don't believe that 6 million Jews were killed in Hitler's gas chambers and ovens,' it would be classed as a crime? It's also a crime in Germany; you're called a Holocaust Denier. That's not free speech, and the people who have enacted that kind of legislation don't believe in free speech. The sixth Plank of the Communist Manifesto is indeed alive and well in Britain and America.

The seventh Plank of the Communist Manifesto calls for the extension of factories and instruments of production owned by the state; the bringing into cultivation of wastelands, and the improvement of the soil generally in accordance with a common plan. We are talking about Corporations here—limited liability companies, artificial entities. Do we have any of those in the West? How about government programmes for the regulation and control of the public lands? Do we have any legislation that deals with the improvement of the soil in accordance with a common plan, such as 'soil conservation districts'?

The eighth Plank calls for equal obligation of all to work and the establishment of Industrial armies, especially for agriculture. Do you have a Social Security number? Social Security has established Westerners into a gigantic industrial army, we are all members of the same group; you cant work without it. Get mum and dad out of the house so that Big Brother can steal their children and mould their minds for the State's use.

The ninth Plank calls for the combination of agriculture with manufacturing industries; gradual abolition of the distinction between town and country by a more equable distribution of the population over the country. This calls for urban renewal, population control and regional planning programmes. Over the last hundred years, the population of people living on the land has decreased significantly. People born in the rural areas have left public schools and gravitated towards the cities to attend colleges in order to train as doctors and, engineers and scientists and the like, and they have then gone of to work for corporations instead of returning to the land. The projection is that by 2015, small farms and businesses in the country will give way to huge corporate farms. Do we have anything like that going on in Great Britain and America? We're city workers and professionals now, aren't we?

The tenth Plank of the Communist manifesto calls for free education for all children in government schools, the abolition of children's factory labour in its present form, and the combination of education with industrial production. This one speaks for itself. Do we send our children to 'State-run brain laundries' or not?

So there we have it. I'm sure you all agree that whether we like it or not, we are all practising communists, underneath the thinnest veneer of capitalism. Scratch that veneer and discover that we are staring into the abyss of state, county and municipal bankruptcies taking place as I write these words. California is right on the cusp of bankruptcy as I write this. A bond and stock market collapse? The bond market can't withstand the economic turmoil that is being unleashed upon it at the moment.

How about the pension system? Do you think you're going to retire on your pension from the police force and live out your golden years on some Mediterranean beach? Do you honestly believe that? I'm here to tell you that the pension system is going to collapse. All of them? No, I'm sure two or three of them will survive. You can just about bet that Government and their pension systems are going to survive, but all private pensions are dead. Are you folks out there on Social Security going to get your cheques? Probably. Are those cheques going to be able to buy anything? Not a chance, but you're going to get every penny you were promised… sort of.

We cannot trace or identify one dime of the $350 billion that has already been spent. We have no idea who got it, we don't know how much they got, and we don't know what they spend it on or where it is today.

BYRON L. DORGAN
UNITED STATES SENATOR FOR NORTH DAKOTA

There was a chap in Germany, in the Weimar Republic, who bought a life insurance policy in 1903 that was worth about 100,000 marks. In 1903, 100,000 marks was worth about £35,000 or $50,000. He paid all of his premiums faithfully until about 1922, when he finished paying off the policy. He cashed it in and then traded it for a loaf of bread. How do you like that? You social security pensioners out there that paid in all those years, that is what you can expect, a loaf of bread. If you're lucky.

Are there going to be more corporate bailouts? Absolutely. This is a fascist regime and you can just bet on more corporate bailouts, at the expense of the taxpayers, who don't have any money anyway because we're all broke, aren't we? But they're going to take what credit we have left and they're going to spend it in our name.

Are we going to see any debt relief for homeowners? None, zero, zilch, zip. In fact, of the first $700 billion the US Government magically pulled out of the hat recently, $350 billion has already been spent. Can you point to one cent that has gone to one homeowner? Just one cent of the $700 billion? If you can identify one cent that went where we were told it was going, please rush, hurry, send me an e-mail and identify the homeowner who received that money.

That money never was intended for homeowners, it was intended for banks, and the banks got it.

No, there's not going to be any debt relief for homeowners. The purpose for putting all of you homeowners in distress is to force you to comply; the last thing they're going to do is to give you any relief. Are we going to have a token recipient in this operation? Oh yes—a token homeowner who is going to get debt relief, and the Government will make a lot of noise about it, like a slot machine bell going off in a Las Vegas casino: Ding, ding, ding, ding, ding. Everyone will get excited. 'Hey, this woman just won over here on the slot machine. Here comes the casino owner now. Wow, he's got the money right there in his hand and he's going to pay the winner. Woohooo, look at that lucky winner, the system really works, now tell everyone not to worry!'

The key to democracy is control over money by the people, not by a secret elite. It's the money that counts. If you lose control of your money, hand it over to people you can't see, you're a slave. That's what you have to remember. Never, ever again, let some secret power elite take control of your money away from you.'

BENJAMIN FULFORD
PROJECT CAMELOT, FEBRUARY 2008

Here's the way this game is being played. Let's suppose I come to you and I say, 'Hey, Bob, let's buy a residential building together, I've got a hell of a deal for you. We've got a £1 million building over here and the owner of the building is bankrupt; he can't make his payments and he's going to lose the building. We can buy it from him for £500,000. All we need to do is put a little partnership together. It will be you and me, and Tony over there. Now, Tony and I don't have any money but what we would like to do is to borrow £5000 from everyone we know, and then you put up £5000 yourself; that'll be our down payment. And then, we want you to pledge your house, because your house is free and clear and we don't own any homes, we are just renters to the bank. Then, we can take over this building. The building, right now, has outgoing payments of £5000 a month and it has a rent structure that is only returning £4000 a month. Oh, and it has a vacancy factor of 50%. We'd also like to renovate the building, so we'd like you to pledge your business and your business inventory for another £200,000 loan that can be paid off at £3000 per month. The rent structure won't support this but we have high hopes that after we renovate the building, we'll be able to rent the other 50% of the flats, even though our tenants are moving out at the rate of 20% a month and we're only renting out new flats at the rate of 10% a month. We're going to be about £2000 a month short in being able to service these two debts, so we want you to cough up the money from your business and your savings to cover that. Now, here's the good bit, we'll all share equally in the profits of this wonderful investment!'

How does that grab you, friends? That's what your Government is doing in your name. You're partners, taxpayers, remember? These are the business deals being made for you. How much money are you making out of those deals? Are you doing well? The people of America and Great Britain have lost their minds; they're just absolutely insane—or at least the 62% who believe the Government is going to bail the economy out and who believe we're going to have a short recession and then it's business as usual.

Is there going to be a recovery? Yes, of course there is, there's going to be a *manufactured* recovery in 2010, pay attention and watch it happen. How do I know that? It's what they did last time. As I've said, there is an objective here, there is a goal that Government, business and industry and the establishment have. They have a role for you and they want you to join in and play along. To make you play, they have to put a little pressure on you. So things are bad and are getting worse—right on their schedule.

It's a proven winner, and the 'Illuminati', the people in the seats of power around the world, have had nothing but success working this scam for the last 2000 years. It has worked perfectly every time, so they don't see any reason why it's not going to work this time around as well.

Of course, they never catch everyone in the trap. You might be the most cunning fox who ever graduated from Cunning University, but you can't catch every hen in the hen house. While you're cornering the sleeping hens, there are those of us able to make a run for it and learn from your attack.

You can't expect any rational or workable solutions from the Government—they will always be vague and ambiguous. For instance, Obama said recently that a stimulus package is required and that stimulus package will produce 4 million jobs. Talk about vague and ambiguous. Where did he get the number 4 million from in relation to an $800 million stimulus package? Does that mean that if we spend 1.6 trillion, that you'll get 8 million jobs, or if you spent $400 billion you'd get 2 million jobs? Where did he get his numbers and from which historical source? When has this ever worked before? What were the dates, what were the numbers, what were the outcomes? How much did the stimulus cost and was it economically viable? Did it pay itself off over time? There's never anything concrete coming from Government— they've already decided that it will follow the doomed path of spending to revive the economy, which only ever wastes and misdirects resources. It was only America's suspiciously-timed entrance into WWII that rescued the US economy from the great Depression, so you can expect much more inflation and much more economic distress with lower economic output. Unless a miracle happens, like a sudden, spontaneous outbreak of freedom, the Federal Reserve and the Bank of England abolish themselves, or common sense becomes epidemic in the west, you can be sure the coming years will be bleak.

As a voter, you have to choose between trusting to the natural stability of gold and the natural stability of the honesty and intelligence of the members of the Government. And, with due respect for these gentlemen, I advise you, as long as the Capitalist system lasts, to vote for gold.
GEORGE BERNARD SHAW

You only have one choice as far as I see it, and that is protect your stream of income by buying gold and silver. Precious metals offer you protection against currency depreciation; it's a hedge against inflation for whatever wealth you have left at the moment. The golden rule here is never risk more than you can afford to lose.

This bailout scheme that is going on around us at the moment makes all the sense in the world to the banks, and I don't harbour any grudges with the bankers. After all, they've got wives and children and mortgages and bills to pay like everybody else, it's just that I don't want to pay their bills for them, that's all. I make my choices in life and when I make a bad choice, I lose. When I lose, I learn. Unless you've got some inside information and you can sidle up to the pig trough like the bankers are doing in Washington and London, then maybe you ought be thinking about a way of hanging on to what you've got because hyperinflation is my bet.

Considering the fact that all of the other fiat currencies around the world, the British pound, the Japanese Yen, the Euro, the Swiss franc and so on, are all just as rotten as the dollar, what is your best alternative for stockpiling and safeguarding your capital and your savings? The answer is gold and silver. Obviously you can hold gold and silver yourself and liquidate it whenever you need it, as the hyperinflation progresses. More and more you will be able to use the gold and silver directly as currency.

The value of paper money is precisely the value of a politician's promise, as high or low as you put that; the value of gold is protected by the inability of politicians to manufacture it.
SIR WILLIAM REES-MOGG

Metallurgists have determined there's seventeen times more silver in the Earth's crust than there is gold. Bankers come along and, of course, they don't want to work to get this precious metal out of the earth, they want people like you and me to do that and they want us to deliver the gold and silver to them. When you have the exclusive power to create money that the slaves of the world must labour for and surrender all that we produce to get, you get some unique opportunities the rest of us don't. You don't need to do anything for profit. Why work for a profit when you can create money? What and whom can't you buy with the unlimited money you create?

There are teachers, preachers, politicians, news media, standing armies, police, and of course, all the slaves necessary to work the plantation—I guess you could even buy the world and tell the rest to get off it! But wait, if you did that, who would do the work, your bidding, build your toys and enhance your lifestyle, enrich and reward and service your high standard of living? Who would feed you? Would you really want to plough lumpy fields? Tend cattle and engage in slaughterhouse activities, mine minerals under ground and risk cave-ins, work in sweat shop factories? No, it's much easier to create out of thin air the money the slaves are willing to work for.

So what do they have to offer us in order to pay us to take the gold and silver out of the ground? Nothing, because they're all lazy parasites. That's precisely why paper money is created: to obtain the labour and wealth of others without payment. They convinced us that we should trade our gold and silver to them for this paper money. It was a hell of a good deal for the bankers; I admire them for coming up with that program because it pays very nicely. Before the introduction of paper money, if you were to ask how much one-ounce of gold was worth, the answer would be seventeen ounces of silver, and that's because for every ounce of gold in the ground, there are seventeen ounces of silver. That's what we call weights and measures.

The bankers came along and they had a little different take on that, they called it 'value'. They printed up a $17 bill, then handed it to the gold miner and said, 'This $17 bill is equal to one ounce of gold,' and the miner, not knowing much about values and weights decided it was a good deal. He took the $17 bill and traded it with the farmer saying, 'This $17 bill is equal to one ounce of gold, so how many bushels of wheat can I get?' The farmer said he could have however many bushels it came to; and so on, down the line. Slowly but surely, over time, we exchanged weights and measures for 'value', which is a commercial term.

These bankers are real masters at commerce. Today, in the management of gold and silver, we don't trade seventeen ounces of silver for an ounce of gold, what we do is trade the silver for dollars. Or pounds, or euros, or Japanese yen. In other words, we are valuing the silver based upon the banker's valuation of paper money. What we have done is reduced our gold and silver weights and measures to value, and there are folks out there practicing arbitrage and making a huge return from this set-up. They speculate in dollars versus GBP and Yen in the currency markets and make significant profit, then they take that profit, measured in value, in the form of paper, and trade it for wheat, corn, beans, honey and oil. And that's called the modern economy.

All of us are involved in it and now we are using plastic credit cards, cheques, discount cards and all forms of 'value' rather than 'property'—gold and silver coin—to make our trades.

The 'value' of gold today is about $900 an ounce and the value of silver today is about $13 an ounce. So as you can see, as they say in economics, there is a ratio of the value of silver to gold. If we divide 900 by 13 we find the ratio today is 69 to 1. So if you take an ounce of gold to a Gold broker he would give you sixty-nine ounces of silver for it, minus his commission of course. Remember, out in the real world there are only seventeen ounces of silver for every ounce of gold, but once you get the bankers in here making paper money and manipulating the markets and converting people over to saving through value, they can actually decide how much your gold or silver is worth. They give you paper for your deposit of gold and they have an exclusive monopoly on making this paper, and if you get caught making it, it's called counterfeiting. They can have an ounce of gold in the warehouse and put out two pieces of paper—two warehouse receipts—or four, or eight, or sixteen. We're all sitting out here thinking that when we've got one of these receipts, it means we've got one of those gold coins in the warehouse. Sometimes we come to find, when inventorying the warehouse that you've got sixteen receipts out there but you've only got ten ounces of gold, which means that if everyone takes their receipt into the gold warehouse, six people are going to be bitterly disappointed. That is why there is the told adage that goes 'short bankers are hung from tall trees.'

The question is, would you rather have a lifeboat on Titanic or a receipt for a lifeboat on Titanic?

The monetary managers are fond of telling us that they have substituted 'responsible money management' for the gold standard. But there is no historic record of responsible paper money management... The record taken as a whole is one of hyperinflation, devaluation and monetary chaos.
HENRY HAZLITT

Historically, when you look at silver against gold, you'll see a long-term value ratio of about sixteen or seventeen ounces of silver to one ounce of gold. However, there were a couple of times in the 20th century when the ratio went as high as 100 to 1, which means that the price of an ounce of gold would be 100 times greater than the price of an ounce of silver. Right now we are in one of those peaks, with a ratio of 69 to 1, which is abnormally high. Based on historical precedent, my prediction would be that the price of silver and gold—at some point in the near future when these metals come back into their own as money—is going to go back toward the long-term average of 16 to 1. My plan would be buy silver—

real, physical silver, not a paper receipt for some promised silver that may or may not exist—while it's still historically cheap. If the ratio moved in the other direction, I'd start acquiring gold, which would then be historically cheaper than silver, and maybe switch some of my silver to gold.

Am I advocating that you should sell all of your stocks and bonds and buy silver? Not at all, I don't know anything about you so I can't tell if that's good for you or not—and nobody can be certain of just how much price-fixing fire-power the paper banking system has left. I'm just letting you know what I plan on doing.

To understand money you first have to understand why money exists. If there's no form of commercial trading going on, then money simply isn't necessary. The very fact that money exists is proof we live in a commercial world. The word 'commerce' means 'trade' and trade requires energy for things to happen, to move. Before machinery, the only way to move things was by man's energy; labour. It doesn't matter what you buy, where you bought it or when you bought it, it couldn't possibly be in your possession if there was no human labour involved. In other word's, nothing could have been created had a man or woman not first accessed the raw materials, every thing currently found on Earth. The finished product is considered to be an 'asset', the true value of the asset being the man hours of labour put into bringing the item into finished form and delivering it to the market place.

The people who are not involved in the manufacturing process are involved in making sure the roads are clear, the electricity flows, the water flows, and the food grown by the farmer gets delivered on time. These are called exchanges—specifically, exchanges of labour for someone else's labour. However, this is not the case today. Today we have people's labour being exchanged for cheques as payment for the labour 'pre-given', making it pre-paid. You have to work first to get paid second. Although there is technically an exchange of labour for paper, the perception of the value of money is misunderstood by almost everyone but the banksters. The only reason money is in existence and in your pocket, purse or bank account, is because you had to work to get it, steal it or win the lottery. In other words the money called 'legal tender' is backed by the labour of the people or it simply would not exist, it could not exist.

In 1931-33 by order of the Privy Council and subsequent Banking Acts, money was declared no longer redeemable, which effectively meant the banks were no longer responsible for buying it back—and they haven't been since. The very place that issues the money doesn't even want the stuff, since the banks know it has no value, and that it represents the labour you gave in exchange for it. It's not the money you owe that's important to the banks, it's the assets you create that they have or hold title to that they really want at the end of the day. The asset has far greater value than the piece of paper or cheque you get paid with, or the money you allegedly owe for it. The simple fact is, money is backed by nothing more than our faith in it, and the assets we exchange it for.

Since money is only backed by our labour, it could be said then that people are assets. In fact, no doubt you've heard a company say that its employees are its greatest asset. If a company has no employees, it can't have any assets. Human assets come before material assets because it's man that crafts the materials into assets.

People are the only energy assets, until the Government can create a sentient, obedient machine to do the same job, which brings us to the root cause of our problems today, as national debts around the world increase at an exponential rate. The bankruptcy of the corporate Governments in 1927/1933/1935 made it impossible to pay any debt with real substance backed money and legal tender was 'valueless' yet it became the only means to pay. This made it impossible for anyone to eliminate a debt, and no debt has been extinguished since. Today, we can only pay debt with other debt instruments. Effectively, this adds up to double debt, and there is no real 'discharge' of the original obligation. This aspect is the cause of the nation's annual national debt.

Contrary to popular belief, a negative value plus another negative value only equals more negative value, yet according to accounting principles, once a debt instrument is used to make payment for a previous debt, the books show a zero balance. But a bankrupt nation's accounting books can never be balanced to zero, as long as banks maintain the power to create money (legal tender) out of thin air and control accounting entry credit. Banks create money (legal tender) and they, therefore, own that money.

Consequently, anything purchased with the bank's money belongs to banks. People use the banks private tender (property), as a medium of exchange, exchanging the bank's property for other property, making the latter property that of the banks. In other words, if you take the bank's property and exchange it for a third party's property—a retailer for instance—all you have done, in essence, is acted as a buying and selling agent for the other two parties; the retailer and the bank. What people are really doing is exchanging one owner's property for another owner's property, never actually owning anything; we're simply middlemen, who receive no value, other than the 'equitable right of use' of the asset while it is in our possession.

The corporate Government bankruptcies were declared because there were no more assets available that were acceptable to the banks in order to make the interest payments on the exorbitant loans. To compensate for this lack of valuable assets, the Governments were persuaded to pledge the future labour production energy of the people, knowing full well that the assets created by the people would be exchanged happily for paper money, specifically, Debt. The Governments take the titles to the goods manufactured or brought into the country and use these titles as collateral pledges for more borrowing capabilities, creating even more debt.

Everyone awake? Pay attention to this:

The holder of a Title is the owner/controller of the property for which the title was created. When our parents were cunningly coerced into registering our births, the Governments took title to the child, and gave the parent a 'certificate of birth' in exchange for it.

All births registered are registered with the Registrar General, who is located near a port of entry. A child comes down the birth canal (a maritime term used for hundreds of years) where it then comes to berth at the port, under Maritime jurisdiction.

We enter Maritime jurisdiction when we leave the waters of our mother's womb. When a ship comes to port it must be entered on the Registry, if the owner of the ship never comes back for the vessel, the owner of the registry will claim it for the port, which is exactly what occurs with human birth registrations. Our parents register the birth with the Ministry and the Ministry then becomes the holder/owner of a name very similar to yours, yet very different. In Admiralty, any time you give someone something of yours—property—it is deemed you give full right and authority to control it unless you specify limitations, which of course is never mentioned upon the registration of a human birth. The property our parents pledged as collateral was our 'name'. The Government now holds your 'name' and is deemed owner of it and, as such, they can then speculate and determine your future asset output, which it can then take to the bank as a security to borrow more money. These securities are commonly known as bonds. Bonds represent future liabilities, things that haven't happened yet, but hopefully will. Court cases are financed in a similar fashion, We're charged for something that has not happened yet, until we refuse or dishonour, the bond then becomes a 'Bill', being an antecedent debt and a valuable consideration in that instant.

This is effectively why we're all bonded—bonded into debt and involuntary servitude. As soon as a birth is registered it is automatically filed as an asset and bonds are created to allow for the borrowing of money at that time, to be paid back by you later, when you are old enough to enter the work force, usually at eighteen years of age. Although your actual title is held in the county of your birth it is only warehoused for inventory reasons and is ultimately held on behalf of the Government. Think of it as a pawnshop of sorts.

The county, after having received the allegedly freely given pledge of the title from your parents, then further pledges it to the Government so it can borrow funds from the banks. This is how the game is played; the sequence of events may vary slightly but the outcome is the same. Remember, if you neglect to reclaim your property from the pawnshop, they own it, and as the owners they can do whatever they want with it, and they do. That's why the County has the authority to pledge your name unbeknownst to you. If you don't return to collect your property, clearly, you must not want it. And the Government takes full of advantage of this 'silent approval'.

The Government offers the (positive) assets—almost everything produced or imported, pledges, titles, collateral to the banking cartel—so that the Banks can fund the system by injecting debt currency. The assets are offered to the central banks as security to cover the loans, as in any loan transaction. In exchange for the pledge of the assets, the banks issue debt (negative) currency to the Governments and Corporations. The Corporations use the money as an exchange for the labour given by its employees, which means the assets created at the manufacturing level are already paid for but are never owned by the very people who make them. The corporations use the pay cheques given to its labourer as a liability to offset income and reduce income tax on the sales of the goods manufactured. The Distributor and Retailer do the same; they reduce their income by applying the cost of the product as a tax-deductible expense. The labourer who did all the work making it possible for the Corporations to make a profit, however, is paid with a negative-value piece of paper and pays income taxes on the full amount, with no 'expense' deductions.

In other words, the Corporations do not pay for anything but gain everything at our expense.

We may be slaves to the money masters, the Corporations or the banksters but who are the puppets who entertain us slaves with talk of being able to affect this predetermined pantomime, puppet show? The politicians.

Once most righteous people get to Congress and Parliament, and they see the filth and perversion that goes on, they get out. You can't send an honest man to Congress and Parliament any more than you can put a good apple into a barrel of rotten apples and expect the good apple to make the rotten apples good; the rotten apples will invariably make the good apple go bad. You can't put a good man in Parliament and leave them there for any period of time and expect them not to be tainted by the process. These bad apples are being motivated by vanity, jealousy, lust, greed, and fear to facilitate the new world order agenda.

The economic climate we're currently experiencing is not an accident, it's being done deliberately with premeditated forethought; it's a part of a program to meld all the nations of the world under a one world government. It's a done deal, you don't need to be concerned about voting for this chap or that chap to prevent it. The Republicans and Labour Party are for it, the Conservatives and the Democrats are for it, The Communists are for it, the Socialists are for it, the Nazis and the Fascists; everybody in the world is for it, everybody wants it. So if you're saying God help us from this new world order, you must be some kind of right wing, rabid, reactionary, radical minority; probably a terrorist that needs to be watched and dealt with.

Now there are a few of us that are opposed to the New World order. I don't know how many there are, 5 million, 10 million, maybe even 20 or 30 million but we're not organised and we're not going to change anything in the current paradigm that is our programmed, fear-based mind-set.

Take Responsibility... look it up for yourself. Search engine paths regarding topics addressed in this chapter:

Argentina financial collapse
Art Rolnick
Bank
Bond Market
Cash

Communist Manifesto
Currency
Debt
Deflation
Derivatives
Federal Reserve
Fiat currency
Freeman on the land
Gold
Gold standard
Great Depression
Hyperinflation
IMF
Inflation
Monetary system
Money
Precious Metals
Robert Menard
Stock Market collapse
Weimar Republic
Zimbabwe financial collapse.

THE BREATHING TAX

Temperature went up significantly up to 1940, when human production of CO2 was relatively low. Then, in the post-war years, when the industries and all economies in the world really got going, and human production of CO2 just soared, the global temperature was going down. In other words, the facts did not fit the theory.

PROFESSOR TIM BALL
DEPARTMENT OF CLIMATOLOGY
UNIVERSITY OF WINNIPEG

Picture the scene: You've left the house forgetting you've only got 5 units of credit in the carbon bank (owned by *famille* Rothschild, coincidentally) which is communicating with the RFID chip in your right hand—the one you queued up to get inserted back in 2010, remember? It's a good 30-minute ride back home where your Family Carbon Credit Charger™ is situated, and you know that once your 5 remaining Carbon Credits® run out, you're going to light up like a Christmas tree on the Carbon Debtor Detector Unit™ within one of the hundreds of Carbon Police vehicles patrolling the city.

You begin to take shallower breaths and hold them for longer. You're getting a little dizzy but you know that if you can make it to the Pay As You Breathe® City Carbon Credit Top Up unit a couple of streets away, you'll be just fine.

The Pay As You Breathe® rate is 3 times higher than the direct debit rate, of course, and you resent having to pay that much for something that was free only two years ago, but thinking about that upsets you, and getting agitated is only going to have you breathing harder, so you push it to the back of your mind. Nevertheless, you pick up the pace in order to get there before your remaining three credits run out. You can just about make out the City Carbon Credit Charger™in the distance, despite the fact your vision is now beginning to blur due to lack of oxygen.

You make it with half a Carbon Credit Unit® to spare and let out a huge sigh of relief, which of course uses up the rest of your credit. You then spot a passing Carbon Police patrol car turn on its light-bar and do a screeching u-turn in the middle of peak traffic. You touch your right hand to the receptor pad on the City Carbon Credit Dispenser™ but instead of charging your credit, it flashes a message telling you to remain where you are as someone will be along to assist you shortly. Sure enough, the patrol car stops right alongside you and a Carbon Revenue Collection Agent steps out and approaches.

'Afternoon, citizen. I see you've just run out of carbon credit. Please pop your hand on the unit there, charge up and I'll pretend I didn't see it this time. After all, we're not monsters, you know.'

You've seen that seemingly compassionate smile before, when your friend Bob was in the same position last week. And you remember the multiple tazering he got when it was revealed that he'd had his chip deactivated by a backstreet mobile phone vendor. You hold your breath and nod emphatically while rubbing at the receptor pad as though your life depended on it. The resulting high-pitched beeps arouse the agent's suspicion and he scans your hand with his Citizenwatch 5000™, to discover that you have several outstanding parking tickets and your credit has been suspended.

'I'm afraid you're going to have to accompany me to the station, sir. Do you have anyone we can inform of your incarceration?'

You wish you'd stayed at home and paid those bloody tickets, instead of demanding proof of claim that the tickets actually applied to you, a non 'person', living man on the land, but all of that is forgotten as you slowly lose consciousness in the back of the Police car.

Just before you pass out, you hear, 'Sir, you are now in contravention of the Exhalation Act 2011. You have the right to remain silent…'

Bearing in mind that we humans exhale CO_2 at a rate of 450ml per minute and we're supposed to be cutting down our output to save the planet, it stands to reason that the carbon tax should surely be extended to breathing.

Whether it is on CNN or the BBC, hardly a newscast goes by that the phrase, 'global warming' (recently softened to the more vague term, 'climate change') is not prominently featured. The subject of Global warming has only been around for the past fifteen years or so, and the first reports merely stated that the Antarctic ice caps were melting and the temperature around the world was rising.

Not many people thought much about it at the time but the momentum of the diatribe has been increasing exponentially in the past five years. We are being aggressively sold on the global warming programme now. We've had Al Gore winning a Nobel prize recently for his hot and heavy participation in the debate. Discussions on the possibility of shutting down the majority of our power plants, which will result in the 'useless eaters' paying a great deal more for our electricity whilst using a whole lot less of it are a key feature of the programme. That's not very good news, is it?

Politicians are a crafty bunch; they don't just start selling something without a purpose behind it. It is promoted by the tried and true method of, 'We need to protect you people from yourselves, you're burning up too much electricity, and in the process you're putting too much carbon dioxide into the atmosphere. As a result of that you're causing global warming and its going to flood the world and it's just going to be terrible, so we're going to save you from it.' Sound familiar? Bless them; they're trying to save us, again.

Trouble is, I get really nervous when politicians want to save me. It never works out well.

We have politicians attempting to give us national identification for our livestock—somehow or another they figure that will save us. There's Hillary and Barack over there in the States who want to give you socialised medicine in order to save you. When your 'wards' are in danger, you need mandatory health care. And they will force you to swallow their medicine.

I don't deny that you people are sick, but I do deny that you need health care insurance, and I deny that socialised medicine is going to solve your health problems. There is a solution but that's not it. This global warming issue has a solution as well, but shutting down the power plants isn't it. So, the politicians have a plan to deal with global warming and—of course—they're telling us it's going to cost money. Right away, anyone with two brain cells to rub together would put two and two together and see that the very reason that we're 'fighting global warming' is because the politicians want more money. Politicians never have enough money, have you noticed that?

These good folks that are advocating a solution to global warming evidently don't believe that nature—or God, if you like—is in control of planet Earth, or that nature can determine what the temperature of the earth ought to be. For my part, I don't know what the temperature ought to be; I haven't got a clue. I didn't arrive on planet Earth until the late 60s but I've noticed that between then and now, things have been going along pretty well. I've noticed that from time to time some years are warmer than others, some summers are hotter, some winters are warmer. Scientists spend a lot of time, effort and energy gallivanting around the world these days (on carbon-spewing aircraft, no less) taking temperatures, and we're told there's 'an average…'

I'd like to suggest that back in the early 1800s nobody was out measuring the temperature. As far as I know, back in the late 1700s nobody was measuring the temperature, or back in 800AD, or 800 BC, or 3000 BC; I don't see any historical records where people were running around measuring the temperature, wringing their hands in great despair and crying out to their gods, 'Oh God, save us from global warming.' But now all of a sudden, hardly a day goes by where it doesn't feature in almost every broadcasting medium.

The news channels have sent correspondents down to Antarctica and up to the North Pole, producing special programmes on how the ice is melting, which we can't deny because they've presented us with satellite pictures showing us what the north polar region looked like in 1960 and what it looks like now in 2009. Sure enough, there is a great difference in the amount of ice that was visible between the two pictures. I want to point out to you that the difference in the amount of ice coverage over the North Pole in January is greater than it is in July. I don't know when they were taking these satellite pictures and they're certainly not specific about when they were taken so—right away—my curiosity is piqued.

About half the ice in the polar region melts in the summertime, did you know that? If you look at the 'before' pictures, showing the coverage of the North Pole, they clearly show the entire Antarctic Ocean covered by ice, all the way down to the latitude of the Aleutian Islands. If you look at the 'after' series of pictures, literally half of that coverage has gone, which is exactly what you would expect between January and July. They never said 'Here's one set of pictures taken in January and here's another set of pictures also taken in January years later,' and they haven't shown us a series of pictures taken every January between the year 1990 and 2009. A little suspicious don't you think? They're not lying to you, as such, they're just not telling you the whole truth, which is basically lying by omission. They're not here to edify you, to give you all of the facts, so you can make an informed decision; their job is to doctor the story, to get you to come to the conclusion that man is responsible for global warming and the melting of the polar ice caps.

We are told that it if all these ice caps melt into the ocean it is going to raise the oceans by a significant percentage and flood the Earth. It is true there is a lot of ice down in Antarctica, and it's also true there is a lot of ice up in the North Pole. It's also true there's a lot of snow and ice in Greenland and in the Himalayan Mountains, but if you gathered every drop of fresh water from all of the land-locked lakes in the Lake District, from the Great Lakes, Superior, Michigan and all of the others, and melted all of the snow and ice in the world; it will only increase the volumes of the oceans by 1%. Bear in mind that the oceans are wide and they're very deep, they cover a little more than two thirds of planet Earth, and not all of the one third left is covered with water and ice; most of it is desert and mountains. It's true that one percentage rise is not going to be good for those people down in Key West Florida or the Maldives, but I sincerely doubt it's going to be a worldwide disaster.

Speaking of Greenland, do you know why it's called 'Green' land and not 'White land'? Give it a moment's thought. A chap called Leifr Eiríksson founded it around 980AD, when we were in the middle of the last great warming trend. On the way to New-foundland, the Vikings passed what we now know as the 'world's largest island' and it was green; there were trees, there was grass and vegetation, so they named it Greenland. The clue is in the name; it does what it says on the tin. I just thought I'd pass that on to you for consideration.

The World Health Organization (WHO) says humans are seriously affected by climate change, that climate change is a global threat and that measures must be taken to combat it. Meanwhile the UN are predicting the average temperature of the world could rise by 6.3°C by the end of this century and that an average rise of 3°C could cause floods in Asia affecting seven million and cause food shortages affecting more than 100 million, so, therefore everyone must participate in the fight to protect the global environment.

I'm inclined to agree, everyone should participate in the fight to protect our global environment, but not because of human-caused global warming, not because Global warming is harmful to the environment and not because the climate models are predicting the end of the world as we know it.

There are two documented periods in history, during the Holocene Maximum in 6000BC and the Medieval Warm Period in the 1500's, where man-made fuel burning, carbon dioxide-producing machinery was not prevalent and non-existent, respectively, yet the temperatures during these periods were much higher than they are today. More recently, the economic boom and industrialisation after the Second World War increased carbon dioxide production and output, and yet global temperatures started to drop from 1940 for more than 30 years. So, using a little common sense, the only conclusion I can come to is that global warming is not related to the amount of carbon dioxide in the atmosphere.

Certain scientists are paid professional whores. There, I said it. They haven't always been whores but I've been observing science and scientists for some time now and—prior to 1990—if a scientist told me that the world was upside down I'd have believed him, because he was a scientist. But then I started paying attention and noticed a very important factor: you can take any subject in science, I don't care what it is, and there will be scientists who will be for it and there will be scientists who are against it. I reject that nonsense. That's not science; that's opinion and propaganda. That is exactly the opposite of what science is and what it stands for.

Science, by dictionary definition, is 'knowledge' and knowledge is absolute. Its like maths—$2 + 2 = 4$, $4 + 4 = 8$, and $8 \times 8 = 64$, remember? Math is absolute and everyone agrees that it is. Real science is absolute and there ought to be the same consensus amongst scientists as there is among mathematicians. Medical doctors have all been to college and all have letters after their names; they're certainly smart people—you'd think all of those big brains, unified by a burning desire to fulfil their Hippocratic oath, could come to an agreement over the cause of cancer, or any subject matter concerned with cancer, wouldn't you?

Now, when one scientist comes along and says the world is warming and another scientist says the world is cooling, and a third scientist comes along saying there's no change, you don't have to be a rocket scientist to realise that they can't all be right. Don't get me wrong, I like science, I'm not opposed to science or scientists, I'm just opposed to scientists with an axe to grind, scientists that lie, and scientists with a personal opinion that they then call 'science'. Oh, and scientists on a corporate or government payroll, both of which—if you stop to think about it—covers pretty much the whole bunch of them.

Ninety percent of all the scientists who have ever drawn breath on planet Earth are alive right now. That's simply because as the population grows, the number of scientists grows. All of these scientists have to have jobs, so who the hell is it that employs these people? The answer is Government.

By the time a child hits fifth grade, he's brainwashed into believing that if he does anything but go to college he'll be a complete failure in life. That's where all of us blue-collar chaps are—we're all failures in life; we didn't go to college, we didn't get a degree and we didn't become a scientist. We're all out there driving trucks, fixing pipes, building houses and doing the worthwhile work. Friends, we could live out the rest of our lives without a climatologist, a palaeontologist or an orthonologist. Just try living without a carpenter, an electrician or a plumber for a while and let me know how that works out for you. You'll begin to get tired of that outside loo in no time at all, particularly in January in northern England.

So the child decides he doesn't want to be a failure in life and he does go to college. He gets his science degree and then goes to work for a University, studying something for the Government, which is probably being paid for by tax income. He has high ideals and great ideas about making a valuable contribution to society but once he's got his feet under the table, and he's earning a nice crust examining frog sperm and whatnot, he's told in no uncertain terms, 'We have an agenda; we have a predetermined outcome that we are looking for. We are going to use science, were going to use scientists, and we're going to use money. If you want funding next year and the year after, if you want to continue in your chosen field here at the University, then you'd better come up with the right research paper. And if you don't, there's not going to be any money for your department next year.'

These major government agencies, whether it's the FDA, the Department of Agriculture or otherwise, are all controlled, directly or indirectly by the Committee of 300, and they all have agendas and policies. These policies have to be met by the employees that work in these institutions, and any scientist or doctor who runs counter to the agenda will be shown the door. Government employees who become iconoclasts and whistleblowers get fired, or they get demoted, or promoted into the basement where they're not going to be heard or be a problem to the official policy. I challenge any scientist working for a government institution to rebut that. You can bet your life that when Big Pharma wants a predetermined outcome, they buy it, and the politicians in Washington and London will pay for whatever predetermined outcome they need to perpetuate their current agenda.

For example, lets take genetically modified food. It's been touted, its been sold, it's being made a part of public policy, yet the science is bad. In fact, there isn't even any science to it—it's a predetermined political outcome, using science as the buzzword to make all of us believe that it has been studied in depth and it is perfectly safe, when the exact opposite is the truth.

One of global warning's main advocates, who denied me via email the right to quote him, and who was predicting global cooling just a few years ago, admitted he's willing to misrepresent the facts if it will stir up the public over the correct causes. Misrepresent means lie. The correct cause, in his estimate, is his opinion that global warming is caused by man-made carbon dioxide emissions; he wants to persuade you to his view and he's willing to lie in order to do that, if it will stir you up and get you excited about it. Someone pays his wages every month, and he is delivering the reports that his boss wants to read and put into the news media. He will do as he's told, say what he's told to say and he'll keep his mouth shut about everything else, or he's out of a job.

Another classic example. Mark Klein, a retired AT&T employee was recently interviewed on television regarding his knowledge of NSA wiretapping. From about 2003-2006, the National Security Agency went to all of the big telephone companies and created a contract whereby they could monitor all telephone and e-mail communications. Klein was one of the technicians who did all of the stages of work on the project and he knew of the agenda—that the NSA was listening in on calls in violation of the fourth Amendment, and that it was an illegal spying operation on the American public. He was asked, 'Did you go to any public authorities at that time and report what you knew.' Klein said that he didn't. When asked why not, Klein replied, 'Because I was afraid I would lose my job.' Klein waited until he got his 20 years in, until he got his retirement locked in by law, and then he went public.

The Scientists that are on the opposite side of the global warming argument are the chaps that have already taken their retirement, or are so secure in their positions that they're not concerned about being fired. The majority all rely upon those government contracts, government jobs, and they will follow the party line. Forget about freedom of speech, it doesn't exist where science is concerned.

Our local weatherman can't predict the weather for this week with any degree of accuracy, let alone for the next hundred years. I'm not knocking weathermen, they actually give us some pretty good information. The other day, for instance, they said was going to rain, starting late in the afternoon and, sure enough, at 6:30 PM it started raining. They said there was a storm coming and it was going to rain somewhere between about half an inch and one inch, so I brought my washing in from the balcony. Well, there were thunderstorms in the area, they were right about that, and they were right that it was going to start late in the afternoon but they were wrong about the amount of rain; it probably only rained about a quarter of an inch all night.

They're generally pretty good and I don't often complain about them, but when a chap tells me there's a 70% or 80 or 90% chance of rain... well, let's think about this one for a minute; If it rains, he was right but if it doesn't rain he was also right, isn't he? Hell, I'm no climatologist but—despite years of public school indoctrination—even I can flip a coin and tell you there's a 50% chance it's going to rain tomorrow. There's a 50% chance it's going to rain tomorrow 365 days of the year. When I hear the weatherman come on and say there's a X% chance of rain, I have to ask myself, I wonder how many people out there actually believe this fool? I wonder if that chump actually believes his own propaganda? Even if he says there's a 90% chance of rain, and it doesn't rain, he's still 100% right. It just fell into his 10% margin for error.

Predictions of accelerated increased temperatures are wildly exaggerated; it's just pure hypothesis, and saying the temperature may rise is not predicting the future, it's not science, it's guessing. 'May' means 'maybe' in this case. For anyone to say the temperature on planet Earth may rise or fall over the next hundred years is the equivalent of the weatherman saying there is a 50% chance of rain tomorrow. The UN says the average temperature of the world could rise by 6.3°C by the end of this century. That is true. Now, let me give you my prediction; the average temperature of the world could decrease by 6.3°C by the end of this century. Both of those statements are true and historically correct because the temperature of the world has increased and decreased by 6.3°C centigrade over the last fifteen hundred years.

Where's my PhD, dammit? Send it, I qualify.

I concede that global warming is occurring but the truth is, over time, global warming and global cooling has been occurring as a matter of natural cycle.

In June of 1991, in the Philippines, Mount Pinatubo erupted. It was quite an explosion and it went on for a couple of years. During the process, Mount Pinatubo gave off a little carbon dioxide. When I say 'a little' I'm actually understating it somewhat because the actual amount was reported to be more carbon dioxide than all of the activities of mankind throughout recorded history. Let me just clarify this; one eruption lasting two years put more carbon dioxide into the atmosphere than all of the coal, oil and wood burning activities of mankind, from the beginning of time to last night. All the carbon dioxide that has ever been created by the hand of man pales into insignificance when we consider one volcanic eruption. It is true that we're putting a lot more into the atmosphere than we ever put there before but the CO2 produced by power plants and from the burning of coal and petrol is a pimple on a whale's backside in comparison with a volcanic eruption. It reminds me of a flea crawling up an elephant's leg with rape on it's mind; the idea is stupid at the outset and borders on insanity. If mankind didn't emit one more particle carbon dioxide, if we stopped altogether, it isn't going to change the climate one iota. Even if we doubled the output of carbon dioxide right now it still wouldn't be significant. It would be very significant to the plants but not to you and me or the temperature of the planet. And I'd like to take this opportunity to point out there is more than one volcano in the world.

Asserting that carbon dioxide causes global warming makes about as much sense as fanning a fire to cool its heat. The amount of carbon dioxide in the atmosphere isn't very much to start with. Water vapour makes up 95% of the greenhouse gases and it's an essential element; without it, the planet would be too cold to inhabit. As the global warming theory of the greenhouse effect would have it, infrared rays hit the surface of the earth and are reflected back to heat the layer of greenhouse gases in the troposphere, which would suggest that the temperature should be significantly higher up there but both satellite and weather balloon data show no significant change in temperature. So it's not the moisture in the air, which makes up the lion's share of greenhouse gases, that is the culprit. On the contrary, more moisture in the air results in more snowfall, which, in turn, means more polar ice.

The oceans are actually the largest contributors of carbon dioxide; as they heat up, they give off CO2 and then reabsorb it on cooling. The atmosphere is mostly made up of nitrogen at 78.084%, and oxygen at 20.9476%, leaving carbon dioxide, helium, carbon monoxide and all of the other gases present making up the 0.9684% that's left over. Carbon dioxide only makes up 0.0314% of the 0.9684%, so all of the plants on the planet live off a gas that makes up less than one half of one percent of all gasses in the atmosphere. The plants trees and vegetation take in carbon dioxide, which they need for their survival, and put out oxygen, which we need for our survival; so there is a symbiotic relationship going on here. As an aside, I feel compelled to point out here that when plants are grown in controlled environments and exposed to extra carbon dioxide, guess what, they thrive and grow faster and stronger, so I'm working for an increase in CO2, which will make the world's forests healthier and more robust, allowing them to support more wildlife. Seems like the way to go, doesn't it?

Models of climate change don't take all of the potential variables into account, like the sun's influence, for instance. If we had been told that sunspots caused global warming, they would be more 'on point'. Sunspots have been increasing over the last ten to fifteen years and many scientists believe it's the sun spot activity that is causing global warming. Did Al Gore put that into his book? If he did, then I missed it.

The increases and decreases in temperatures on earth correspond with changes in the magnetism and energy output of the sun. Using records of solar magnetism going back a thousand years, hypothecated though they may be, we can see that the sun's periods of low magnetism and lower energy coincide with the major changes in the Earth's climate. More recently, the decline in temperature from the 1940s through to the mid-70s coincided with a decline in the sun's magnetic activity. According to current information, temperatures are rising now and—guess what—there is significant magnetic activity in the sun at the moment. Go figure.

You can't say that CO2 can drive climate, it certainly did not in the past... CO2 clearly cannot be causing temperature changes, it is a product of temperature, it's following temperature changes.
PROFESSOR IAN CLARK
DEPARTMENT OF EARTH SCIENCE, UNIVERSITY OF OTTAWA

By examining the quantities of CO2 found in ice core samples, Professor Ian Clark has shown that an increase in the earth's temperature does coincide with an increase in carbon dioxide but it's not CO2 causing an increase in temperature; it's the rising temperature that causes an increase in CO2 production and is several hundred years delayed.

A new term has been coined to describe those of us who aren't buying any of this man-made global warming nonsense; 'Global Warming Deniers'. Like the Holocaust deniers—those who don't believe six million Jews were killed during World War II—when the propaganda machine gets cranked up, if you deny it, if you're a skeptic, then they have to brand you with a label that makes you feel bad and has you ostracised. The objective here is to belittle you, to make fun of you. They are trying to show that you're stupid, you're dumb, you're uninformed, and—most of all—you're out of step with the majority. Please, send me an e-mail and tell me when the majority was ever right about anything—let me know, would you? I'm still hanging on with bated breath for the majority's correct opinion on World War I, or World War II or, for that matter, any historical event that has transpired. The truth is usually locked up in some little group, or some odd chap, a lone voice in the wilderness, some iconoclast who stands firm and says, 'Hey, listen, let me tell you how this works.'

Dr. Ignaz Semmelweis is a good example here. He woke up one day and dared to assert that all of the deaths in the labour wards at the time were being caused by a lack of hygiene on the part of the doctors and surgeons and suggested infection was most likely spread from the cadavers that were being autopsied to the mothers in the maternity wards. His simple suggestion, 'We need to wash our hands,' was ridiculed, and Dr. Semmelweis was locked up in a sanitarium soon afterward, and yet here we are today—surgeons are required to scrub up before every operation. I sometimes wonder that if Semmelweis could see us today, would he be holding a grudge about the straitjacket and the electroshock treatment, or smiling contentedly to himself and considering the years of forced sedation as a fair price to pay for the quantum leap in hospital hygiene.

This warming debate is similar to every other political issue, like gun control, birth control, the 'right to life' or the 'right to choose'. There is a segment of society on one side of the issue and a segment of society on the other side. Of course, the 'people in the know' capitalise on our beliefs and they collect a lot of money. What we're doing here is creating another one of these 'right to life versus right to choose' scenarios, in which millions of people will line up on one side or the other and send their dues into their chapter, group or organisation. Someone in Congress, for instance, proposes some new gun-control regulation, so the National Rifle Association sends out 5 million letters to NRA members, telling them to send in their funds to help fight this ridiculous policy. The money floods in, producing hundreds of millions of dollars in revenue for these organisations and, of course, if you're a member of the National Rifle Association it's 'money well-spent'. On the other hand, if you are a member of the gun control crowd and some chap in Congress proposes a liberal policy, they send out millions of letters to their members, which produces of hundreds of millions of dollars for their organisation. This goes on and on and it doesn't make any difference whether its abortion, right to choose, gun control or the Next New Thing Today, Global Warming. So far we don't have chapters and groups on either side of the debate but it's coming, mark my words, sit back, relax and watch it coming.

You can rest assured that the powers that be are going to play this propaganda game in the press and ultimately they're going to succeed. You can bet your life that Al Gore, Barack Obama and Gordon Brown, the compromised scientists, Fox News and the BBC are all in favour of it, all of them want it; and you're going to get it. They propagandised you over the war in Iraq until you finally said, 'You know, I think we need to go to war in Iraq.' So the powers that be got their way and you woke up four or five years later kicking yourself, didn't you? In the same fashion they're going to propagandise you on global warming, then one of these days you're going to vote for a global warming solution which will give them the power to put tax on petrol and they'll spend that $250 billion on enslaving you even more. And once again, you'll wake-up 10 years from now, overcome by a powerful sense of déjà vu when the Next New Thing Today is announced.

Once a statute gets passed, it's almost impossible to repeal it—that's just the nature of the beast. You know, these folks aren't going to be satisfied with the one-dollar-tax, they're going to be back for a 10% increase, and then a 15% increase. It's like the income tax; once they get the damn thing in there, they'll just raise it a little bit every year. 'We still have the big problem of carbon dioxide in the atmosphere, so we need to increase the tax.' Pretty soon it will be two dollars on the gallon. This is a worldwide proposition. For those of us living in the United States and Great Britain who are sitting here saying, 'I can't make ends meet now, never mind when these taxes go up,' most of the people in the developing world live on two dollars a day and they want to raise the price of petrol for those people by a dollar a gallon too. Can you see the devastating results that this is going to have on the poor of the world? This is a death sentence for the poor. While you and I in our countries are going to be inconvenienced, it's going to make the difference between living and dying for people in the Third World. Of course that fits in with Global 2000 and the proposal that we will reduce the earth's population by 90% over the next 50 years.

Keep your eye on the ball now. The ball is a tax on fuel. I don't know about the rest of the governments around the world but here in the UK and over there in America they're talking about a carbon tax; they want a tax on petrol of around one dollar—70 pence— per gallon. In the US they're using 6 billion barrels of oil per year, which will amount to a new yearly tax income for the US government of $252 billion.

They're not going to raise the tax on petrol by $1 straight out of the chute, that's just the proposal and it's so outrageous that they want a dollar a gallon tax, a carbon tax. You're going to resist it, you are going to fight it, but there is a psychological modality that has been used by the communists over the past hundred years and it is 100% foolproof, it works every time—because it appeals to human nature.

Human nature is motivated by vanity, jealousy, lust, greed and fear. If you are unable to control your five motivators—all five— you can rest assured that somebody will be pulling your strings and you will dance to their tune. It's the way all salesmen motivate their customers to buy. It's the way insurance companies sell you a policy. We're going to jerk your chain and you will respond accordingly.

The system has worked very well for the Communists in the past. Joe Stalin had it down to a fine art, and Adolf Hitler used it perfectly against Neville Chamberlain. What you do is you come up with an outrageous demand, like, 'we want Poland, Czechoslovakia, Austria, Italy and Romania, and if you don't meet our demands, we are going to go to war with you and we're going to give you a very bad day.'

Neville Chamberlain runs over and he says, 'Now look, Mr Hitler, you've got to understand that we can't give you all five of those countries over there. Hell, we'll happily go to war with you before that happens.' So Hitler tones it down a little and says,

'Well, okay, what is your best offer?'

Chamberlain says, 'We'll give you Czechoslovakia.'

A little while later Hitler returns with,

'Now we want: Poland, Denmark, Netherlands, Lithuania, Romania and Austria.'

Again, Chamberlain jumps up and says, 'Oh God, no, no, no Mr Hitler, if you do that we'll surely go to war.'

'Alright, what are you offering this time?'

'You can have Austria and Poland.'

And Hitler says, 'Have a nice day.'

So, in the same fashion, the Government makes an outrageous demand like, 'We want a dollar a gallon for this carbon tax.' Of course we jump up and down and say, 'God, no, we'll revolt before you get that much.'

'Okay, what's your best offer?'

'Ten cents.'

The Government accepts and then enacts the legislation accordingly, with a provision written into the Act that they can raise the rate any time they want. Then a little later it'll go to 20 cents, 30 cents, 50 cents and then a dollar. Before long it becomes $2, then $5 and so on, much like the Income Tax. You're going to get a $1 a gallon carbon tax and you're going to have a solution to global warming rammed down your throat whether you like it or not. Eventually...

When discussing the little ice age and global warming, we have to bear in mind that the dates are approximate. We can't say that in 1326AD, on the 17th of March at 4.30PM, the Little Ice Age began, and it ended on 9th December, 1806 just after breakfast; it's not an exact science—but it's pretty close. Because of dendrochronology—the study of tree rings—along with the study of sediments on the ocean floor, particularly where volcanoes run into the ocean, we can actually come up with some hard science.

There was a significant period of cooling that occurred after a warmer North Atlantic era known as the Medieval Climate Optimum. Pack ice began increasing in the North Atlantic, as did glaciers in Greenland and three years of heavy rains paved the way for a period of freezing temperatures in Northern Europe. Since this occurred in historical times, and since Earth shows a propensity for cyclical behaviour, we may infer that it has probably occurred in prehistory as well. How many times, we don't know, but we do know of two. We have historical records of the warming period from 800-1300. In addition, we have the physical measurements we can make today and compare with those historical records. We can then extrapolate that into the future and theorise that if the world does warm up in the future—as occurred between 800 and 1300—what are the likely results? It will probably have identical results to what occurred then. It was something less than catastrophic then, so why would we think it could be catastrophic today?

The point regarding the Little Ice Age is that it takes 3-400 years for the global warming and cooling trend to work itself out. Historically, the temperature variations have been as much as 3-8 degrees centigrade; we have documented evidence of it. So when scientists tell you that we could have a 2-3 degree temperature rise over the next hundred years… so what? It's already happened and the world didn't come to an end the last time or the time before that, when it rose more than two or three times more than the doomsayers are telling us is going to occur in the next hundred years.

A hundred years ago when we were measuring temperatures, we were measuring them in rural areas; today we take measurements in metropolitan areas. These metropolitan areas have a higher average temperature because of the concrete and asphalt. You have to go out into the countryside, where you don't have the radiation of heat. When you get into your car on a sunny day and wind up the windows, it gets hot in there pretty damn quick because of the radiation effect of the sun's energy on that car. Steel heats up in a hurry. If you were trying to take average temperatures in a car compared to somebody else taking temperatures outside the car, they are obviously going to be greater inside the car. Taking temperatures inside a city is going to give you a higher reading than outside the city. It's just common sense. That being the case, they're still taking those temperatures inside the cities, in the same place they were taking them 100 years ago.

Readings being taken in the southern hemisphere are not going up or down; there is no global warming in the southern hemisphere. Any global warming that has being going on over the last century has happened in the northern atmosphere, so climatologists are now divided and don't seem so sure that global warming is occurring globally.

It's been suggested that a solution to global warming would be to spray dust particles into the atmosphere with jet aeroplanes. A bit like what they are doing already, but instead of spreading protozoa and cancer-causing chemicals that harm us, just spread dust. The sun's rays would hit the dust, bounce back out into space and it would cool the earth off. It's been estimated it would cost about $2 billion every year. By all accounts you could cool the earth by 2 degrees using this method.

Now I'm acutely aware that it sounds a lot like science fiction and you're probably asking yourself 'Is there any merit to that idea?' There certainly is—in fact, it's already been done. It wasn't accomplished with jets; it was done by volcanic activity. Throughout the Little Ice Age the world experienced heightened volcanic activity. When a volcano erupts, the ash reaches high up into the atmosphere and it spreads to cover the whole earth. This cloud blocks out some of the incoming solar radiation, leading to worldwide cooling that can last up to two years after an eruption. Sulphur, in the form of SO2 gas, is also given off and when this gas reaches the stratosphere, it turns into sulphuric acid particles which reflect the sun's rays, reducing the amount of radiation reaching the Earth's surface.

The 1815 eruption of Tambora in Indonesia blanketed the atmosphere with ash. The following year, 1816, came to be known as 'the year without a summer' when frost and snow were reported in June and July in both New England and northern Europe. So the ash can circle the earth and cool it off, which gives credence to the idea of spreading dust particles in the atmosphere. I don't know whether it would take ten aeroplanes to do this or five hundred but the estimated cost would be around $2 billion a year. Seems cheap at the price, compared to the $250 billion a year we will be paying in carbon taxes.

I remember seeing a recent report on CNN, where a correspondent was chatting with a scientist and announcing that the polar bears in the Hudson's Bay area were decreasing in numbers. Now, again, this report is probably true. After all, some of what they tell you is the truth, some of it is an ordinary lie, some of it is a damn lie, but all of it is propaganda.

Contrary to the reports we're receiving, polar bears are not dying out because of global warming and they are not becoming extinct, nor are they even threatened. There are thirteen groups of polar bears in Canada, eleven are increasing and the other two are decreasing in population, all based on local factors. So there are two groups of polar bears in Canada that are in decline, let's accept that as a true report. However the other eleven groups are increasing in numbers, so if the increase is equal to the decrease then we actually end up with more polar bears. If it isn't, then it's about the same and nothing has changed. But the purpose behind the reporting of the decrease in the two groups is to promote the idea of man-made global warming. Again, they're not giving you the whole story; another deception by omission. They don't report about the polar bears in Alaska or Siberia at all—are they decreasing? How many groups are there over there? How many in each group? I don't know. And when I say I don't know, how the hell can we make an evaluation, a determination or a decision based on insufficient facts?

The statement that global warming is wiping out the polar bears is inconclusive, we don't have enough facts to make that determination. Besides, it's not worldwide; it's only in Canada. You can rest assured that if there was a decline in polar bear population in

Siberia or Alaska, they'd be over there to report on it. Even the scientists concede that they don't know exactly why these two groups
are in decline. It could be mercury poisoning or any other number
of reasons. It could even be that the female polar bears in those two
groups all look like a bulldog chewing a wasp, and the male polar
bears have particularly high standards. Or maybe the males have
just decided to become celibate or 'self sufficient'. Who knows?

On April 6th, 2006, a group of leading scientists came forward to
question the so-called 'consensus' that the Earth faces a 'climate
emergency'. In an open letter to Canadian Prime Minister Stephen
Harper, they declared that the science is crumbling from underneath man-made global warming promoters.

*Observational evidence does not support today's computer climate models,
so there is little reason to trust model predictions of the future... Significant scientific advances have been made since the Kyoto protocol was created, many of which are taking us away from a concern about increasing
greenhouse gases. If, back in the mid-1990s, we knew what we know today
about climate, Kyoto would almost certainly not exist, because we would
have concluded it was not necessary... it was only 30 years ago that many
of today's global-warming alarmists were telling us that the world was
in the midst of a global-cooling catastrophe. But the science continued to
evolve, and still does, even though so many choose to ignore it when it
does not fit with predetermined political agendas.*

EXCERPTED FROM AN OPEN LETTER TO CANADIAN PRIME MINISTER STEPHEN
HARPER
FINANCIAL POST, APRIL 06, 2006

According to the paid professional whores in the mainstream
media, the ice cap over in Antarctica is melting and shrinking,
but that's not what the scientists are telling us—the scientists who
are on-site, on-the-job, making day-to-day calculations, observations and readings. The scientific literature says man-made global
warming is BS, so somebody is lying. From my perspective I can't
tell you who is telling the truth and who isn't, but I'm highly suspicious, especially when I see there is a $250 billion carbon tax head-
ing our way. It does offer a clue about who might be lying though.
Hell, for $250 billion, I'd lie!

In order for us to pass the legislation, to get you to pay a dollar
or a pound more for a gallon of petrol, we've got to scare the living hell out of you. We've got to get you so psyched-up that you're
willing to sign on and stand in line to pay your money.

The tried, tested and proven modality for achieving political ends: you demand a gigantic slice of the pie, knowing full well that you're not going to get the whole thing.

I come to you and say, 'Give me half of your pie. And if you don't, we're going to get into a big, nasty fight and you'll probably get hurt.'

'You're not going to get half of my pie.'

'Then get ready for the fight.'

'Well, okay, instead of the fight, maybe I might give you a smell of the pie.'

'A smell? Put your dukes up.'

'All righty then, I'll give you a piece of my pie but I'm not happy about it.'

So you give me an eighth of your pie and I walk off. Here's what the net result is: it's your pie, I don't have any claim on it, I'm not even entitled to look at your pie, but because of my threats and my blustering and my demands, I walk away with one eighth of your pie, with your consent. And we used your knife to cut it.

We don't want to fight, we only fight when we actually have to, when the fight-or-flight response kicks in. Human beings do not naturally like confrontation. Well, at least 95% of us don't—5% of us do, and that's because 5% of us are extroverts, and the extroverts are the movers and shakers in the world. So that 5% comes to the other 95%, the majority of us, and make demands upon us. When these demands are made, we don't want a fight or a confrontation, so when it comes to race, politics, religion, the subjects and topics that are so divisive, we would rather go along to get along than have a fight that will settle the matter once and for all. In order to bring peace, we say, 'Well, maybe they've got a point and maybe we should listen.'

The news media is the lapdog of politics, it doesn't have anything to report on unless they go and talk to the Police or the fire department. Just take a look at your evening news. What are they reporting on? They're talking about police reports, fire department reports, and the political reports. They go down to the city council and the mayor's office hoping for a story to fill a time slot. That's what your evening news is all about—it's a canned program that repeats itself day after day. Oh, and a little sports and weather. All we're dealing with here is the weather news, that's all global warming is, a story to fill a time slot in the weather news section.

Propaganda is made up of this constant repetition; global warming is real, global warming is here, global warming is a catastrophe waiting to happen—on and on and on and on and... pretty soon we begin to believe it, and lacking the courage, the fortitude to confront or cross-examine our accuser, we go along with it.

Our opponent is very wise, he never brings the confrontation down to an actual fight; he's just threatening the fight until we finally back off. He pushes you as far as he can and he backs off when you give him some of what he's asking for. Then he goes away. For a while. He'll return on a different front at a different time, with a new agenda, and makes the same outrageous demands. Lather. Rinse. Repeat.

Anyone who goes around and says that carbon dioxide is responsible for most of the warming of the 20th century has not looked at the basic numbers.
PROFESSOR PATRICK MICHAELS
DEPARTMENT OF ENVIRONMENTAL SCIENCES
UNIVERSITY OF VIRGINIA

Ultimately, when you're out there on the raw and ragged edge telling the truth about what's going on, they have to shut you up. After all, these people spend a lot of money, time, effort and energy putting these fraudulent contrivances together. They're conmen. They got you to buy into the Iraqi war, and now you've got it whether you like it or not. You can sit there and say, 'I'm going to vote the Republicans or the Labour Party out,' but the people behind the scenes don't give a rats rectum one way or the other because they control both sides. It doesn't make any difference at all to the Committee of 300 who the hell sits in the White House or Downing Street. Barack Obama and Gordon Brown will just follow their instructions, as did Bush, Blair and Clinton. If they get belligerent, if they ever balk, then the Committee will just take care of them in the same way they did JFK. And that will be the end of that argument.

We've been deceived before, we're being deceived now, and at some point in the future—I don't know over what and when—but I predict, our government is going to lie to us again. And the vast majority are going to believe those lies and continue to be deceived.

Unfortunately, thanks to public schooling, common sense isn't prevalent anymore. Government has convinced us that global warming is real, and they did it by telling us that we've got 'consensus'. Global Warming is real, but Global Warming being caused by the burning of fossil fuels and power plants is a lie. Let me remind you of the numbers…

Take all of the power plants burning coal today, all of the train-loads of coal that are burned in homes, all of this coal that puts carbon dioxide into the atmosphere—it amounts to 6.5 gigatons of CO_2 per year—it's measurable and undeniable. Now take all of the vegetation and plants biomass in the world that is dying and also releases carbon dioxide—it amounts to 150 gigatons, and is also measurable and undeniable. Got it?

Now IF—notice the big IF—carbon dioxide caused global warming; all we're doing is adding to the problem by 4% a year, which is inconsequential.

Remember Mount Pinatubo? It put more carbon dioxide into the Earth's atmosphere in that two-year period than all of the activities of mankind from the beginning to the present day.

It is often said there is a scientific 'consensus' to the effect that climate change will be 'catastrophic' and that, on this particular question, 'the debate is over.' The claim of unanimous scientific 'consensus' was false, and known to be false, when it was first made; that the trend of opinion in the peer-reviewed journals and even in the UN's reports on climate is moving rapidly away from alarmism.

Where did this claim of consensus come from?

David Miliband, Environment Minister of the United Kingdom, was greeted by cries of 'Rubbish!' when he told a conference on climate change in Spring 2007 at the Holy See, that the science of climate and carbon dioxide was simple and settled. Miliband was merely reciting a mantra that has been widely peddled by politicians such as Al Gore and political news media such as the BBC, which has long since abandoned its consti-tutional obligation of objectivity on this, as on most political subjects, and has adopted a policy of not allowing equal air-time to opponents of the imagined consensus.
VISCOUNT MONCKTON OF BRENCHLEY
'CONSENSUS?' WHAT 'CONSENSUS?'
AMONG CLIMATE SCIENTISTS, THE DEBATE IS NOT OVER
SCIENCE & PUBLIC POLICY INSTITUTE, 19 JULY 2007

Let me point out here that Ron Paul never got equal time in the 2008 debates and—as a result—you never heard what his story was to any effective degree. Where these debates are concerned, once the Democrat/Conservative and Labour/Republican candidates are chosen, you're not going to hear anything of any consequence from any other candidates but those two. And that's because the two major parties finance, support and promote those debates—the other splinter parties do not, which means they will not get equal time. Therefore, we never get an opportunity to hear any opposing views in Britain and America.

It makes all the sense in the world and I don't blame the two parties. After all, if they are paying for it —they sure as hell aren't going to let the Socialists, Communists, the Greenies or anybody else in. When it comes to science—knowledge— I think it would serve all of us to listen to the other side before we saddle ourselves with this carbon tax. One dollar per gallon is significant but, in the scheme of things, we're already paying round $3-$4 per gallon for petrol, so what difference is it really going to make?

My petrol tank holds about 30 gallons, so when I fill up at four dollars a gallon, that's $120. So what difference does another 30 make to me? It's not going to break me. I mean, if I've got $120 to put in my tank, I've probably got another 30 in my pocket. The chap who's back it is going to break is the chap who's only got $10. When he goes into the petrol station and he wants to buy petrol at five dollars a gallon, he can only get two gallons. Friends, that's what's going to bring famine to planet Earth because the poor people also have to have oil energy and they're struggling at the moment as it is. You raise that tax by a dollar a gallon— it's going to be a burden on Americans and Europeans but it's going to break the backs of India, Indonesia and Africa. Those people are going to starve to death as a result of it.

The claim of 'consensus' rests almost completely on an flawed and now-outdated single-page comment in the journal Science called *The Scientific Consensus on Climate Change* (Oreskes, 2004). Naomi Oreskes, a historian of science with no qualifications in climatology, described the 'consensus' in a very limited sense, quoting as follows: *'Human activities... are modifying the concentration of atmospheric constituents... that absorb or scatter radiant energy... most of the observed warming over the last 50 years is likely to have been due to the increase in greenhouse gas concentrations.'*

Oreskes' interpretation of 'consensus' falls into two parts. First, she states that humankind is changing the composition of the atmosphere. This statement is isn't in question because measurement has proved that the concentration of carbon dioxide in the atmosphere has risen over the past 250 years to such an extent that CO_2 now makes up almost 0.01 per cent more of the atmosphere than in the pre-industrial period. However, on the question whether that change has any detrimental climatic importance, there is no consensus, and Oreskes doesn't state there is.

The extent of a claimed consensus that dangerous human-caused global

warming is occurring is unknown and the claim of consensus is unsup-
ported by any objective data. However, this is irrelevant because by its
nature any consensus is a product of opinions, not facts. Though consen-
sus determines legal and political decisions in most countries, this simply
reflects the number of persons who interpret data in a certain way or who
have been influenced by the opinions of others. Consensus does not confer
accuracy or 'rightness.' Scientific matters are certainly not settled by
consensus. Einstein pointed out that hundreds of people agreeing with him
were of no relevance, because it would take just one person to prove him
wrong. Science as a whole, and its near neighbour medicine, are replete
with examples of individuals or small groups of researchers successfully
undermining the prevailing popular theories of the day. This is not to say
that individuals or small groups who hold maverick views are always cor-
rect, but it is to say that even the most widely-held opinions should never
be regarded as an ultimate truth. Science is about observation, experiment
and the testing of hypotheses, not consensus.

JOHN MCLEAN
FALLACIES ABOUT GLOBAL WARMING

'Consensus' is propaganda. There is no consensus, there hasn't been a consensus, and no one has claimed to have consensus except Al Gore, the media and the politicians. There is no consensus among scientists. The reason for that is that scientists all know the truth about global warming; it doesn't make any difference what side the scientist is arguing for, he knows the truth of the matter. I will go so far as to assert that Al Gore may claim to believe his own propaganda, but he also knows the truth. That's called fraud. Fraud is when you know the truth and then espouse something different, and when someone knows something is false and they tell it to you as a truth, that is nefarious and it's done with an evil intent. The people involved in this lie all know the truth, because the science is out there and you can rest assured that the propo-nents of this lie are well aware of it; both sides of this argument are fully informed of the other side's positions.

I, personally, am convinced that Al Gore has read all of the argu-ments against global warming and was fully informed when he wrote his book and made the phony documentary. I am also as-sured that Al Gore is no idiot; you don't become Vice President because you're stupid. He's a very bright man, a very intelligent, articulate chap; and I do not believe a single word he says.

Electricity is a good clean source of energy and the production of electricity has been a great benefit to mankind. Let's be realistic— our standard of living comes from energy and this whole concept of 'man-made global warming' is an attack on electric power, because the number one emitter of carbon dioxide is coal-fired power plants. The ultimate end here—taking Global 2000 into account—is to reduce the earth's population by 90%, and they know that by reducing the consumption of energy, they can reduce the earth's population. This is the dark side of the global warming debate. Make no mistake about it, the advocates of global warming will ultimately win out in the debate, that's the tragedy of it.

They've got propaganda, and propaganda is a powerful force. Except over the awake and aware.

Suggesting that global warming is caused by carbon dioxide in the atmosphere is absolutely ridiculous. Carbon dioxide is a beneficial gas that benefits plant life, which is ultimately beneficial to all animal life on the planet. It would be like saying oxygen in the air is harmful to the environment. Carbon dioxide is a good gas, there's nothing wrong with it, the more the better. If they were saying carbon monoxide was the culprit, maybe they'd have something to argue about.

Global warming today is not as great as it was on two prior occasions. From 800AD to the present we've had three cycles of global warming and global cooling, and so far that global warming has not been as great as it was during the last two occasions; it didn't spell doom to the inhabitants then and it doesn't today. In the early part of the second millennium, some 800-1000 years ago, temperatures on the earth were higher than they are today. You can rest assured that the Arctic Ocean was having longer summers and warmer winters and that the Eskimos living out there at the time we're probably wondering what the hell was going on then but, sure enough, as nature would have it, the Earth cooled again and all was well.

We're in a long-term trend of global warming which began around 1800 and it's still going on. It's going to continue going on. How hot is going to get? I don't know. Is it going to rise another 3 degrees? If it does, it will match the warm period in the Middle Ages.

It isn't the carbon dioxide that is causing global warming, it's the global warming that causes carbon dioxide; they've got it exactly backwards, and if there was ever a scientific proposition put before the general public that was more fallacious than man-made global warming, write me an e-mail and tell me what it was. I'm telling you there is an objective in mind; it's the carbon tax. Nobody wants to hear that humans don't cause global warming, it just doesn't sell. There's a payday at the end of all this nonsense and that payday is $250 billion a year in taxes.

The concept of man-made global warming isn't bad science; it isn't even science, its just pure, naked politics—nothing more, nothing less. As for me, I'm buying a bigger pair of carbon shoes, so I can leave a bigger footprint.

Keep your eye on the ball.

I do believe in Global Warming, but I don't believe that humans CO2 is causing that warming.
PROFESSOR TIM BALL
DEPARTMENT OF CLIMATOLOGY
UNIVERSITY OF WINNIPEG

Take Responsibility... look it up for yourself. Search engine paths regarding topics addressed in this chapter:

Al Gore
Carbon Dioxide
Carbon Tax
Climate Change
David Miliband, Environment Minister of the United Kingdom
Global Warming
Greenhouse Effect
Holocene Maximum
Little Ice Age
Medieval Warm Period
Mount Pinatubo
Polar Ice
Professor Ian Clark, Department of Earth Science, University of Ottawa
Professor Tim Ball, Department of Climatology, University of Winnipeg
Rising Sea Levels
Ron Paul
Sulphur
Sunspot Activity
Tambora
Volcanic activity affecting climate
WHO World Health Organization.

THE DEVIL'S EYE

Television is the greatest and most pervasive hypnotist and propaganda tool ever conceived, and is the most powerful weapon of psychological warfare in history. It teaches people what to think, but not how to think, and has given modern man a totally false perception of society, of the world, and of each other.

Our society is the most manipulated and controlled in history because of the programming and conditioning we're all exposed to by virtue of mass media and public education. We're living in a virtual reality, a totally controlled environment created by and benefiting only the controllers.

The most powerful special interest in Washington today is the media. Not only do they give money and lobby, and do all the things that industries and companies do in Washington, but they of course control whether a politician's mug gets on the tube. Now that's power — that's the ultimate power in the political realm, controlling perceptions.
CHARLES LEWIS
FORMER 60 MINUTES PRODUCER

The media has become the fourth branch of Government.

The majority of households in the West own at least one television, and we spend almost half our lives watching one. The average Brit and American soaks up nearly five hours of TV a day. For most people, television is not only considered a member of the family, it's one of the most important members, it runs the household and is invariably a main feature in the room, with all chairs pointed in its general direction. It's often used as a baby sitter and as the main source of information. In effect, the television has come to represent a religious altar before which the nation worships, an oracle to whom they bring daily tribute.

Using television, TPTB have succeeded in creating a distracted, deluded, divided and class-driven society, suffering from historical amnesia, and who are completely oblivious to the true reality of their surroundings. Television, via nonstop indoctrination, nourishes a media-driven obsession with collecting meaningless trinkets, fashions and possessions, and shapes how the viewer sees themselves as part of humanity. Most of all, it has robbed people of their ability to think critically and objectively. You would be hard put to find a human quicker to criticise and ridicule anyone who offers any alternate viewpoint than a television viewer addicted to Fox News.

Anyone who challenges the prevailing orthodoxy finds himself silenced with surprising effectiveness. A genuinely unfashionable opinion is almost never given a fair hearing.
GEORGE ORWELL

I'm sure many of you are familiar with George Orwell's book, *1984*, in which he warned that people were in danger of losing their freedom of mind without being aware of it happening because of psychological, emotional and intellectual manipulation—mind control. That world of 1984 arrived unnoticed in Britain, America and elsewhere, because people were conditioned not to notice it. Many people don't think about the things that affect them subconsciously because—generally speaking—they don't know what to look for until someone comes along and starts pointing things out. Only then can they see how unseen forces influence us all without our conscious awareness. In fact, the ultimate control is controlling people without their conscious awareness.

The mind control issue is not a new one—it's ancient. What's different about the times we live in is the technology that allows for the execution of the principles and techniques of hypnotic programming, and mind control on a massive scale to influence the thinking and behaviour of large numbers of people.

Many people—especially young people—unquestioningly accept the reality that is presented by the media. There's a reason why television networks, the music industry and various other media companies have 'programming' departments. The programming with which we are constantly assaulted throughout our lives conditions us—it programs us to a particular world view. Popular culture, films, television and music carry messages about how society works and how people should behave, so, entertainment is not value-free, it's not pointless and it's not harmless—it has ideological content.

We may consider it 'normal' because we were born into this system of lies and deception. In fact, deception has become part of the social framework of society, and because we were born into this situation, and our parents were born into it and suffered from it, we don't know any better. Although there's a qualitative difference between something as seemingly harmless as *Sesame Street* and the number of violent video games like *Grand Theft Auto*—whether or not it's coming from public broadcasting channels or commercial entities, it's all 'programming'. Even this book is programming— the pertinent question is has the media been created to educate and empower or deceive and control?

Ultimately, the person who is broadcasting determines the context. In other words, consider the source.
We falsely think of our country as being a democracy when it has evolved into a mediaocracy; where a media that is supposed to check political abuse, is part of the political abuse.
DANNY SCHECTER
FORMER CNN AND ABC NEWS PRODUCER

You ought to ask yourself why we're so obsessed by being entertained—distracted—from our daily lives. Television is the perfect means and mechanism for the transmission of propaganda, because people consider it a break from the grind of daily life, and, every day, sit down, tune in and 'switch off'. All we know is that we feel relaxed, and the day's worries fade away as we watch our favourite evening broadcast. How often have you heard someone say, 'I just want to watch a movie and give my brain a rest?' How is it that we often find ourselves slack-jawed and glued to the television set, even if we have no idea what is on the screen and have no interest in it?

What compels you to stare, night after night, at all the glittering hokum that has been deliberately put together for you?
J.B. PRIESTLEY

Despite the fact there may be other people in the room, we find ourselves being drawn to the glowing box in the corner. It's a physiological response—the television is literally plugging into the human nervous system through the ocular nerve. Think back to when you've watched young children sitting watching television, they have a glazed, vacant look in their eyes because they are in a trance state, a hypnotic state of mind.

It's significant that television has the ability to do this. It doesn't matter what you're watching, although the image on the television screen seems to be static and stationary, it is actually flickering. We don't see it consciously, but subconsciously the flickering effect, the repeating visual pattern of the flicker, brings about the trance state. You may have noticed the effect in old films where they have a TV set on in the background and there will be a black roll bar going up and down the TV screen—the camera hasn't compensated for the flicker rate. The roll bar effect is basically a visual representation of what is going on. The longer a person watches television the more easily the brain slips into alpha frequency; a slow steady brainwave pattern in which the mind is in its most receptive mode. It's a natural state—we go in and out of it during the day. It's the dreamlike state we experience just before we drift off to sleep at night or just as we wake in the morning; there's minimal conscious mental activity going on and the subconscious is wide open for programming at that point. The conscious capacity for analytical and critical thinking is paused and images and suggestions can be embedded directly into the mind without your involvement. You can be told what to think by scripted news readers, told what to buy, what to wear, where to go, and kept otherwise distracted by sport, meaningless celebrity gossip, and a barrage of sex and entertainment—ever more frequently punctuated these days by messages of fear, and warnings of looming terror.

When we're presented with a piece of information, and we are in a fully switched-on, awakened state, we have the opportunity to make the choice if we're going to accept whether or not a piece of information is true. When we make the decision, that information is filed away in our memory with the file identification that we have accepted or rejected it as true. If the analytical mind is bypassed, then someone else can put a tag, a code or a subheading to the file that can be activated at a later time, by a jingle or a logo, for instance.

The first order of business for any advertiser or propagandist is to create the circumstances that will induce the state of mind that is favourable to the reception of their message, the hypnotic, fully receptive state of mind. Large corporations that control the world's economy programme the minds of millions of would-be robot-like employees. Once programmed, we return day after day to our repetitive, non-interactive jobs, after which we return to our television masters for new programming. Of course, after making a pittance, we need to know how to spend our money. We're flashed images of cars and toys and all sorts of things that we're told we need. We think we're discussing our own thoughts, but when the conversation is really analysed, we're usually not. The discussion revolves around what show we watched last night, or sport, or something we learned from the Discovery channel, our feelings towards the opposite sex, or 'the war on terror'. Whether we realise it or not, what we're discussing—and 98% of what we think we know about anything—has been taught to us by the television or by print media that is wholly owned and controlled by a handful of corporations.

The basic principle behind hypnotic programming is to get the subject to focus the attention of their conscious mind on one of the five senses. In the case of television we are obviously talking about sight and the flickering image, or sound—any repeating sound pattern will induce the trance state—the perfect example being trance music played at raves.

You may have noticed that the rate at which transitions or cuts happening in film and—more important—adverts is speeding up. The pace is getting more and more frenetic; a trend that has its roots in the MTV music video genre. A slow, sustained message gives the viewer a chance to think and use discretion, whereas a fast-paced presentation with multiple cuts, edits and flashing symbols doesn't allow time for anything other than absorption. Quick cuts, going from one shot to another, causes a corresponding chemical reaction in the brain, which inevitably releases endorphins, having a drug-like effect on the viewer. A child sits in front of the TV and watches the quick cutting and fast paced cartoons, music videos or children's programming and can sit still due to the induced trance-like state and the consequent endorphin rush from the chemical reactions in the brain.

Television has changed a child from an irresistible force to an immovable object.
LAURENCE J. PETER

When the TV is off, or they are away from the set, many children are fidgety and restless and can't focus because they're searching for the same kind of drug effect they get when they're sitting in front of it. Television programming disturbs a child's brain chemistry to such a degree that it can cause addictive patterns of behaviour. Allowing children under the age of three to watch television can undermine their linguistic and social development and put them at risk of health problems, including autism and obesity. And let's not forget Attention Deficit Disorder, which was unheard of prior to television.

In any totalitarian movement, regardless of where it occurs, the programming is directed at the children, because they are the future. Capture the minds of the children and you've captured the nation. That's why the mass media is so important, why entertainment is so very important; it is creating a unified mind-set amongst the entire population. Storytelling is the oldest means of transmitting information in society—there's very little difference between primitive man sitting round the flickering light of the campfire, telling stories of how things work, what's right and wrong, how society should behave, and modern man sitting in front of the flickering electronic campfire being told the same through storytelling, drama and music.

Television is not the Truth. Television is god-damned amusement park. Television is a circus, a carnival, a traveling troupe of acrobats, storytellers, dancers, singers, jugglers, sideshow freaks, lion tamers and football players. We're in the boredom-killing business.
PADDY CHAYEVSKY

You may be interested to know that, in Romania, Amusement parks are called *Parc de distractii*—that's 'distraction park' to English speakers. They also still call commercials 'propaganda'. A spade remains a spade there, but only until the US gets around to rectifying it.

How often have you bought something and then wondered what on earth possessed you afterward? It is affectionately known as an 'impulse buy'; I think we've all had that kind of experience. It's a common everyday illustration of being compelled to make a purchase based on a conditioned response that has been programmed into us, to have a preference for a particular product. That is the whole point of programming—whether it's by an advertiser or a propagandist, there's really no difference between the two; one sells products and the other sells ideas—ideas about Globalisation, or the new World Order, or the need for a new means of dealing with society's economic ills.

I know the secret of making the average American believe anything I want him to. Just let me control television. You put something on the television and it becomes reality. If the world outside the TV set contradicts the images, people start trying to change the world to make it like the TV set images…
HAL BECKER
MEDIA EXPERT AND MANAGEMENT CONSULTANT, THE FUTURES GROUP

The whole point is to install in all of us a conditioned response where we'll jump when they say, without thinking, and with a preference for a particular idea or product. At the beginning of news broadcasts, we have the repetitive graphics moving back and forth and the dramatic jingle, reinforcing the trance state. The news broadcaster looks directly into the camera and into the eyes of the viewer, having a very deep impact in terms of driving information in; it makes the information transfer very personal, and is another well-known hypnotic technique.

If you think about it, whenever you hear news broadcasters speak, you realise that—regardless of their ethnic background, whether they're black, white, Hispanic, Asian or Oriental—they all have a similar way of speaking. Newscasters all sound a certain way—they all have the same rhythmic speaking style associated with the spreading of true, factual information—a speech pattern noticeably similar to that of a hypnotist.

People have been conditioned to accept this format as 'the way true factual information is presented'. Generally speaking, the new, incoming newsreaders tend to mimic their veteran peers in terms of the accepted style, and if their own speech pattern is at odds with the traditional form, consultants may be brought in to correct diction, breathing, body language and tweak any other presentation issues until the desired presentation is achieved. News anchors are chosen because of their ability to deliver the message, not necessarily because of their journalistic achievements, and they become veteran 'anchors' because, whilst they are invariably very malleable, they are— often unknowingly—excellent hypnotists, and are recognised as such early on.

They're then established as a respected, authority figure, which encourages the audience's acceptance of the information. The news 'programming' begins with the statement concerning the news headlines, Here is what the news is going to be. Then we get the news story itself, This is the news. Finally, at the end of the program, we get a reminder of the main headlines, then, to drive it home, And that was tonight's news.

Essentially, you're hearing the same story 3 times in the space of 30 minutes. The repetition of the information—over and over again—is what builds the conditioned response so that whenever we are presented with the information again we'll accept it automatically without thinking about it.

The famous radio broadcast of Orson Wells' rendition of H.G Wells' *War of the Worlds* is an interesting example in this context because the adaptation was made in order to present the story as a news broadcast. There was an anchor person, there were journalists in the field reporting on new developments, there were outside 'experts' being brought in to comment on what was happening. The combined effect being that people actually thought Martians were invading New Jersey, and it caused a panic that took almost 48 hours to subside, even after it was revealed to be a stunt.

A similar event happened in 1949 in Ecuador. There was a presentation of *War of the Worlds,* done as a news broadcast. Only this time, when the public found out it was a fake, they burned the radio station down. We could learn a few things from those people; we could do with being a little more proactive in standing up for our own sovereignty on a number of levels, not the least of which is our mindscape.

Freedom of mind is the first freedom from which all other freedoms are derived, and if we don't have that, then we're in a lot of trouble.

We're subject to pressure from all sides and placed under enormous strain; with the pressure of psychological warfare along with the control of information, the manipulation of the economy and the destabilisation of jobs, most people don't know whether they're coming or going and ultimately end up calling to the Government for help. So, of course, Government comes forth with the draconian solution that they've wanted to implement all along and the public, having demanded it, embraces it.

We're feeling the effects of a scientifically-induced nervous breakdown, which makes it highly likely why, we see the eruption of mass shootings, school shootings and other kinds of unusual behaviour.

And it happens sequentially; one or two major events will happen, followed by a lull, then more chaos. Using the Hegelian Dialectic, they create a problem, then crisis-manage the problem to a predetermined conclusion which the public celebrates, and which couldn't be accomplished without the psychological preconditioning of the population in order to facilitate the changes. The manufactured crisis is always followed by a concerted push toward more restrictive legislation to control people's behaviour. The thrust toward gun control in the US after the Columbine incident, The Patriot Act and The Anti-Terrorism Act following 9/11 and 7/7 being classic examples.

Sixty years ago, eighty-six small corporations—who all competed to deliver the best and most informative news—ran the media in the western world. Today, it is run as a well oiled, very streamlined, and tightly controlled machine owned and operated by only six corporations, who now control all major western mainstream television and print media. With the current rate of corporate growth, that number is soon to drop to three corporations.

A handful of us determine what will be on the evening news broadcasts, or, for that matter, in the New York Times or Washington Post or Wall Street Journal…. Indeed it is a handful of us with this awesome power… And those [news stories] available to us already have been culled and re-culled by persons far outside our control.
WALTER CRONKITE

We have to keep in mind that all of these media corporations have extremely close ties to major financial institutions and arms manufacturers, which immediately poses huge questions regarding the objectivity and reliability of any information presented by these corporations. Can you say, 'Conflict of interests?' If that wasn't bad enough, each of these corporations get their news from only one of two sources; Reuters or The Associated Press. These two organisations serve as the international news corps, and channel all information down to the networks.

To cut a long story short, mainstream news is controlled by a tiny, elitist clique, which is why there is very rarely—if any—negative press about the World Bank or the international banking cartels reported by the mainstream media. It's why the majority of people have no idea about *Codex Alimentarius* or the real effects of fluoride and simply do not know how the world and it's corrupt money system is really run.

These commercial entities now vie with the government for authority over our lives, they are not a healthy counterweight to government, they are as big as or bigger than government and they work closely with government.
MARK CRISPIN MILLER
PROFESSOR OF MEDIA STUDIES
NEW YORK UNIVERSITY

These corporations are not answerable to the people, only the politicians can regulate them, and politicians can be bought with campaign contributions so large that the politicians will allow unregulated corporations to go about their business eliminating less powerful voices until there's only one voice left.

We have massive problems with what I call a legal corruption all over America, where the system has been gamed by various powerful interests. And it is all disclosed, of course, but no one reads it and the media doesn't

> *generally report it. So this is a wink-and-nod exercise with rampant cor-*
> *ruption, and the American people, in a very interesting way, viscerally*
> *understand that things are corrupt.*
>
> CHARLES LEWIS
> FORMER 60 MINUTES PRODUCER

Most of the mind control we're experiencing is not subliminal; it's not as subtle as we would think. It's more about being inundated with false data, such as 'Everybody knows depression is a chemical imbalance,' or 'Everyone knows schizophrenic is genetic,' 'Everyone knows America is right, no matter what,' 'Everyone knows schools want what's best for kids,' and so on. Of course, there's also the Fear, fear, terrorism, terrorism, pandemic-swine-flu-get-vaccinated-or-DIE! nonsense—there's nothing subliminal about it, it's overt, in-your-face, propaganda-style, old-school mind control.

Perception control is emotional control is mind control.

One of the main methods used to manipulate and control is very simple and basic; the control of information. If we don't have all the facts on any particular topic then our judgement is going to be no better than the quality of our information. It's very easy to change the meaning of an event or a speech through editing. Research done during the first Gulf War in 1991 suggested strongly that the more people watched CNN news broadcasts about the war, the less they knew about the war. Right now, for instance, we're being indoctrinated by a specific line of propaganda called 'the belief system of the aggressor' which is basically the United Kingdom and the United States of America justifying their position regarding Iraq or Iran. We're never told the truth about the buildup, what's really been going on in the background; the dirty history. And we're certainly never given details about the decision-making process or, crucially, what the real consequences of the war will be. All we're getting is 'This is a great little war, shock and awe, we're kicking this bad guy's ass.' The more you watch the mainstream media's slant on war, the more ignorant you get about the country we're raping and pillaging.

How often have you wondered what your wife, husband or your partner, or your boss, or the chap sitting across from you on the bus is really thinking? We all take it for granted that we'll never really know for sure. After all, our thoughts are our own—private and unreadable by anyone else. The right to keep your thoughts locked up in your brain is one of the most fundamental of being human—until now that is.

Neuroscience research into how we think and what we're thinking is advancing at a blistering rate, making it possible for the first
time in human history to look directly into the brain and to read
out the physical makeup of our thoughts; to read our minds. The
specialised use of MRI scanning, fMRI (functional MRI), makes it
possible to see what's going on inside the brain while people are
thinking.

Neuroscientist Marcel Just and his colleague Tom Mitchell of
Carnegie Mellon University, have combined fMRI's ability to look
at the brain in action with computer science's developing power to
sort through massive amounts of data—to see if they can discover
what happens in the brain when people think specific thoughts.

An experiment was conducted where they asked subjects to
think about ten objects—five of them tools, like a screwdriver and
a hammer, and five dwellings, like an igloo and a castle. Just and
Mitchell then analysed the activity in the brain for each.

The classic expectation—that they would discover a simple data
stream from one particular area of the brain—was completely
wiped away when they realised that instead of a simple flash of information presenting itself, a veritable lightning storm of synaptic
activity occurred in different areas. Charting the sequence of this
activity was the key.

When you think of a screwdriver you think about how you hold
it, how you twist it, what it looks like, what you use it for and
perhaps the time you dropped it point-down on your toe, and
each of those connections show up in different places in the brain.
When we think 'igloo', for example, neurons fire off in a different
sequence, making specific object identification a matter of crunch-
ing the numbers on a computer, presumably with an eye towards—
following the logical progression of all science—making it possible
to interpret any thought taking place in the human mind.

It's not that when you think of a hammer it is identical to when I
think about a hammer, there are characteristics to deal with. It may
be that I've had a bad experience with a hammer and you haven't,
which would produce slightly different readings, but the similari-
ties are close enough to identify the thought. In real-time tests, subjects were placed into the MRI scanners and shown a series of 10
items and asked to think about each one for a few seconds. Within
minutes, the computer—unaware of what pictures the subject had
been shown, and working only from the brain activity patterns as
read out by the scanner—could identify what the subject had been
thinking about, ten out of ten times.

Of course, TPTB aren't satisfied with just identifying a thought about a hammer, and neither is neuroscientist, Professor John-Dylan Haynes at the Burnside Centre in Berlin. He's using a scanner, not just to identify objects people are thinking about, but to read their intentions. Subjects were asked to make a simple decision, whether to add or subtract two numbers they would be shown later on. Haynes found that he could identify what they had decided to do based on activity readings taken from the small area in the brain that controls intentions. If a person is planning to add or subtract, the pattern of activity is different in both cases.

Throughout history we've never really been able to force someone into revealing information; we know torture doesn't work that well because the subject will say anything in order to stop the pain, and persuasion doesn't work that well because most people eventually realise they're being manipulated. If someone can read my intentions, we need to discuss who might be able to use that technology in the future; whether we're going to let the Government do it or whether they are going to let me do it.

If I have two children and I come home one day and my car is banged up and both of them deny responsibility, am I going to be allowed to drag them off to the local brain imaging 'lie detection company' and get them scanned to find out which one is going to pay for the repairs? A company called No Lie MRI is already offering lie detection services using brain scans, charging $10,000 per scan. The technique is still not proven but—in the meantime—Haynes is working on something he believes will be even more effective; using scan results to figure out where you've been.

Using footage from a video game, Haynes created an experiment in which the subject is taken through several rooms in virtual-reality houses. The subject is then placed into the scanner and the computer is able to tell what environments he or she has seen based on brain activity readings. It's being touted as a potential tool for police in the case of break-ins, or being able to tell if someone has spent time in an 'Al Qaeda' training camp, for instance.

Haynes claims that the German national security agency has approached him for the use of the technology, and there are companies that are considering these kinds of possibilities and using them. In India recently, a woman was convicted of murder after an EEG scan of her brain allegedly revealed that she was familiar with the circumstances surrounding the poisoning of her ex-fiancée.

Forgetting for a moment what we now know about our 'person' and the distinction between the legal entity and the living man or woman, and forgetting that we're never obliged to do anything, despite the obligation we may infer in the language of 'legalese', and considering that most people have no idea what their rights are and how to enforce them, could the legal system force us to take one of these tests? You might say, 'I have a 5th amendment right, the right to remain silent. I don't have to incriminate myself,' but that civil right only prevents the Courts from forcing you to testify against yourself. They can still force you to give DNA or a hair or blood sample, even if that would incriminate you. So, here's the big question; if you can brain image me and take information directly from my brain, with or without my knowledge or permission, is that testimony, or is that simply another case of taking a sample of DNA, blood, semen and other things they can demand over my objection?

They can and do use unlawful force, when we refuse to get on our knees, but the 'legal system' hasn't decided on the hi-tech information-extraction issue yet. For now, it's impossible to force someone to have his or her brain scanned because the subject has to lie still and co-operate but that could change.

There are several other technologies that are currently being developed that may be able to be used covertly and even remotely. For example, they're trying to develop a beam of light that could be projected onto your forehead that would penetrate a couple of millimetres into the frontal cortex. Receptors would then decode the signal that is bounced back and—as the story goes—the beam is imperceptible, so it could be done without your knowledge. They can't do it just yet, but they're working on it.

Those who manipulate the organized habits and opinions of the masses constitute an invisible government, which is the true ruling power of our country.
Edward Bernays
assistant to William Paley, founder of CBS

Essentially, what we're talking about here is the sort of technological ability seen in the 2002 film *Minority Report*, based on a science fiction short story written in 1956 by Philip K. Dick. Imagine a world where companies could read our minds. Light beams may be a bit far off, but fMRI scanning is already being used to try to figure out what we want to buy and how to sell it to us. It's a new field call Neuro-Marketing and one of its pioneers is a London company called Neurosense Limited, which already has clients such as Unilever, Intel, McDonald's, Procter & Gamble, MTV and Viacom using its services.

The field is growing rapidly; there are already about 92 Neuro-Marketing agencies worldwide. Of course anyone with a modicum of integrity would question whether it's ethical to scan the brain for commercial purposes. Besides that aspect, Neuro-Marketing's ego could well be writing cheques it can't cash. If you image my brain and you say TheAntiTerrorist craves chocolate and I say 'No, I don't,' are you going to believe the brain imaging result over my declaration? You can only do that if you've proven that that particular part of the brain lighting up means—in all cases—that I crave chocolate. What a lot of these people seem to be doing is simply imaging the brain, and then declaring what the results mean, never proving that the result actually translates into behaviour.

When neuroscientists show a brain scan, we just believe it; after all, 'neuroscience' just reeks of credibility, doesn't it? We're being told that this is the area where people add and subtract, and that is the area that deals with this or that thought—they could tell us anything and we'd just suck it up. In any event, as brain imaging continues its progress and finds its way into the courts, the market and who knows what other aspects of our lives, be wary and get ready with your tin foil hats. Just and Mitchell have already uncovered the signatures in our brains for kindness, hypocrisy and love, which is awe-inspiring and terrifying at the same time. They assert there will be a machine that will be able to read very complex thoughts like *I hate so-and-so* or *I love the opera,* not in twenty years but somewhere between five to ten years.

You only have to look at the US Patents issued in the last decade to realise the leaps being made in mind-control technology. Take this one, for instance:

NERVOUS SYSTEM MANIPULATION BY ELECTROMAGNETIC FIELDS FROM MONITORS
Document Type and Number: US Patent 6506148
Estimated Patent Expiration Date: June 1, 2021
Abstract: *Physiological effects have been observed in a human subject in response to stimulation of the skin with weak electromagnetic fields that are pulsed with certain frequencies near ½ Hz or 2.4 Hz, such as to excite a sensory resonance. Many computer monitors and TV tubes, when displaying pulsed images, emit pulsed electromagnetic fields of sufficient amplitudes to cause such excitation. It is therefore possible to manipulate the nervous system of a subject by pulsing images displayed on a nearby computer monitor or TV set. For the latter, the image pulsing may be imbedded in the program material, or it may be overlaid by modulating*

*a video stream, either as an RF signal or as a video signal. The image
displayed on a computer monitor may be pulsed effectively by a simple
computer program. For certain monitors, pulsed electromagnetic fields capable of exciting sensory resonances in nearby subjects may be generated
even as the displayed images are pulsed with subliminal intensity.*

Computer and TV monitors can be made to emit weak low-frequency electromagnetic fields simply by pulsing the images displayed on the screen. Effectively, the ½ Hz and 2.4 Hz sensory resonances can be used to manipulate the nervous system of the subject sitting in front of the monitor. Kewl.

And here's another fine mess we'll be exposed to, no doubt:

*METHOD AND DEVICE FOR PRODUCING A DESIRED BRAIN STATE
Document Type and Number: United States Patent 6488617 (Issued on
December 3, 2002).
Estimated Patent Expiration Date: October 13, 2020
Abstract: A method and device for the production of a desired brain state
in an individual contain means for monitoring and analyzing the brain
state while a set of one or more magnets produce fields that alter this state.
A computational system alters various parameters of the magnetic fields
in order to close the gap between the actual and desired brain state. This
feedback process operates continuously until the gap is minimized and/or
removed.*

The human body has an electromagnetic energy field that both surrounds and passes through it. Countless studies have been done on the subject and countless books written, and there are millions of people around the world who work to develop and strengthen their energy field every day. In China alone, there are millions who start their day by practicing the martial art of Tai Chi or Chi Kung in order to achieve this.

The system of acupuncture is also based on an understanding of this energy field, which the Chinese refer to as Chi (chee), the Japanese as Ki (kee), and what the people of India refer to as Prana.

For some years now, modern medicine has been using electromagnetic fields to increase the healing process of broken bones in the body to encourage bone cell growth.

*An unbelievable and highly classified psy-ops program utilizing 'Silent
Sound' techniques was successfully deployed. The opportunity to use this
method occurred when Saddam Hussein's military command-and-control
system was destroyed. The Iraqi troops were then forced to use commercial
FM radio stations to carry encoded commands, which were broadcast on*

the 100 MHz frequency. The US psy-ops team set up its own portable
FM transmitter, utilizing the same frequency, in the deserted city of Al
Khafji. This US transmitter overpowered the local Iraqi station. Along
with patriotic and religious music, psy-ops transmitted 'vague, confusing
and contradictory military orders and information. Subliminally, a much
more powerful technology was at work, however. A sophisticated electronic
system designed to 'speak' directly to the mind of the listener; to alter and
entrain his brainwaves, to manipulate his brain's electroencephalographic
(EEG) patterns and thus artificially implant negative emotional states
—- feelings of intense fear, anxiety, despair and hopelessness were created
in the Iraqi troops. This incredibly effective subliminal system doesn't just
tell a person to feel an emotion, it makes them feel it. In short, it implants
that emotion in their minds.
ITV News, 23 March, 1991

Television emits electromagnetic radiation, the larger the screen—or the cathode ray tube—the greater the radiation. I would consider making new rules about how close your children are to the TV while they're being mesmerised by Barney the dinosaur.

The fMRI scanner seems insignificant, considering it's been proven to be much easier to induce desired brain states in an individual, using magnetic fields or micro-electric currents, than to scan the brain and attempt to decipher the signal using computer programs. If there is technology available that is really capable of extracting information from someone's mind, why are the military still resorting to torture in Abu Ghraib and Guantanamo? Perhaps water boarding is just more fun. Bloody mind-reading killjoys.

Silent Subliminal Presentation System
Document Type and Number: United States Patent 5159703 (Issued on
October 27, 1992)
Estimated Patent Expiration Date: December 28, 2009
Abstract: A silent communications system in which non-aural carriers,
in the very low (ELF) or very high audio-frequency (VHF) range or in
the adjacent ultrasonic frequency spectrum, are amplitude- or frequency-
modulated with the desired intelligence and propagated acoustically or
vibrationally, for inducement into the brain, typically through the use
of loudspeakers, earphones, or piezoelectric transducers. The modulated
carriers may be transmitted directly in real time or may be conveniently
recorded and stored on mechanical, magnetic, or optical media for delayed
or repeated transmission to the listener.

The use of subliminal technology first came to public attention in the 1950s, with the publication of Vance Packard's book *The Hidden Persuaders,* in which it was revealed that the American industries were researching subliminal technology in order to influence people to buy their products. At the same time an experiment was being conducted in a film theatre in New Jersey in which a message was flashed on the cinema screen for 1/30th of a second every five seconds, 'Drink Coke, Eat popcorn,' and sales increased dramatically during the duration of the film. Certain B grade horror movies were also experimenting with subliminal techniques, flashing words like 'blood' at a certain frequency or using barely audible sounds of an angry hornets nest to elicit an emotional response.

There was an immediate public outcry against this, and rightly so. The public recognised that this was an instance of an invasion of the privacy and sanctity of one's mind, the influencing of one's mind—without conscious awareness or consent—to buy goods and services. Congress got involved and there was a discussion about passing laws, but—after a while, and because the populace are so easily distracted—the commotion died down.

Even if legislation had been passed regarding subliminals, enforcement was a major issue. The very nature of subliminals is that they're undetectable—well below the threshold of conscious awareness. The message is presented so quickly or so faintly that we're not consciously aware of having seen or heard anything. Someone would have to sit and inspect every frame of film, or every second of sound tape, and that just isn't practical. So nothing really happened. Despite the public upset, many people are under the impression that we have been protected from subliminals ever since, though in 1998, the December/January issue of *Civilization Magazine,* the official publication of the Library of Congress, contained an article declaring that the use of subliminals is part and parcel of our everyday life.

Bear in mind that patents are usually applied for after the technology has proven itself to be commercially viable using working models. It is quite typical that by the time new scientific knowledge is mentioned in the mainstream media, it's already been tried and tested, usually years or even decades before we get a whiff of it.

This Silent Subliminal Presentation System technology needs much more bandwidth than the analogue signal can offer to be put into practice, which would explain the need to switch exclusively to the digital signal in 2009. Think about that for a moment. Why are our governments so keen to give us a clearer and more highly defined television experience, friends? Why on earth would they be so concerned about the visual quality of our televised entertainment that Congress and Parliament would pass statutory legislation, without a referendum, mandating that the HD conversion takes place, and then subsidise up to 90% of the related cost by offering discount coupons and wotnot?

I decided to look into this transition and why they are doing it. My first instinct was to see if there was any connection between the digital transition and RFID chips, and I wasn't particularly surprised when I found the link.

The RFID chip is manufactured by Applied Digital Solutions and known as Digital Angel.

Applied Digital Solutions merged with AT&T back in 2001. In 2008, the FCC (Federal Communications Commission) had an auction of the 700mhz spectrum of the digital signal and AT&T bought enough of it to cover more than 87% of the US population. One of the problems that Applied Digital Solutions was having with these chips included the limitations caused by the readers having to be in close physical proximity to them in order to receive the information. Now it seems they'll be able to read data from chips wherever a digital television signal can be picked up.

Applied Digital Solutions claim to have sold 9 million dollars worth of this technology to the United Kingdom's Ministry of Defence to replace current technology that will be obsolete soon due to changes in satellite monitoring technology. By all accounts, they'll be able to turn these RFID chips on or off remotely without having to worry about where a reader is located. It would seem the distance won't be a problem for them for much longer.

If a significant percentage of the public rejected the digital transition, and simply refused to go along, they'd switch back to analogue faster than you can say Tin Foil Hat. They need you to absorb your daily dose of propaganda, deception and lies. Without it, you might actually start to wake up to the nonsense that is going on around you, and we can't have that, now can we? There's also lots of encouragement to get digital radio these days—and in the United Kingdom, at least, the target date of 2015 has been set to get rid of the old analogue radio broadcasts.

The media is the most powerful entity on earth. They have the power to make the innocent guilty and to make the guilty innocent—that's power. Because they control the minds of the masses.
Malcolm X

Comcast has openly admitted they're currently installing cameras on their new cable boxes which would make use of body-form-recognition software, in order—so the sales pitch goes—to provide custom-tailored service, and custom tailored advertising. The boxes would be able to tell who is in the room based on the shape of their body, enabling them to customise programming to fit our individual requirements.

The software would also be able to distinguish between a child and an adult, and would adapt security settings appropriately. Anyhow, it's all in the experimental phase, so they say…

A major corporation wants to place cameras that can track your movements in your own home. Where's the harm in it? Cue catchy jingle:

It's personalised, secure and efficient!
Now you can leave your fat, dumb kids
at home with the Comcast Cable Caregiver!

If the television craze continues with the present level of programs, we are
destined to have a nation of morons.
DANIEL MARSH, 1950

Whoever controls the programming controls your programming, and if you have children who watch television, whoever controls the television has at least some control over what they think, what they want, what they'll like and dislike, and how they'll grow up to view the world. We need to maintain our mental sovereignty to the highest possible degree. We have a duty to ourselves to be highly selective about what we allow our minds to be exposed to and—crucially—what we allow our children to be exposed to. They are the future. Using the television as a baby sitter and giving malevolent strangers the power to shape your child's mind is an irresponsible, lazy and obtuse way to raise a child.

The best thing you can do to inform yourself and immediately improve your wellbeing, your health, and your intelligence, is to turn off your television set; except perhaps for thirty minutes of news a day, just to keep track of the propaganda being fed to the general public. For a better and more informed perspective, get your news online from independent websites—and go to many sites from differing countries and sources, to compare the same story from a variety of perspectives.

You've been told that the Internet is an unreliable source of information—that really depends on how well you trust your own discernment, intuition and ability to think for yourself. The Internet is simply the world's largest mirror held up to humanity, reflecting life back at you. It's true, there are many phoney websites and red herrings thrown into the pot, but there's also a lot of very reliable information from very reliable sources, if you look in the right places. A bit like life itself when you stop and think about it.

If you're able to be media-free for extended periods of time and disengage yourself from the frequency of chaos, anxiety, stress, distraction and general hustle and bustle, you begin to get clear; you begin to listen to your intuition and live a freer, more joyous life—a life you design, rather than a life designed for you.

Take Responsibility... look it up for yourself. Search engine paths regarding topics addressed in this chapter:

Applied Digital Solutions
Associated Press
Burnside Centre Berlin Neuroscience
Chi
Codex Alimentarius
Corporations controlling mass media
Digital Angel
FCC Federal Communications Commission
GWEN Towers
HAARP
High Definition Television conversion
Josef Mengele
MRI
Marcel Just Carnegie Mellon University
Media Controls the Masses
Method and device for producing a desired brain state United States Patent 6488617
Mind Control
Minority Report 2002 film
MK ULTRA
Nervous system manipulation by electromagnetic fields from monitors US Patent 6506148
Neuro-marketing

No Lie MRI
Philip K. Dick
Prana
Professor John-Dylan Haynes
RFID
Reuters
Rothschild
Silent Sound technique
Silent Subliminal Presentation System United States Patent 5159703
Silent Subliminal Presentation System technology
The Hidden Persuaders Vance Packard
Tom Mitchell Carnegie Mellon University
Analog to digital conversion government funding
Electromagnetic field
fMRI
Subliminal advertising.

THE PEOPLE'S REPUBLIC OF DEMOCRACY

I have wondered at times what the Ten Commandments would have looked like if Moses had run them through the US Congress.
RONALD REAGAN

Freedom is something that we in the Commonwealth and in America take for granted. We're all just as free as birds, aren't we? We know that to be true because we learned it in our public schools. However, I've lost count of the number of messages I get from people who complain about the freedoms they have lost or that they ought to have.

I'm reminded of the quote by Johann Wolfgang von Goethe:

None are more hopelessly enslaved than those who falsely believe they are free.

That's one of those profound statements that you run across every once in a while that holds more truth than meets the eye.

We use the word 'freedom' liberally. Almost every time you saw Bush Jr on TV, the word would just fall out of his mouth. He would constantly attempt to wax eloquent about freedom, voting, the right to choose and democracy. Meanwhile, over here in Blighty, we've got Gordon Brown speaking of regime change in order to protect the freedom of British people, and so on. Hillary Clinton and Obama want to give you good Americans compulsory health insurance, and you should be as pleased as punch that your government cares about your freedoms and your health so much that they're about to force you to buy health insurance—it's for your own good, you know. They make sure you've got driving insurance to protect you and everyone around you, so it only stands to reason that you should have health insurance. After all, you hardly know what's good for you and you should be glad there are many smart people in Parliament and Congress figuring out how to keep you safe and healthy.

You may recall Mel Gibson's last scene, playing William Wallace, in the movie *Braveheart*—he is being mercilessly tortured, is clearly broken and in his final moments of life, just before he dies, he manages to find the strength to scream FREEDOM…

A very dramatic and emotive ending to the movie, I'm sure you'll agree.

I don't know about the rest of you around the world, but here in Britain and America, freedom is something we learn about early in life. We're told about our grandparents fighting in two World Wars for the freedoms that we have today and in America, in particular, you're taught to be very 'patriotic' at an early age. I'm not against patriotism at all, I'm just pointing out that everyone is really quite excited about freedom these days and I'm left wondering, does anyone know what freedom really is?

A friend of mine in the States was in court recently discussing 'rights' during one of his many cases. He preached a sermon for the Judge about this right and that right, the constitution, freedom and one thing and another, and the Judge listened patiently but ruled against him anyway. As he was leaving, the Judge noticed him walking by in the hallway and said, 'Mr Ellis, have you got a minute?'

My friend, seeing an opportunity for an interesting discussion said, 'Judge, for you, I've got all day,' and followed him into his private chambers. The Judge expressed his admiration for the way my friend handled himself in court and they discussed the case briefly, but eventually got round to the topic of rights. The Judge said, 'I notice that you claim you have a lot of rights, and you talk about rights extensively in your legal writing.'

My friend replied, 'Yes sir, I'm concerned about my rights and I'm concerned about the erosion of those rights.'

'Well, how many rights do you think you have?'

There was dead silence while my friend mulled over the question. Eventually he had to concede that he didn't know.

'To the best of my knowledge, as an American citizen, you have around 1100 rights that are available to you.'

My friend was amazed at this and said he thought it was closer to around one hundred.

'No,' the Judge replied, 'if you have a Social Security number you have what are called 'Civil Rights' as opposed to inalienable rights, and there are at least 108 of those. Then of course you have your constitutional rights to life and liberty and the pursuit of happiness. And then you have the Ten Commandments, those give you certain 'common' rights'. The Judge went on to list several more and then revealed a secret that very few people seem to know...

'Whether you have 1100 rights available to you or not is irrelevant and immaterial because the only rights that are ever available to you at any given time are the rights that you can claim. And if you don't claim that right, it does not exist for you.'

A good example of this is vaccination. Here in the UK, vaccination is still voluntary, although probably not for much longer. However, in the US it is compulsory in most States via 'laws of general applicability' (in other words, they apply to everyone). Let me rephrase that: they apply to everyone but there are 'exceptions'. There are always exceptions written into these statutes because they have to give you a back door. If there wasn't a back door available, they could be accused of violating your American Constitutional rights—the constitutional right to practice religion, for instance.

So, if Government came along and said everyone has to have vaccinations, those religious groups who believe vaccination is a desecration of the temple of God, and that it's a sin, would have their rights to free exercise violated. As a result, under the American constitutional system you have to make allowances for these people. There are also medical conditions to take into account. Taking the recent mandate by Governor Perry in Texas as an example, all females in the state should be vaccinated with the anti-viral cancer vaccine. Let's suppose there's just one female in Texas who is allergic to this vaccine for medical reasons, she has some sort of immune response condition like lupus, and this vaccine would injure or possibly even kill her. Would you presume that she has to line up and take that vaccine anyway, even though it's a medical threat to her life? Of course not. Her doctor would probably write some sort of note, an excuse would be made and she can go to school without it. So we've two obvious exceptions, religious and medical. Could you qualify for one of those medical or religious exemptions? Typically, if you're a Catholic, Protestant or Jew, the answer is no, and if you're in good health, the answer is no, so you just line up, shut up and get your shot like everybody else.

Where did the Governor of the State of Texas get the power to order you to go and get this vaccine? He got it from the birth certificate—when you registered your child and gave him to the state. When the Governor of Texas says, 'I want all of the children in Texas under the age of 18 vaccinated with this vaccine,' what you're dealing with here is the doctrine of *Parens Patriae.*

Parens patriae—'Parent of his country'— is used when the government acts on behalf of a child or mentally ill person. It refers to the 'state' as the guardian of minors and incompetent people.

The State, who owns your children, has the power to do that. And here is the strange part, they never tell you about that. Why should they? To do so would be to give up their power.

Parens Patriae is a Latin term and if I used that term with the average Joe, he'd probably say, 'You do that and you'll have to clean it up!' He hasn't got a clue what it means, the public schools never taught him, so he doesn't know what he's involved in when he gets a marriage licence or birth certificate. There really is nothing quite like a man who is a slave but believes he is free.

Let's take a look at Webster's dictionary and see what freedom is:

A quality or state of being free; liberation from slavery, imprisonment or restraint; exemption from necessity; exemption from extraneous control; choice and action as freedom of will; ease; boldness of conception or performance; freedom from care; liberty; licence; the power or condition of acting without compulsion; the power to act or speak or think without externally imposed restraints; immunity from an obligation or duty.

Of all of the people who are arrested every day and taken into the police station, photographed and fingerprinted and have their DNA sample taken, I wonder how many question or challenge the alleged powers of their captors? They complain about it, but they don't actually know where the lines are drawn in the sand. They can see that their freedom of action is being taken away from them, that they're being compelled to do something they don't want to do and they relate that to freedom and complain about losing their rights. Nobody has taken your rights, you gave them away, you surrendered them. Nobody is taking my picture, fingerprints or DNA against my will or over my objection, because I know the difference between a law and a statute, because as a responsible man on the land, I'm obliged to know what the law is and I know how to claim my rights.

There are around 2.5 million laws (statutes) in active status today in Great Britain and the United States, and those statutes are being added to at the rate of around forty-seven pages a day. Friends, every one of those 'laws' impairs your freedom to some degree. For instance, when you want to fly in an aeroplane and some guy pulls you out of the line and says, 'Pull down your pants, bend over, I want to look up the crack of your hoo haa to see if you're carrying explosives.' That's very, very personally intrusive. That is the antithesis of freedom—unless of course you're an exhibition-ist and you want to flash your backside at a complete stranger. Besides those odd people who like to expose themselves, the rest of us wear clothes because we're hiding something, obviously. I always laugh at people who say, 'If you don't have anything to hide, what are you afraid of?' I like to ask them, 'Well. If you don't have anything to hide, what the hell are you wearing clothes for?'

I have a whole load of things I want to hide, and I don't want you to know about them. It's called privacy. It's a wild and crazy idea, but if I told you what I was hiding, it would no longer be private, would it?

We used to have an old saying in this country that went, 'He who is governed best, is governed least.' Have you heard that gem? The moral behind this adage is if you want to be governed 'least', you have to be the most responsible. Freedom demands responsibility.

Let's suppose everybody in Great Britain obeyed all of the traffic regulations—nobody speeds, everyone stopped at red lights and stop signs, everybody drove on the correct side of the road. Let's suppose that everybody in Great Britain obeyed all 2000+ traffic rules, all of the time; why would you need a traffic policeman on the street? Wouldn't they be redundant? Wouldn't they be super-fluous, unnecessary, a waste of time and taxpayers money? Evidently we need 2000 traffic statutes to spell out, with specificity, 'Thou shalt stop at the stop sign'!

The law is written for the lawbreaker, not the law practitioner.

You haven't had your freedom taken, the government hasn't taken any freedoms, liberties or immunities from you... unless you signed them away, threw them away or abandoned them along the way. Government doesn't take your rights from you, you have to surrender them. You couldn't waive one of your rights if you stayed in bed. You have to get up in the morning, you have to go to some agency or other and pick up a pen and sign your name to abandon, surrender or waive any rights, freedoms or immunities. And that's what has happened.

Let's take a look at a licence, do you know what a licence actually is? If we take a look at Bouvier's Law Dictionary, we see that a li-cence is permission to do something that is illegal, unlawful, a tort or a trespass. That legal definition, along with a smidgeon of logic would suggest that anyone who possesses a licence is a criminal by definition. If you've got a licence in your pocket, you're a criminal because you want to commit a tort or a trespass and you have to have someone's permission to do that. So you go to a qualified authority who can give you permission to do this tort or trespass against somebody else. That 'someone else' in this case—whether your religious or not—is God and the Ten Commandments. Remember, all law comes from some religious doctrine or other.

The government are just lining up, encouraging you to engage in criminal activity with promises of protection from the police power of the state.

How about the marriage licence? Do you know what marriage is, lawfully or biblically speaking? Marriage is an agreement with penetration—that's what creates marriage. You don't need a state-licenced preacher or vicar to say any words to have an agreement with penetration—you could do that on a desert island in the South Pacific all by yourselves.

Americans and Brits seem to be abysmally ignorant of the law. We go to public school and we learn how to lay the neighbourhood girls in the back of our cars, but we don't know much about marriage, marriage licences and birth certificates, and the legal consequences that come from them. Then we complain when the social worker comes by and wants to know why your child has a bruise on him and insists there has to be an investigation. Why the hell would the social worker believe that your child had a bruise on him because you beat him? When I was a child I always had bruises on me. Sometimes it was because my father took a belt to me but most of the time it was because I fell out of a tree, or I was out playing and doing something I shouldn't have been doing and I got hurt. People don't consider that the social worker's intervention is solely due to the fact that they have a marriage licence and birth certificates and that the state owns their children.

I know when I say that, people get really incensed. I can't tell you how much vitriolic e-mail I received following my broadcast on Admiralty jurisdiction, where I asserted registered children belonged to the State. Didn't you know that a marriage licence is a privilege from the state and that every child born to a family with a state marriage licence is a 'ward of the State'? Your children are wards of the State in a guardian-ward relationship. When you got the marriage licence, you became a 'Three Party General Limited Partnership'—the boy, the girl and the State. The State then owned one-third of the spoils of the contract. Then you had a child, got a birth certificate and you gave your two-thirds interest to the State, so now the state has a 100% interest in your children—you're just the State's baby sitter. This is why the social worker can come and take your child and place it in foster care—they're just changing baby sitters because as far as they're concerned, you weren't looking after their property well enough.

When a church incorporates, when anyone incorporates, the corporate entity becomes a creature of the state and its officers become agents of the state, and the agents and the officers and the corporations have no constitutional rights. Did you get that? By the way, if you take a licence for anything you lose your constitutional rights for the thing you took the licence out for. If you get a marriage licence, you're waving your constitutional rights to marriage. If you get a driving licence, you're waiving your common law right to travel. If you get a business licence, you're waving your rights to property. It's just a way the law is set up and I didn't make it that way so don't get upset with me, I'm just here to report to you that that's the way the game is played. If you're saying, 'Well, I didn't know that… that can't be true, I didn't learn that in public school…'

Why the hell would a master want to teach his slave the truth about slavery and freedom?

There was a time in Great Britain, the United States, Canada and New Zealand, when you could drive your car without wearing a seat belt, do you remember that? They didn't even put seat belts in cars years ago, never mind make you wear one. Today, if you don't fasten your seat belt, you're going to get a ticket, whether you'd like one or not. And they'll remove some of your property; money. With the seat belt rule, you've one more duty you're obliged to perform. Pretty soon you have another rule that says you have to fasten your baby in a special seat, facing a particular way, in the back of your car. Now I know you may be sitting there thinking, 'You daft bugger, AT, don't you know that it's good for you to fasten your seat belt?' Well, maybe it is. I don't deny that you people are all a lot smarter than I am and you probably know how I ought to live my life better than I do, but that's not the point here. The point is that every time you pass a statute, you have some new restriction, you have somebody who is interfering with your free will, your choice to make up your own mind as to whether you want to wear your seat belt today or not.

Even though it may not be good for someone, their decisions are probably bad and wrong, and they shouldn't make those bad decisions, should we interfere in anyone's life and spoil their day, imposing upon them our will, our wisdom, our brilliance, our better way of life? I'm of the opinion that we ought to leave people alone and let them decide for themselves, but when we do that to others, then those others want to do that to us and soon enough we're all running around in the legislative corridors screaming and calling for new statutes, and more and better laws. Before you know it you have two and a half million statutes and you're saying, 'Oh my god, I live in the People's Republic of Great Britain.'

The bottom line is, the more laws you have, the less freedom you have. The equation works very simply:

The more Freedom you possess the less law you will be subjected to. If you want more freedom you need fewer laws, and if you want more laws then you want less freedom. You have to have, hold and exercise individual responsibility.

Let's try it on this way: I'm not going to fasten my seat belt and I'm not going to buy insurance and I'm driving down the road. I run into a tree and I go through the windscreen and I get hurt pretty badly. Of course someone will say, 'Well, now we have to pay your hospital bills.' Why do you have to pay my hospital bills? Why do you even have to pick me up off the street? There are people out there; I guess we call them 'do-gooders' who seem to be of the opinion, 'If these people aren't smart enough to live their lives the way we think they ought to be lived, then we're going to live their lives for them!'

You see, if I want any health insurance, I'll buy it. I don't want you to buy me any health insurance. If I get ill and I need an operation, just let me die. If I can't afford to pay for the operation myself, just leave me alone. I should have looked ahead, I should have been wise, you know, like you smart people out there who have insurance, but I didn't. I spent my money on wine, women and song. I had a wonderful time. You, on the other hand, were thrifty and diligent and you gave up the wild women and cigarettes and the Jack Daniels and you bought health insurance. God bless ya. When you get ill, you can go over to the hospital and you can have that bypass surgery or liver transplant or whatever it is you need. I don't blame you for choosing how you wanted to live, that's what I think everybody ought to do, and that's why I'd like you to leave me alone, and let me do for myself. Let me look ahead, and let me think for myself. Let me decide whether I want to fasten my seat belt or not, and get out of my face. Let me decide whether I want to buy insurance or not. I know it's a crazy idea but that's what freedom is all about; it's you making choices for yourself.

I have been accused of advocating anarchy in the past. Well, somewhere between 'anarchy' and 'police state' there is freedom and normalcy. Anarchy is total lawlessness, which is what you've got over there in Baghdad, and then—here in Great Britain and the United States—we have 'police state'.

I'm advocating something in-between.

If you want to be free, you have to have *'exemption from extraneous control, the power of the will to follow the dictates of its unrestricted choice and then to direct the external acts of the individual without restraint, coercion or control from other persons.'* We talk a lot about freedom in Great Britain and America but *'the power of the will to follow the dictates of its unrestricted choice and to direct the external acts of the individual without restraint, coercion and control of other persons'* is practically unheard of in our countries.

Do you know what a franchise is? A franchise is 'freedom or immunity from some burden or restriction or the like; a particular privilege conferred by Grant from a sovereign or a government and vested in an individual or individuals; a positive right to do something otherwise legally incompetent.' You've got a McDonald's franchise, a Burger King franchise, and you have a franchise tax board in California. They're giving you something that's otherwise legally incompetent, something that is otherwise illegal. So what was it you people out there in California wanted to do that you have to pay the state of California a bribe or an income tax for? Have you ever stopped to think about that? Let's say I want to go and open up a restaurant and call it McDonald's and I don't want to have to pay McDonald's any franchise fee, but I want to capitalise on the name. After all, it's a very popular name. I want to call my restaurant McDonald's because if I call it McAntiTerrorist's, no one is going to come in. No one's ever heard of my restaurant.

All of you wonderful people recognise the name McDonald's though because they advertise a lot. I don't want to pay McDonald's anything, I don't want to go through their training programme and I don't want to do anything that McDonald's does—I just want to use the name McDonald's. Of course, McDonald's would have every right to come to me and insist that I pay their franchise fee and conform to all of their rules and regulations.

California and the United Kingdom are telling you the same thing, friends. 'If you want to join the California club, the UNITED KINGDOM club, or the CANADA club, if you want the franchise benefits that we offer you here then you have to subscribe to our franchise… but if you do that you lose your freedom.'

I'd rather lose the benefits and take my chances of limited success with my McAntiTerrorist restaurant, and keep my freedom. How about you? And we have this 'democracy franchise' going on at the moment. We've got Gordon Brown and Obama saying, 'We want to go over to Iraq and offer them the benefits of our democracy—we have to make the world safe for democracy.'

> *Be Nice to America… or we'll bring democracy to your country.*
> GEORGE W. BUSH AS QUOTED BY LT. GEN. RICARDO SANCHEZ,
> LATELY TURNED INTO A RATHER POPULAR BUMPER STICKER

Did it ever occur to us that maybe the other people in the world don't want us coming over there telling them what kind of government is best for them? Has it ever occurred to we Brits and Americans that maybe if we just kept our nose out of Iraq and minded our own damn business, maybe they could sort out their own government?

Lets suppose they can't, let suppose those people can't figure out what kind of government they ought to have. How does that impact us over here in London? You see, I don't care if those people over there ever have an election again. You might be sitting there thinking, 'AT, you're totally insensitive.' You're right about that. You see, a part of the thing called freedom is 'mind your own bloody business,' keep your nose out of other peoples lives, leave them alone and let them make their own mistakes.

I know it's a bloody heavy burden for Christians in America and Great Britain to let other people make their own mistakes but that's because they're so much smarter than everybody else. The UNITED KINGDOM and UNITED STATES Corporations have troops in 132 countries around the world—just to show them how much we love them, and how much we want to guide them and direct them, so that they don't make mistakes; so they can live the 'good life' like we do here in Britain and America. When we do that, we restrict their freedom, we get in the way of those people doing what they want to do. We call it freedom and democracy, but they call it tyranny, they call it occupation and they don't like it. That's why we've got problems in Iraq. If we were to mind our own business and leave those people alone, they'd probably kill each other, they'd probably have a big civil war and raise hell over there but who are the Americans to preach to the world about civil war? You had a big one of your own, in which about 650,000 people were killed. I don't think anyone here in London or over there in New York would be too happy about the Russians or the Chinese 'visiting' and preaching how we ought to love one another and how we ought to conduct our own political affairs.

Franchise isn't the way to get more freedom.

There's another word that I think we ought to get really familiar with and that word is 'privilege'. Do you think privilege has anything to do with freedom? A privilege is *'a right or immunity granted as a peculiar advantage or favour; a 'personal' right in derogation of a 'common' right; a 'special' right or immunity; a franchise or a patent.'*

So, a privilege is a franchise, it is something that can be given to you, and can be taken away. I remember when I was a child, when someone asked me who's bicycle I was riding, I would say, 'It's my bike.' One day, my dad got cheesed off at me about something and said, 'You're staying home for a week, no television and you can put that bicycle in the garage and walk for a week.' Who's bike was that really, friends? Yes indeed, that was my daddy's bicycle and he could give me privileges and he could take them away in a heartbeat. Social Security is like that. Social Security is a social welfare scheme, it is a privilege, and parliament can terminate it tomorrow morning at 9AM if they so choose. You might have paid into it for a long time but that doesn't mean you're going to get anything out of it.

Then there is a thing called 'limited'—in other words, restricted; bounded; prescribed; confined within positive bounds; restricted in duration, extent or scope.

'Restricted; bounded; prescribed...' that's what happens when you get a driver's licence. You become restricted, bound and circumscribed. The traffic policy enforcement officer tells you what you can do and can't do. He stops you at a roadblock and says, 'I'm going to search your car,' or 'Get out here and walk along the white line,' or 'Breathe into this machine.'

It's what happens when you get on an aeroplane, 'Bend over and let me look up the crack of your hoo haa.'

That's not freedom, that's tyranny.

Limited lends itself to 'limited liability'. Before we get to limited liability, let's take a look at what 'liability' is.

Liability: *'A state or quality of being liable; that for which one is liable, such as one's obligations or debts; opposed to assets; bound or obliged by law or submission to other forces; answerable; exposed to danger or risk of something undesired.'*

A liability is something that is undesired. You're liable for the income tax, you're liable for the Social Security taxes, and you're liable for prosecution for not fastening your seat belt. You have a liability if you don't perform on all 2000 of these traffic rules and regulations, liable to have your children taken away from you if you don't follow all of the child welfare and protection statutes and send them to public school, or have them vaccinated with cat vomit and monkey spunk.

Limited liability is basically insurance. You don't want to be strictly liable for all of the damages that you may cause somebody out there, so you buy an insurance policy, like a homeowner's policy, and that way when I come over to visit, slip on your steps, fall down and break my ankle and sue you for £1 million, you can sit there and say, 'No problem, AT, I'm protected—I'm in safe hands with Norwich Union, because I've got homeowners protection.'

The truth of the matter is you got insurance because you didn't want to be responsible for me coming over there and slipping on your steps, because you were too cheap to throw a little salt out there and protect me. Or because your child was out there digging holes and I stepped into one of those holes, fell over and broke my leg. You don't want to be responsible for filling in your holes and putting salt on the steps, you'd rather buy an insurance policy. As an aside, for those of you who put any value in the Bible, the Scripture strictly prohibits limited liability. Limited liability is about shirking responsibility and is therefore the opposite of freedom. If you come to my house and slip on my steps, I have to pay for those damages. You might be off work for a few weeks and I might have to pay your wages for that time. That's what strict liability is all about. I accept that responsibility. The more responsible I am, the more money I can save and the more freedom I can exercise.

Another interesting word is 'immunity'. Immunity is 'exemption from any charge, duty or tax; the state or power of resisting the development of a given disease, infection or micro organisms.'

I'd like to have a lot of immunity. If you're immune, you're exempt. I'd like to be exempt from the traffic policeman, compulsory vaccinations, compulsory seat belt laws, insurance legislation, taxes, and diseases.

Finally, we come to the word 'property'. Property is the holy grail of law and is founded upon the biblical law 'Thou shalt not steal.' Without 'thou shalt not steal,' you couldn't own any property. If you had freedom, you would have property, because freedom is an attribute of property. Most of us, when we think about property, think about the, chair, the car, the house; the tangible thing, But there is another form of property, which is tangible and intangible. You see, property can also be intangible and a right is an intangible property.

My right to life is an intangible property. You can't see it, hear it, taste it, touch it or feel it, but I own it, it's mine, it exists, and you can't have it. If you take it from me, it's a theft, and it also violates 'thou shalt not kill,' for which there is a penalty. There is no such thing on planet Earth as a law without a penalty, because if you've got a law without a penalty, you don't have a law, you have a suggestion. Laws are not suggestions, laws have teeth, they have penalties, they have consequences, and they have results. Do you always get caught? No, of course not. Sometimes you can be driving ninety miles an hour and get away with it, especially if you've got a radar detector on your dashboard. I'm not suggesting that you can't break a law without getting caught, we all do that, I'm just pointing out that if you break the law you run the risk of the consequences.

Property is *'the exclusive right to possess, enjoy and dispose of a thing; ownership in a broad sense; any valuable right or interest considered primary as a source of wealth; that to which a person has legal title; the thing owned; an estate; an attribute common to all members of a class, thus sweetness is a property of sugar.'*

Rights of and by themselves are properties. If you have a right to vote, then that right is a property right even though voting of and by itself is a franchise. So you have a right to that privilege.

Then we have 'absolute property' and personal property. Absolute property is 'the sole and exclusive right and possession of movable chattels.' So you think your car is your property? Tell that to the police officer when he tells you to get out of your car and that he's going to have it towed away. You don't own your car. Take a look at the title to your car, it doesn't say title, it says certificate of title.

Look up the word certificate in a law dictionary and you will find a certificate is just evidence that a title exists but you don't have it, because the actual title is vested in the state. So a car is chattel property but it's not yours.

We're practising the first plank of the Communist Manifesto, which calls for the abolition of all right to property. We have an equitable interest in the state's property, or the bank's property but we certainly don't own it.

Oligarchy? A government resting on a valuation of property, in which the rich have power and the poor man is deprived of It.
PLATO, *THE REPUBLIC — BOOK VIII*

In trying to assess the issue of law-enforcement, the courts, the prisons, the crime, the rehabilitation, the death penalty and cruel and unusual punishments, there's been a lot written—and much more is going to be written in the future—but one point all of us seem to agree on is that crime is out of control and something should be done about it. We call our nations the free-est on earth and we refer to Russia and China as police states, but when we analyse the facts they tell us a different story.

America holds more people, per capita, in jails and prisons than they do in Russia or China. Did you know that? America has more people in prison than any other country in the entire world, including South Africa, which used to be the Number One Police State. Compared to the US, Russia has only a third the number of people imprisoned. In reality, the people of America and Great Britain are living in a police state; totally unaware of it and therefore, totally unconcerned about it.

NAME THIS NATION…

- *It has locked up more of its citizens than any other nation on the planet.*
- *It has also locked up a higher percentage of its citizens than any other nation on the planet.*
- *It has locked up more of its citizens than any other nation in the written history of this planet.*
- *It has imprisoned its own citizens - without any charges filed.*
- *It has imprisoned its own citizens - without any access to legal counsel.*
- *It has imprisoned its own citizens - without any access to family.*
- *It has imprisoned its own citizens - without any habeas corpus.*
- *Almost all its imprisoned citizens are in prisons run by corporations, not the government.*
- *It's the only first world nation that still has a death penalty.*
- *It has been proven to have 'secret' military prisons of torture in other nations.*
- *It claims that its brutal torturing of men, women, and children - is 'legal'.*
- *Its citizens have seen the visual proof of the torture - But yet, they 'allow' it to continue.*
- *Its own military/intel people have made it clear that most were innocent of any crimes.*
- *It spies on its own citizens, without warrants.*
- *It spies on its own citizens, without just cause.*
- *It spies on its own citizens, against its own laws.*
- *Incredibly, it refers to itself as 'the land of the free'.*

MICHREL L. STANDEFER
THE OLD HIPPIE'S GROOVY BLOG

There is very little difference between our governments and those of China or Russia... let's test that statement, shall we? Do Russia and China have national identification cards? Here in Great Britain and over in the United States they're pushing for an ID card, and they hope to have it in place by 2010 but, friends, we have already had a national identification card called social security since the 1930s and most of us carry drivers licences around in our pockets. When the policeman stops us and says, 'Where's your ID?' you whip it out and show him. You use the drivers ID to cash cheques and do business with it nearly every day of your life. You have been 'identified' and numbered like a cow in a pasture and you wouldn't leave home without those documents. You're not quite sure what would happen if you did leave home without them but you're afraid to leave home without them. Try it some time, just leave your identification at home, don't take any identification with you whatsoever and just go about your day and see how you feel. There was a time in Britain and America when people didn't have ID. Imagine how it used to be in the 1800s, travelling without a social security number, no driver's licence, no one is taking pictures so you have no picture ID. You could go from England to France without any personal identification, except perhaps for the family bible. Can you imagine trying to do that today?

Do you need a driver's licence to drive in Russia, or China?

Can they build on their land without government approval?

Are they subject to searches on their public roads?

Do they have a portion of their wages stolen?

Do you have to get permission to work where and when you want to in Russia or China? I don't know if you do over there but you certainly do in our fair countries, don't you? You have to have a National Insurance number and a P45 form in Britain.

Do you have to register your guns where you live? Can you 'pack heat' anywhere you want, when you want? I don't know if you can walk around with a gun stuffed under your armpit in downtown Beijing or Moscow. I'm told those are police states, so I would imagine you couldn't. Of course, you Americans can still own a gun but not without a permit from your Master. Remember, if you have to get a permit from your Master, that's a franchise, it's not freedom. Freedom is based on the choice, do I want to carry a gun or not?

I imagine you have to register your vehicles in China too. You'd expect that in China because they're police states but, again, there was a time in our countries where you didn't have to do that.

The brutality involved with beneficent socialist welfare police states, such as with the KGB or the Gestapo and the like, usually comes along a while after the regime is in position, so you don't have to worry about your feet being caned for filming a police officer just yet.

After all this time, the Russians haven't rejected the Ten Planks of the Communist Manifesto, and they've never accepted a Bill of Rights or the Ten Commandments. We Brits and Americans used to accept the Bill of Rights and the Ten Commandments, but now we've rejected both and have adopted all Ten Planks of the Communist Manifesto. I think Communism has won the day.

If the Chinese were ever to collect on all of the property and bonds they now own—the interest they now own in America—and they were to move in and take over the American government and impose on you Americans the terrible dictatorship that you're so fearful of, I don't think they'd change anything from what you already have. You've already got the perfect police state, you've got everything in place there that the police state in China has, so I really don't think you're going to notice very much difference in your everyday way of life.

There has been a sure and steady erosion of rights, privileges and immunities in the way we exercise our lifestyles, but the question arises, is this done because the government came in and put a gun to your head and used constraint or coercion, threat or force or violence? Or, is it the case that the government made offers to you, and you accepted those offers and you have enslaved yourself by way of your own hand or your own mouth? Has this been imposed upon you against your will and over your objection, or are you the cause of your own injury? I contend that the latter is the modality that we Brits and Americans have used to become feudal serfs. I don't think the word slave is quite correct. Bond servitude is probably the better legal term to use. We're not actually slaves, we're bondservants, since bond servitude is an ancient modality that goes back to the Mosaic Law at Mount Sinai. Bonded servitude is always accomplished by the free will and consent of the bondservant.

The more irresponsible a society becomes, the more tyrannical it becomes. The more responsibility you and I exercise, the freer we're going to be. That's the bottom line. It doesn't make any difference where you are in the world, citizens of any country who are controlled in this way are not free, they're living under tyranny. And it doesn't matter whether or not we have a better deal than the Russians or the Chinese; both of our systems are tyrannical by definition. The only difference is the level of tyranny being used and how well the people understand the system they're under.

The Chinese and the Russians and others understand that they live in tyranny, while we Brits and Americans have been convinced that it can't happen here, even though it quite clearly is happening, and right under our noses. We recognise it as tyranny in those other countries, but here in our own country, we call it 'law and order'. Nevertheless, a police state is a police state is a police state. There must be a simple solution that will free us from this mess of crime and punishment. A solution that stops us from punishing the innocent while making sure the guilty get what they deserve.

The system we're under at the moment only manages to cause scorn for the law in general and our prisons are simply schools where petty criminals are taught advanced crime rather than being institutions for rehabilitation. If someone loses their property, the criminal loses his freedom, but he never makes amends to the victim, and the taxpayers are cheated out of their money to support these human warehouses we call prisons. The beneficiaries of this system aren't the victims, they're the barristers, lawyers, Judges, prison guards, policy enforcement officers and the government, and they literally thrive off the system. Crime really does pay, and very well. What's worse is that not only does the victim lose by having his property taken, but he also loses even more—in taxes—to the prison industrial complex to feed, clothe and shelter the thief.

How many broken homes, divorces, fines, prison terms and shattered lives must there be in the name of law and order, just for the benefit of the law enforcement growth industry? How many people get their livelihood from this business? How many agencies are created by legislatures, city councils and Parliament, just to deal with crime? The truth is it we have no idea, really, how many 'persons' work in the 'business' of law enforcement, taking into account the sheer number of police, solicitors, barristers and Judges, not to mention the social workers, bailiffs, secretaries and the like, but each and every one of these people is looking for 'crime.' They're looking for lawbreakers, they want to apprehend somebody and then punish that somebody in order to justify their employment. The building inspector is looking for building violations; Social security man is looking for dole cheats. They're all looking for somebody they can apprehend, bring to justice, prosecute, punish and put in prison.

It seems as though it's the purpose of government to build a system of law and order, a system that is so big that everyone will either be employed by the enforcement agencies, or they'll be warehoused in the law enforcement agency's prisons.

It would also appear that the citizens are being used by government to further that agenda. This industry is nothing more than a business made up of law enforcement agencies. The customers—the people of the State—are in a business relationship with these government agencies. Like any business, this industry needs more and more customers to continue to grow and prosper, in order to justify its existence and size to the people, in order to obtain more funds to further that growth.

The cycle goes something like this:

We're told that we need to have more laws. New statutes are proposed to parliament. Parliament then passes those statutes, and creates a criminal act where there wasn't one before—wearing green socks on Wednesdays, for instance. So the Government now has more statutes to enforce, and therefore needs more employees to enforce them. The government appeals for more funds, due to the increasing crime rate caused by this legislated crime of wearing green socks on Wednesday. The funds are made available, and more employees are hired by these governmental agencies. More employees now have to justify their existence, and as a result, have to find, or trick, more 'customers' into committing more and more of these so-called crimes. In order to control more of these so-called crimes, now we need another law.

That's what you're buying; you're buying more crime.

Barack Obama says he's going to put 100,000 more policy enforcement officers on the streets of America. Well, those hundred thousand policemen, on average, are going to arrest someone every day. That's 100,000 more arrests everyday. Lets say 94%, 94,000, of those arrests are going to be convicted. Those 94,000 people, if they go to prison, are going to need beds, food and clothing. And that's why you have more people in prison in the United States than you have in Russia or China, because you want more and more law and order, and the more law and order that you buy, the more people you're going to imprison and therefore the more people you're going to have to support in those prisons, through taxation. The more policemen you employ, the more Judges you're going to need, the more barristers and lawyers, secretaries and support staff and prison guards. You have to get up in the morning and go out and vote to buy all of this law enforcement—you're not having this imposed on you, friends, you're going out there and actively buying it, supporting it. You want it, you desire it, and you demand it. And any politician who won't give you what you want is 'soft on crime' and you're going to vote him out.

We've put an iron collar around our own necks in the form the law-enforcement growth industry.

The real party of interest is the insurance company. It's the insurance company that wants you to lock your car, it's the insurance company that wants you to lock your house, it is the insurance company that wants you to fasten your seat belt, it's the insurance company that wants you to fasten your child into the special seat in the back of the car. The insurance company wants you to be compelled—by law and by force and violence if necessary—to pay insurance premiums, and then they don't want to pay any of the claims. It makes all the sense in the world; I don't blame them— it's just business—but why would you and I want to pay for such a system? It's the insurance companies that stand to lose profits from your oversight, and therefore it's the insurance companies that want you punished when you fail to perform. The insurance companies are the ones that lobby for the legislation that uses the police power of the state to enforce private interests, private business, decreasing claims and increasing profits of their insurance companies. That's what is behind all this nonsense.

The traffic courts provide another example of government protecting private interests. Who cares if a person 'speeds' down the open road, especially if that person's car is the only vehicle on the road? If we're at home and asleep, do we really care? But statistics show that 'speed kills', with consequently increasing claims at the insurance window; which causes an increase in operating costs, and therefore, a decrease in profits.

As long as you want insurance, as long as you wallow in insurance, you can kiss your freedom goodbye. If you don't want to be individually responsible for your actions then somebody else has to be and whomever else that's going to be is going to seek to limit his liability. When he seeks to limit his liability, he's going to do it in such a way that it is going to infringe on your rights, privileges and immunities. That's the way life has always been, it's the way it is today and it's the way it's going to be in the future, unless... you want freedom. The cost? You have to be responsible for your own actions.

But we Americans and Brits don't want to be responsible for our actions, therefore, we have to do as we're told and shut up.

The Government needs to control the people and generate revenue, so the first thing they do is they put a licence out there and tell you that if you get the licence there are many benefits. Of course, you want the benefits, so you get the licence. There is no downside; it's all plus, until they get everyone licenced. Once everyone is licenced, they introduce all of the taxes that go along with it. It's a bit like income tax...

When income tax was first enacted, only the super wealthy were affected. It started out at 1%, then 2%, 8%, and finally we're where we are today. The camel sticks his nose in the tent, then his shoulders, and pretty soon the camel is in the tent and you're out in the sandstorm. It's the way it works, over a period of time.

The National Security State uses fascism to protect capitalism while they say they're protecting democracy from communism.
MICHAEL PARENTI

Let's look at the traffic legislation to show how we've enveloped ourselves in tyranny.

At the turn of the century when Common Law was in use, imagine two horse-drawn carriages approaching each other. They collide head-on, killing three horses and injuring three children in the carriages. The driver of one of the carriages is killed and the damages are in the hundreds of pounds. So who sues whom, and how much do they sue for? Who was the damaged party? Was one driver drunk? Was the other driver speeding? Who was negligent? Is there a third-party insurance company involved in the action?

In common law, this case would be very costly in terms of time and effort and energy and money to litigate, but both parties have rights so the issue has to be decided in court, and a jury has to decide the law as well as the facts in the case. That's the common law at its finest.

When the 'horseless carriage' appeared on the scene, the insurance companies saw a way to make billions in premiums if they could keep claims to a minimum. As more cars appeared on the road, accidents increased because of the increased speed of the cars compared to the horse drawn wagons and carriages, and, consequently, the losses to insurance companies increased. So somewhere, someone in the insurance business said, 'We're having a lot of claims on these horseless carriages—how can we cut costs and increase profits?'

One of the biggest problems they had was determining the liability that you have in accidents. Since there were no rules of the road, and only common sense prevailed without written rules and regulations, it was very difficult to determine and attach responsibility. Was anyone speeding? There were no speeding laws then, other than the basic law of reason and prudence. Was anyone drinking or drunk? Well, there weren't any laws against drinking and driving, so could you show that the chap who was drunk caused the accident? Did anyone cross the centre line? There weren't any laws to tell either driver which side of the road to drive on. Did the drivers have insurance? There weren't any laws compelling a driver to have insurance. Were the drivers licenced? There weren't any licensing laws.

This doesn't mean that the common law didn't work, it just didn't work as efficiently as the insurance companies thought it ought to work—or at least not as common law relates to making profit and gain.

Now we can begin to see the alleged need for traffic laws. You and I didn't need a speeding law, the insurance company did. You and I don't need a seat belt law, the insurance company does. Who is it that really needs these traffic laws? The courts and the insurance companies need them. The insurance companies need the traffic laws for economic reasons and the courts need them to speed up cases and litigation. Whether the travelling public needs traffic laws for their health, safety and protection was not, nor is it now, nor will it ever be, the prime motivating factor in the passing of traffic or any other laws.

Commerce, money and profit is the prime motivator for enacting laws (statutes), and all of the statutes that come out of your legislature are commercial laws that deal with the commerce clause. Legislators don't pass laws that say, *thou shalt not commit adultery, thou shalt not kill, and thou shalt not steal;* legislators pass laws that benefit this or that company, this or that industry—it's simply to do with trade, commerce, business and industry affecting some public interest.

Private business interests proposed new laws through various governmental agencies and lobbyists and the legislators were tricked or bribed into believing it was in the best interests and general welfare of the citizens. The desires of private interests became statutory law.

In the early days, these rules were not enforced as criminal statutes with pains and penalties, because there were common law protections, and it didn't appear that anyone had lost rights. When a loss or damage occurred, there was no loss of rights because the common law would simply use the statute as evidence to establish fault.

If one were to Judge these men (legislators) wholly by the effects of their actions and not partly by their intentions, they would deserve to be classed and punished with those mischievous persons who put obstructions on the railroads.
HENRY DAVID THOREAU

The insurance industry has a huge financial interest to protect, so the money they spend is spent to make more money. Since there's no financial interest in 'rights', there's rarely any resistance to these new rules and regulations. Nobody makes money out of rights; they make money out of selling insurance premiums. So every time a controversy comes up, you can rest assured the insurance company will be there with the legislature to testify at all the committee hearings.

Who's going to be there to testify concerning your rights? You're certainly not, you're at work, you're on holiday, you're doing something else. That's why you have 2.5 million statutes, because there are many industries, many businesses, and thousands of campaigners in Congress and Parliament lobbying for these laws that make them money. Whether it's the pharmaceutical industry selling drugs to the National Health Service, or it's the insurance industry selling insurance policies to you and everybody else, if there is money to be made, they'll be in there talking to the legislature about enacting a law that's economically viable and makes money for that industry.

The global economy has become like a malignant cancer, advancing the colonization of the planet's living spaces for the benefit of powerful corporations and financial institutions. It has turned these once useful institutions into instruments of a market tyranny that is destroying livelihoods, displacing people, and feeding on life in an insatiable quest for money. It forces us all to act in ways destructive of ourselves, our families, our communities, and nature.
DAVID C. KORTEN
WHEN CORPORATIONS RULE THE WORLD

The police state imposed on the Chinese people by force is no different than the one we Americans and Brits have imposed upon ourselves today, except for the fact that we paid to have our rights taken in favour of contracts with benefits. The Chinese, at least, saved some money. However, we still have our rights, they're still there to claim, and we can reject limited liability, perpetual slavery and debt whenever we want to accept responsibility for our actions and debts. The Chinese can't.

When our governments pass the Patriot Act and the likes of the Anti-terrorism Act in the UK, those acts just open the door. Once those Acts are in place, they can be amended from year to year and they can bring down on you a reign of tyranny that will make Joe Stalin and Adolf Hitler took like Sunday school teachers. That's what you can get used to, that's what you can expect. And you've already approved it.

There aren't many people who want to trade their slavery and apparent safety for the conscientiousness of the life of a free man. But for those few men and women who want to be free, the choice is theirs. Every person who wants to be free can free himself or herself, but no one else can free them. The masses prefer security; social security, limited liability, and the satisfaction of having others control their lives. If you want to be truly free and claim your rights, you're obligated to defend them—and with your last breath, if necessary.

> *¡Prefiero morir de pie que vivir siempre arrodillado!*
> EMILIANO ZAPATA SALAZAR

Take Responsibility... look it up for yourself. Search engine paths regarding topics addressed in this chapter:

Anti-terrorism Act
Drivers Licence
Freeman Movement
Immunity exemption from charge duty tax
National ID Card
National Insurance Number
Parens patriae
Patriot Act
Police man versus police officer
Social Security Number
Ten Commandments
UNITED KINGDOM corporation
UNITED STATES corporation
Birth certificate the state owns your children
Business license
Democracy

Franchise freedom or immunity from restriction
Legal versus lawful
Limited liability
Making the world safe for democracy
Marriage certificate Three Party General Limited Partnership
Medical exemption from vaccination
Police state
Property law
Religious exemption from vaccination
Rights and priveleges
Seat belt law
Statute versus law
Statutory law
Terrorism
The Communist Manifesto.

CHASING A SMELL

Once upon a time, there was everywhere and nowhere, everything and nothing, just pure consciousness experiencing being conscious. After an indeterminable amount of 'time,' simply experiencing being conscious became a little monotonous, so consciousness decided it would be nice to have a conversation about being conscious.

Consciousness divided itself in two and although both parts were aware they were one, discussed the experience of being conscious. The conversation was captivating for a while but—inevitably—it became cyclic and dull.

'Let's play a game,' said one half, 'Let's pretend that being over there is more important than being over here.' So they did. They spent 'time' moving back and forth, despite already being everywhere and nowhere at once. The mental exercise, suspending disbelief and discussing whether or not they were where they were, was thrilling, for a 'time' but, as before, it got repetitive and predictable. 'I know,' said the other, 'Lets pretend that if I get over there before you, I win.' So they did.

They raced back and forth and took turns at 'winning' and they congratulated each other and the game was exciting and interesting, and 'time' flew by. They divided and split and multiplied over and over, mitosis and cytokinesis, increasing the odds and making the race more and more exciting but, eventually, even that became a little dull. 'Let's make it so that if I win, I really win and if you lose it means I'm better than you are.' The others smiled and said in unison, 'That's just silly, I am you.' They laughed for an eternity, then. 'Okay, let's pretend that if you lose, you forget that you are me…'

So the game took a fascinating turn and we have been playing it ever since. When you finally remember who you are—when you know that we are all one—this game ends and we can begin a new adventure.

Every now and then, you get a sense of it, a whiff of it, when you make what we call a spiritual connection with another soul—another part of The Whole—when you find yourself speaking the other's thoughts in the middle of a conversation, or when you think intently about someone you know and they phone you a few minutes later. Like chasing a smell, it's there powerfully and for a moment you know you can follow it to the source effortlessly, but then it's gone and you're left sniffing the air trying to get back on track. There it is, only fainter this time. Now stronger. Then it's gone once more. When the knowledge of our oneness turns from a simple belief in our heads into a knowing that we carry in our very souls—when we remember who we really are—I believe we'll return to Source and begin anew.

The last few years have been a particularly enthralling part of the journey for me. Those of a more pragmatic nature would probably dismiss the synchronicity I've experienced during this time as coincidence but I'm acutely aware that I'm on a very particular path of discovery. I have some idea where it leads, but the main thing is that it feels inevitable. And good. And right.

I used to be a pragmatist; airy fairy ideas didn't sit well with me, they weren't grounded in anything I could make much sense of. Eventually, I found myself increasingly surrounded by airy fairy people who would say particularly irritating things like, 'Yes, but what were you thinking just before you hit your thumb with the hammer?' Or 'In my last life, you were my cat.' I liken it to discovering there's a mosquito in the room as you curl up under the duvet for the night. You try to ignore it and you manage it for a while but you know that at some point it's going find a way in and give you something to scratch in the morning, so, you get out of bed and smash its head in with a slipper. Ah, peace and quiet. You hunker down for the night and another one whizzes past your ear.

After a while, you somehow find yourself leafing through the pages of a book you wouldn't normally give the time of day to and—Bob's your uncle—it's all downhill from there. Though downstream might be a better description.

I now feel like I'm floating downstream—a hell of a lot easier than impersonating a salmon, which is what I feel I've been doing up to this point. A corner has been turned, some burden has been lifted from my shoulders, and I know I've shifted my focus from a reality that manifests limitations to one that manifests freedoms.

I'm convinced at a fundamental level of the power of the individual. I believe that we create our own reality, and we're personally responsible for the lives and experiences we have. Everything you have in your life right now is something you created, and everything that is going on in the world right now, we created collectively. Most people don't like to acknowledge this truth, because it would mean embracing the concept that we create the abuse, or the lack, or the suffering in in our lives, or in the world as a whole.

We're all connected, yet solely responsible for our personal actions. We are all one, yet we all have individual desires. Everything I do, everything you say, everything we think affects the entire universe. What happens to one happens to the all, and what happens to all, happens to the one. It doesn't get any more airy-fairy than that, does it? Yet, it makes complete sense to me now and is proving to be increasingly true as the days go by.

If you're familiar with Mastery or eastern philosophy—Zen Buddhism and the like—you'll know that when the initiate approaches the Master, seeking enlightenment, the first thing the Master tells them is, 'I have nothing to give you. You have everything you need. I have nothing to teach you. There is nothing I can teach you that will give you enlightenment.'

Typically, the initiate takes that to mean 'Oh, he's challenging me. He just wants to see how committed I am to my actual enlightenment.' So the initiate stays on with the Master, and the Master proceeds to throw the initiate into a series of exercises and asks him questions that he answers but there's never a right answer. And because he's answering he's never getting it—he's never practicing Mastery.

Looking for a connection to your greater self—your higher consciousness—in the 'wisdom' or leadership of others, you are not accessing the part of you who remembers who you really are.

Being one with Source, the greater consciousness, is something you practice in every moment, it is not something you can establish or achieve because you're already there, and if you are not, it is only because you are resisting it. You ARE the greater consciousness. The only way you disconnect at any moment is by not taking responsibility, by living as though you are a victim to your situation or circumstances.

Never confuse responsibility with culpability—they are two entirely separate things. No one is culpable. Everyone should be responsible. That the two are so often used interchangeably is evidence of old programming that you can consciously choose to change.

When people are told, 'You should take responsibility...' they most often hear, 'Accept punishment for *"fill-in-the-blank"*.' As a result, most people spend so much of their time and energy running from the former (culpability) that they rarely stop and embrace the latter (responsibility). Most people live much of their lives feeling like either a victim of something, or a perpetrator of something else. It can be… tiring.

Regarding the amorphous word, *They*—it's used all the time, and the meaning is always different for every person employing the term. Throughout human history there's always been a *They*, whether *They* referred to the ancient Egyptian pharaohs, the Roman ruling class, The Imperial British, the Third Reich, the Czars, the Bolsheviks, the church, who *They* are changes continually, yet the concept of *They* has been a constant theme of the human experience.

The conspiracy theories fuelling the game remind me of a set of Russian dolls, the pertinent question being who's really at the heart of things?

The Queen twists open to reveal George Bush Sr and George Bush Sr twists open to unleash David Rockefeller, followed by a Rothschild, then a slowly descending, nested puzzle of The Black Pope (on a rope), Elvis, The Mafia, The Jesuits and so on. Perhaps the centre *matryoshka* is Homer Simpson. And inside that is a donut. I do get the distinct feeling, though, that if the dolls were all made of foam rubber and were all exactly the same size, you could rearrange the plot sequence anyway you liked, most likely based on whatever you'd read on the Internet the night before.

Considering the ever-decreasing-circle of arguing who is really in charge—who is the inner doll—the truth is, *They* is simply *Other*. The other part of All. And the Game of Other goes on.

What interests me more than the term *They* is the question, what do *They* really want? My answer: *They* want your industry. That's all. And *They* are willing to dangle the promise of eternal life if you work in this one for nothing. Or *They* may promise corporate bonuses, or your name on a public building, or an award, or a statue. *They* may even promise you your 'freedom' if you do what they say. You may think you must give them your obedience, your adherence, your loyalty, the very birthright of your soul, though all *They* really require is your industry.

Any ruling class (minority) sees the seething biomass of humanity (vast majority) as existing to serve and service their needs, and throughout time have developed manipulation into an art form in order to accomplish this goal. If the enticements of jingoism, religion, television—any and all aspects of bread and circuses—don't work, if a sovereign soul ever attempts to try and opt out, *They* do their utmost to corner you like a straying sheep and use every threat they can muster, including hunting you down and gunning you down in the name of their current status quo.

They want your industry. *They* want you to serve and service them, and they'll stop at nothing to achieve this.

There is a secret the Elite would rather the seething biomass not catch on to: *They* run the world like a corporation—to them, it's really *Just Business.*

The tendency is to view the Elite as a shadowy, sinister bogeyman—don't fall for it—think, shadowy, sinister businessman instead. *They* run everything like a corporation, and why not? Nations are corporations, religions are run like corporations, clubs, organisations, secret societies—the ones in charge are simply looking to maintain and hopefully increase their slice of the pie. Pump profits. Feather the CEO's nest. That's all. *Just business.* It's the rest of us who take it so personally, and—believe me—they count on that. They love to keep us angry, agitated, and continually arguing with one another.

So, what happens when a work force gets larger than the job requires? Cutbacks. Layoffs. Where the Elite agenda is concerned, reducing the work force could translate into poisoning the food and water supply, or pushing tainted vaccinations, or the true classic: keeping different cultures schismed, agitated and continually killing each other off. Factor in the huge push towards constantly reminding the population that we are *a cancer on the earth*, we are *responsible for the changing climate*, we are *guilty for the mess we are all in* today, and it all begins to make a strange sort of sense.

We are not dealing with Dr. Evil or Snidely Whiplash, we are simply faced with businessmen. The good news is, *They* have an Achilles' Heel...

Let's say they do indeed manage to fulfil their manifest destiny. They bring world population down, they clear the continental United States and return it to a pristine state to serve as a pleasure park nature reserve, they get their work force down to a 'manageable, cost-effective size'—just enough people to serve and service their needs—say they manage all this—what then?

In the end, people who live simply to dominate and enslave others always eat their own. In other words, they turn on each other.

Dominating others is an addiction they will never be able to lose. In their quest for superiority, when they run out of biomass to torment, they will turn on one another. Small consolation if you and most of the rest of the population has long since fallen as a casualty to their schemes, but in approaching this life on earth as a game, you can turn this weapon in their hand by gaining and maintaining clarity about why and how they play, and what they hope to gain.

Know thyself. Know thy adversary. Adopt and adapt their strategies—not to dominate them, but to keep yourself free. Do everything possible to postpone any sweeping countermoves your adversary may attempt and keep on buying time—perhaps enough time for them to start killing each other off. And, why not? They've been using that particular tactic on us for millennia.

Perhaps it's time to start learning from your opponent.

Having said all that, there is no *They*. All the while you are convinced there's a hidden malevolent entity guiding us all to oblivion, or that the end is nigh, you're distracting yourself from realising that you are consciousness, you are the beginning, the middle and the end, everything and nothing, everywhere and nowhere, I am you and you are me; You and I are *They*.

If you are interested in blazing your own trail, it may be good to remember that all systems of belief are a series of events characterised first by the birth of a good idea. This idea gradually develops into dogma architected by other humans, and finally ends up carved into the rock of *rules-you-must-adhere-to-or-else* by still more humans. The original concept came from a human, just like you. They simply had a revolutionary idea about how the world could work and shared it with other people. Those people then took it and ran with it and eventually developed it into the Rules Carved in Rock.

These good ideas end up as rigid rules primarily because most people aren't convinced of the value of their own ideas and of their own innate connection to Source. They believe they are floundering in an ocean of uncertainty and it can seem much safer to cling to the same rock others are grasping with such apparent fervour, this presumed Rock of Absolute Truth.

Absolutes make people feel safe. Absolutes, to the believer, can't be argued with or challenged. Absolutes seem to be a secure place to hide. And Absolute Truth seems to be different everywhere you go.

Looking closer, Absolute Truth seems to be different for every person you ever meet. Wars are fought over which Absolute Truth is the correct one. Absolute Truth is debated in courts all over the world every day. Many religious texts claim to hold the Absolute Truth, and the debate over which text is correct has been the number one cause of violent death on this planet, as in the long-time favourite game:

I Am Right. You Are Wrong.

How's that working out for the planet anyway? Last time I checked, not so well.

One of the most popular life games is Victim. It's a best-seller and most of us have become so good at it that we've forgotten it's a game. Sometimes we've been playing it so long we've forgotten other games even exist.

There is something seductive about the Victim game. It's expected. It's ingrained. It's currently fashionable. It feels familiar and we know the rules. The bottom line is, are you going to adopt the stance and mind-set of a Victim? Or a Victor? All the subsequent actions of your life will be informed by which choice you make.

If it's all just a game, then we all have a part to play. One of my parts in this story is to be the messenger, a Potentiator of the Mind, if you like. However, I'm bringing a little more than the game obliges me to bring. I am also here to remind you that it is a game.

Speaking of games, a certain sharp cookie and master game player once told a story about Monopoly.

Whilst visiting friends, he was invited to play, but declined. His highly competitive host began to rib him about his ability and whatnot. After a few minutes of taunting, he replied, 'Alright, I'll join in but you won't like how I play.' With that, they set up the game for four people.

After a time, all the players having accumulated property to some degree or other, our hero unfortunately landed on one of his host's very expensive squares and was liable for a heavy tax. The host smiled with glee and put out his hand to receive the monopoly money.

'We can play this two ways,' says our man, 'you can let me go on and we'll forget about the tax, or you can take the money from me, in which case I will give all of my properties to Bob over here, and he will undoubtedly win.'

'You can't do that,' said the host, 'it's against the rules.'

'I'll tell you what,' our hero replied, 'if you can find the rule that says I can't do it, I'll hand over the tax and we'll crack on.'

Of course, the host dug out the rule book and pored through it like a man possessed but—sure enough—there was no rule for or against our hero's tactic. Realising he was beaten, and not being prepared to let anyone else win by default, the host relinquished his right to take the tax and they played on.

Every time our man landed on another's property, he made the same offer and each let him pass untaxed. He eventually won by a long margin, and laughed as he reminded them, 'I said you wouldn't like how I play.'

In defining our game experience by deferring to rules that others have set, and by following those rules to the letter because it seems safer to do so, we risk being bound and hampered by those very rules. The key is flexibility, and trusting your own ability to fly by the seat of your pants. This is a skill that can only be mastered when you realise that you, the player, have the ability to level the playing field just by holding and exercising your own power instead of automatically deferring to that of others.

Games are only fun when you commit. For instance, you can't play a murder mystery game without committing yourself and/or suspending disbelief; otherwise the game is not fun and becomes a case of going-through-the-motions. Your job, in this life, is to play full-out, to play for keeps and commit to the game—to immerse yourself completely, whilst never forgetting that it is a game.

You can tell a lot about the way someone lives their life by watching how they play. Their commitment and their relationship to their own ability and self-confidence is reflected in the way they throw the dice, hold their cards, move the avatar around the board and, most of all, their behaviour when they win or lose.

A fundamental part of enjoying any game is knowing what the rules are and what they are not. I strive to accurately assess my opponent's agenda, and will bend, turn, mould or adapt it to work for me, whilst never compromising the integrity of the game.

You also have far more power if you think of the game as poker, rather than any dice-based game in which 'chance' comes into play. There is no chance involved here—we create it all. In poker—as in life—you're dealt a specific hand and it's what you do with it that determines whether you win or lose. You can bluff, you can attempt to deduce another's hand by card counting, you can manipulate the other players by giving false 'tells'; it's a game of skill, intuition and experience.

WHOMEVER IT IS THAT WINS; IN THE END, IT IS YOU.

I am acutely aware that I'm walking a thin line here; you may think I'm making light of the alarming events going on in our world right now, but in terms of the big picture, they are frivolous because it is just a game. But we're pretending this game is real so we must play full-out—it has to be taken seriously. We have to do all the things we're doing; protesting about 9/11, the war in Iraq, the raping and pillaging of other nations' natural resources and so on.

It is serious but your other job is to take the most empowering perspective on any event. As long as you remember we're playing a game, you are empowered to affect the game as an equal. The moment you forget, you can become victim to the other player's tactics.

You don't necessarily have the power to stop the game right now, as a single aspect of the whole consciousness, unless it turns out that you are the hundredth monkey, but you have just as much power as the banker, if not more so.

There is no one who can insert anything into your experience unless you're vibrating at a level that will allow it in. No one can create in anyone else's experience unless they're open to it. They can come after you with guns and vaccines, fluoride and statutes and any number of things, but unless you are playing the fear game, and vibrating at the low frequency that allows it in, they can't harm you.

We have to ask ourselves why we are being bombarded by messages that induce fear. Fear in terms of frequency is a very slow vibration and as such, allows for easier manipulation. While you're in a state of fear you are more pliable, malleable and suggestible. On the other side of the coin, we have anger; another very low frequency state. Keep in mind that although anger is a fear killer, it still operates in the same low frequency. This is why *They* seem to be able to create more effectively than you can, because we're all hopping back and forth between fear and anger; scaring each other with talk about what *They* are doing and then getting angry about it, never raising vibration long enough to create anything we really desire or anything that can turn the game to our advantage.

While you're listening to the shock jocks, who are also playing their part in the game—wonderfully so and with consummate skill—try tuning in to how you are feeling; if you're fearful or angry or both, you're right where *They* want you. That may suit you for now—though you will get tired of it eventually and move onto something that makes you feel better—like, believing in your own connection to All That Is.

The shock jock's duty in this game is to disillusion you. To Dis-

Illusion, to show you that you are living under an illusion and to wake you from it; to remove your rose-coloured spectacles. To do that, he needs to scare you out of your apathy, using fear and anger as a motivator. It serves its purpose well and those particular players have committed to vibrating at that low frequency for your benefit. But *once you awaken,* your job is to raise your vibration and start creating. If you choose to remain in the low frequency by staying with the shock jocks in the realm of fear and anger, *you will not be having as much fun as you could have playing the game.*

Listen to them, get the headlines, then get out and raise your frequency again.

Without naming names, there are certain shock jocks out there that make me want to go out and do some serious harm, so I avoid them. It's really as simple as that. I'll listen just long enough to get a sense of what's going on behind the curtain and I'll let them play their part—their part being to inform me of what the other players are doing in the game—but as soon as their emotional energy begins to affect mine and bring down my vibration, I leave.

Here's a another secret for you: the 'elite' love to be hated, and we love to hate them—just like Larry Hagman playing JR Ewing in *Dallas.* Everybody loves to hate the bad guy and if the actor is good—as Larry Hagman is—we can often get lost in the game and get caught up in hating the actor. Hate is fuelled by both fear and anger, and the only ones who benefit from your hate, and therefore your self-imprisonment in the lower frequency, is *Them.* The parts of the Whole that are playing the part of the Elite in this game are giving an incredible performance. Perhaps they may even be lost in their parts and have forgotten it's a game themselves, but—like the best method actors—they are playing full-out and are committed to their performances for the sake of keeping the game interesting and exciting.

They may be trying to kill us, but try this concept on for size: you can't really die, you are *eternal.*

Think of it as a game of paintball: you may get splatted, but it just means you have to sit the rest of this game out and wait for the next one.

If you can't wrap your mind around the concept that you are an eternal being, then answer me this:

If this is the only life you have—if this is all there is—do you want to spend it being angry, fearful and miserable all the time? Then why not try using your imagination—remember what that is? The thing your parents, your teachers, your partners continually try to stop or stifle or change when they accuse you of daydreaming, or wasting your life in fantasies, or simply hoping for something better.

It's your imagination—reclaim it. Imagine how powerful you are often enough, steadily enough, with clarity of purpose and singleness of intent and watch your life change. The road to empowerment does not mean controlling others, but rather choosing the thoughts that best affect how your own life unfolds. It's that simple. If you can grasp that whatever anyone else thinks about you is none of your business, then a good 99% of your work is done.

The road to empowerment is the most individual journey of a human life. You set the timetable for development, you choose the way you approach the challenges, you maintain your connection to the greater part of yourself, you do all this. Be constant, be vigilant, be committed to the course you set for yourself. If you need to gain clarity, then factor out everyone else's static, factor out the peanut gallery and concentrate on what you desire to make of your life.

Humans have a hunger to create more and better and different experiences all the time—it's the entire point of being alive. The difficulty comes because people, by and large, are terrified to do it alone, to be the first to try, to stand out from the crowd, to march to the beat of their own drum. They are afraid of making a wrong decision. Or of experiencing embarrassment. Or of being alone.

From my own observations, the biggest fear most people ever have might be the realisation that they are alone. We all die alone. We all suffer pain alone; no one can do either for us. Neither can they know exactly what we see with our eyes or hear with our ears or dream when we sleep, no matter how we strive to communicate those things through poetry, painting, music or blogs. No one knows exactly what you feel, and how you feel it, but you.

To forestall embracing this state of aloneness, we join a church, or a political party, or an online forum, continually checking in on other people's opinions of us and measuring our power according to who wins the online flame war. We form wars against drugs or porn or Republicans or the Tory Party. We lobby, we petition, we march… we do ten thousand things with ten thousand others, but rarely pause to give a moment's credit to the power of the individual. Why is that? Why do we feel so powerless alone? Why do we let this fear hold us down when history has repeatedly shown us that it is the individual, the lone voice in the wilderness, who lets a pebble fall from his hand and starts the avalanche of change.

You are alone. You're alone because you are an individual having an experience called life that is completely unique to you. You're alone because despite the begging, pleading, lying, seducing, dominating or manipulating you may do, you can never really change another sovereign soul. You are alone because the only life you can ever have a lasting effect on is your own. And you know what? That is powerful enough. By far.

Change your thought about your powerlessness as only one person—it's only a belief, and a belief is just a thought we continue to think in a habitual manner. You have the power to change the belief—any belief—and ultimately your life. You have this power. And if you think you don't, then you have already lost the game.

CHANGE THE THOUGHT = CHANGE YOUR LIFE.

You have a connection to the larger part of yourself that no one else can ever touch or violate or take away. Feel it. It's there. Believe in yourself and you will become powerful in your own right.

The human we are hardest on in all the world—without exception—is ourselves. So give yourself permission to smile from time to time. Lighten up. Be easy. Float downstream. Try and have some fun. And if you take anything at all from this chapter, or anything at all from this book, let it be this one mantra:

'I'm in it for the adventure.'

TIMOTHY ANTITERRORIST
21 JUNE 2009

Acknowledgements

Thank you to J.C.R. Licklider, Leonard Kleinrock, Larry G. Roberts, Radia Perlman, Bob Kahn and Vint Cerf for your contribution to the creation of the Internet, and for helping me flourish as the dedicated autodidact I am today.

Sincere thanks to Mary-Elizabeth: Croft & Robert-Arthur: Menard for pointing the way towards freedom. Though the path can be arduous, it's always worth the journey.

Thanks to Dr. Alun Kirby for his generous contribution to *Vaccine Nation*.

Thanks to Danny Shine and Charlie Veitch of the *Everything is OK* series on the YouTube channels, *spiritualentertainer* and *cveitch*; your message is infused with an addictive and invaluable sense of laughter and joy. You have lightened my journey.

Thanks to Stevie T and Huw Thomas for providing a counterpoint and hours of insightful debate.

Thanks to my very good friends, SC, AR, IB, JR, JG, LP & RP.

And to theantiterrorist channel subscribers and to all who have contributed to The Wake Up Call—in whatever role you presented yourselves—I am forever in your debt.

Lightning Source UK Ltd.
Milton Keynes UK
UKOW051435120312

188825UK00001B/18/P